C-281   CAREER EXAMINATION SERIES

*This is your
PASSBOOK for...*

Forest Ranger

*Test Preparation Study Guide
Questions & Answers*

COPYRIGHT NOTICE

This book is SOLELY intended for, is sold ONLY to, and its use is RESTRICTED to individual, bona fide applicants or candidates who qualify by virtue of having seriously filed applications for appropriate license, certificate, professional and/or promotional advancement, higher school matriculation, scholarship, or other legitimate requirements of education and/or governmental authorities.

This book is NOT intended for use, class instruction, tutoring, training, duplication, copying, reprinting, excerption, or adaptation, etc., by:

1) Other publishers
2) Proprietors and/or Instructors of "Coaching" and/or Preparatory Courses
3) Personnel and/or Training Divisions of commercial, industrial, and governmental organizations
4) Schools, colleges, or universities and/or their departments and staffs, including teachers and other personnel
5) Testing Agencies or Bureaus
6) Study groups which seek by the purchase of a single volume to copy and/or duplicate and/or adapt this material for use by the group as a whole without having purchased individual volumes for each of the members of the group
7) Et al.

Such persons would be in violation of appropriate Federal and State statutes.

PROVISION OF LICENSING AGREEMENTS – Recognized educational, commercial, industrial, and governmental institutions and organizations, and others legitimately engaged in educational pursuits, including training, testing, and measurement activities, may address request for a licensing agreement to the copyright owners, who will determine whether, and under what conditions, including fees and charges, the materials in this book may be used them. In other words, a licensing facility exists for the legitimate use of the material in this book on other than an individual basis. However, it is asseverated and affirmed here that the material in this book CANNOT be used without the receipt of the express permission of such a licensing agreement from the Publishers. Inquiries re licensing should be addressed to the company, attention rights and permissions department.

All rights reserved, including the right of reproduction in whole or in part, in any form or by any means, electronic or mechanical, including photocopying, recording, or by any information storage and retrieval system, without permission in writing from the Publisher.

Copyright © 2025 by
National Learning Corporation

212 Michael Drive, Syosset, NY 11791
(516) 921-8888 • www.passbooks.com
E-mail: info@passbooks.com

PASSBOOK® SERIES

THE *PASSBOOK® SERIES* has been created to prepare applicants and candidates for the ultimate academic battlefield – the examination room.

At some time in our lives, each and every one of us may be required to take an examination – for validation, matriculation, admission, qualification, registration, certification, or licensure.

Based on the assumption that every applicant or candidate has met the basic formal educational standards, has taken the required number of courses, and read the necessary texts, the *PASSBOOK® SERIES* furnishes the one special preparation which may assure passing with confidence, instead of failing with insecurity. Examination questions – together with answers – are furnished as the basic vehicle for study so that the mysteries of the examination and its compounding difficulties may be eliminated or diminished by a sure method.

This book is meant to help you pass your examination provided that you qualify and are serious in your objective.

The entire field is reviewed through the huge store of content information which is succinctly presented through a provocative and challenging approach – the question-and-answer method.

A climate of success is established by furnishing the correct answers at the end of each test.

You soon learn to recognize types of questions, forms of questions, and patterns of questioning. You may even begin to anticipate expected outcomes.

You perceive that many questions are repeated or adapted so that you can gain acute insights, which may enable you to score many sure points.

You learn how to confront new questions, or types of questions, and to attack them confidently and work out the correct answers.

You note objectives and emphases, and recognize pitfalls and dangers, so that you may make positive educational adjustments.

Moreover, you are kept fully informed in relation to new concepts, methods, practices, and directions in the field.

You discover that you are actually taking the examination all the time: you are preparing for the examination by "taking" an examination, not by reading extraneous and/or supererogatory textbooks.

In short, this PASSBOOK®, used directedly, should be an important factor in helping you to pass your test.

FOREST RANGER

DUTIES:
Forest Rangers are employed by the State at various locations throughout the State. Forest Rangers perform a wide variety of duties in their assigned geographic area, including forest fire prevention and suppression; forest management and utilization of State and private land; care, custody, and control of State lands; forest insect and disease control; search, rescue, and emergency work; the development of recreational areas and facilities; inspection of gas and oil drilling sites before and during operation; and making mined land reclamation inspections. Forest Rangers are authorized to enforce certain provisions of the environmental conservation law and codes, rules, and regulations of the State. Pursuant to conditions prescribed, they may be required to carry firearms for the express purpose of enhancing their safety and effectiveness in performing duties relating to such enforcement.

As a Forest Ranger you would be required to participate in a formal residential training program. Upon successful completion, you would work in an assigned patrol area, and elsewhere throughout the state for emergencies and special assignments. Forest Rangers perform a wide variety of duties related to overseeing the care, custody, and control of DEC administered lands.

As a Forest Ranger, you would be a sworn Police Officer, authorized to investigate complaints and enforce provisions of the Environmental Conservation Law (ECL) and other state laws in order to protect the State's lands, other natural resources, and the people who use them. You would be required to carry firearms and complete necessary annual training for State certification. Forest Rangers conduct search and rescue operations for lost or injured persons throughout the State; conduct wildland fire management operations including wildfire suppression in the State and when requested for national firefighting efforts; and coordinate and assist in incident response efforts to natural and man-made emergencies and disasters. Forest Rangers educate the public concerning the proper use of public lands and resources; visit schools, fire departments, and organizations to promote resource protection; teach national and state-certified courses to other agencies, volunteer groups, and fire departments concerning search and rescue, wildland fire suppression, and wilderness safety and etiquette; and foster and develop volunteer assistance from the local communities to support the Department's wildland firefighting and search operations. Perform related duties.

SCOPE OF THE EXAMINATION:
The written test is designed to test for knowledge, skills, and/or abilities in such areas as:

1. **Applying written information (rules, regulations, policies, procedures, directives, etc.) in police** situations These questions test for the ability to apply written rules in given situations similar to those typically experienced by police officers.
2. **Memory for facts and information** - These questions test for the ability to remember facts and information presented in written form. You will be given 5 minutes to read and study the information in the Memory Booklet. After the 5-minute period, the Memory Booklet will be taken away. You will then be required to answer questions about the material that was presented in the Memory Booklet.
3. **Reading, understanding and interpreting written information** - These questions test for the ability to read, understand, and interpret the kinds of written information that police officers are required to read during their formal training period and on the job.
4. **Preparing written material in a police setting** - These questions test for the ability to prepare the types of reports that police officers write. You will be presented with a page of notes followed by several questions. Each question will consist of four restatements of the information given in the notes. From each set of four, you must choose the version that presents the information most clearly and accurately.
5. **Natural resources and environment** - These questions test for basic practical knowledge of fish, wildlife and other natural resources; outdoor recreation; forestry and environmental awareness.
6. **Wilderness management and outdoor recreation, tree and plant identification, map interpretation and surveying** - These questions test for knowledge of the principles and practices of outdoor recreation on forest lands and management for public recreational use and other purposes; identification and characteristics of trees and other plants found in the State forests; and understanding and interpreting maps and surveying fundamentals.

HOW TO TAKE A TEST

I. YOU MUST PASS AN EXAMINATION

A. *WHAT EVERY CANDIDATE SHOULD KNOW*

Examination applicants often ask us for help in preparing for the written test. What can I study in advance? What kinds of questions will be asked? How will the test be given? How will the papers be graded?

As an applicant for a civil service examination, you may be wondering about some of these things. Our purpose here is to suggest effective methods of advance study and to describe civil service examinations.

Your chances for success on this examination can be increased if you know how to prepare. Those "pre-examination jitters" can be reduced if you know what to expect. You can even experience an adventure in good citizenship if you know why civil service exams are given.

B. *WHY ARE CIVIL SERVICE EXAMINATIONS GIVEN?*

Civil service examinations are important to you in two ways. As a citizen, you want public jobs filled by employees who know how to do their work. As a job seeker, you want a fair chance to compete for that job on an equal footing with other candidates. The best-known means of accomplishing this two-fold goal is the competitive examination.

Exams are widely publicized throughout the nation. They may be administered for jobs in federal, state, city, municipal, town or village governments or agencies.

Any citizen may apply, with some limitations, such as the age or residence of applicants. Your experience and education may be reviewed to see whether you meet the requirements for the particular examination. When these requirements exist, they are reasonable and applied consistently to all applicants. Thus, a competitive examination may cause you some uneasiness now, but it is your privilege and safeguard.

C. *HOW ARE CIVIL SERVICE EXAMS DEVELOPED?*

Examinations are carefully written by trained technicians who are specialists in the field known as "psychological measurement," in consultation with recognized authorities in the field of work that the test will cover. These experts recommend the subject matter areas or skills to be tested; only those knowledges or skills important to your success on the job are included. The most reliable books and source materials available are used as references. Together, the experts and technicians judge the difficulty level of the questions.

Test technicians know how to phrase questions so that the problem is clearly stated. Their ethics do not permit "trick" or "catch" questions. Questions may have been tried out on sample groups, or subjected to statistical analysis, to determine their usefulness.

Written tests are often used in combination with performance tests, ratings of training and experience, and oral interviews. All of these measures combine to form the best-known means of finding the right person for the right job.

II. HOW TO PASS THE WRITTEN TEST

A. NATURE OF THE EXAMINATION

To prepare intelligently for civil service examinations, you should know how they differ from school examinations you have taken. In school you were assigned certain definite pages to read or subjects to cover. The examination questions were quite detailed and usually emphasized memory. Civil service exams, on the other hand, try to discover your present ability to perform the duties of a position, plus your potentiality to learn these duties. In other words, a civil service exam attempts to predict how successful you will be. Questions cover such a broad area that they cannot be as minute and detailed as school exam questions.

In the public service similar kinds of work, or positions, are grouped together in one "class." This process is known as *position-classification*. All the positions in a class are paid according to the salary range for that class. One class title covers all of these positions, and they are all tested by the same examination.

B. FOUR BASIC STEPS

1) Study the announcement

How, then, can you know what subjects to study? Our best answer is: "Learn as much as possible about the class of positions for which you've applied." The exam will test the knowledge, skills and abilities needed to do the work.

Your most valuable source of information about the position you want is the official exam announcement. This announcement lists the training and experience qualifications. Check these standards and apply only if you come reasonably close to meeting them.

The brief description of the position in the examination announcement offers some clues to the subjects which will be tested. Think about the job itself. Review the duties in your mind. Can you perform them, or are there some in which you are rusty? Fill in the blank spots in your preparation.

Many jurisdictions preview the written test in the exam announcement by including a section called "Knowledge and Abilities Required," "Scope of the Examination," or some similar heading. Here you will find out specifically what fields will be tested.

2) Review your own background

Once you learn in general what the position is all about, and what you need to know to do the work, ask yourself which subjects you already know fairly well and which need improvement. You may wonder whether to concentrate on improving your strong areas or on building some background in your fields of weakness. When the announcement has specified "some knowledge" or "considerable knowledge," or has used adjectives like "beginning principles of…" or "advanced … methods," you can get a clue as to the number and difficulty of questions to be asked in any given field. More questions, and hence broader coverage, would be included for those subjects which are more important in the work. Now weigh your strengths and weaknesses against the job requirements and prepare accordingly.

3) Determine the level of the position

Another way to tell how intensively you should prepare is to understand the level of the job for which you are applying. Is it the entering level? In other words, is this the position in which beginners in a field of work are hired? Or is it an intermediate or advanced level? Sometimes this is indicated by such words as "Junior" or "Senior" in the class title. Other jurisdictions use Roman numerals to designate the level – Clerk I, Clerk II, for example. The word "Supervisor" sometimes appears in the title. If the level is not indicated by the title, check the description of duties. Will you be working under very close supervision, or will you have responsibility for independent decisions in this work?

4) Choose appropriate study materials

Now that you know the subjects to be examined and the relative amount of each subject to be covered, you can choose suitable study materials. For beginning level jobs, or even advanced ones, if you have a pronounced weakness in some aspect of your training, read a modern, standard textbook in that field. Be sure it is up to date and has general coverage. Such books are normally available at your library, and the librarian will be glad to help you locate one. For entry-level positions, questions of appropriate difficulty are chosen – neither highly advanced questions, nor those too simple. Such questions require careful thought but not advanced training.

If the position for which you are applying is technical or advanced, you will read more advanced, specialized material. If you are already familiar with the basic principles of your field, elementary textbooks would waste your time. Concentrate on advanced textbooks and technical periodicals. Think through the concepts and review difficult problems in your field.

These are all general sources. You can get more ideas on your own initiative, following these leads. For example, training manuals and publications of the government agency which employs workers in your field can be useful, particularly for technical and professional positions. A letter or visit to the government department involved may result in more specific study suggestions, and certainly will provide you with a more definite idea of the exact nature of the position you are seeking.

III. KINDS OF TESTS

Tests are used for purposes other than measuring knowledge and ability to perform specified duties. For some positions, it is equally important to test ability to make adjustments to new situations or to profit from training. In others, basic mental abilities not dependent on information are essential. Questions which test these things may not appear as pertinent to the duties of the position as those which test for knowledge and information. Yet they are often highly important parts of a fair examination. For very general questions, it is almost impossible to help you direct your study efforts. What we can do is to point out some of the more common of these general abilities needed in public service positions and describe some typical questions.

1) General information

Broad, general information has been found useful for predicting job success in some kinds of work. This is tested in a variety of ways, from vocabulary lists to questions about current events. Basic background in some field of work, such as sociology or economics, may be sampled in a group of questions. Often these are principles which have become familiar to most persons through exposure rather than through formal training. It is difficult to advise you how to study for these questions; being alert to the world around you is our best suggestion.

2) Verbal ability

An example of an ability needed in many positions is verbal or language ability. Verbal ability is, in brief, the ability to use and understand words. Vocabulary and grammar tests are typical measures of this ability. Reading comprehension or paragraph interpretation questions are common in many kinds of civil service tests. You are given a paragraph of written material and asked to find its central meaning.

3) Numerical ability

Number skills can be tested by the familiar arithmetic problem, by checking paired lists of numbers to see which are alike and which are different, or by interpreting charts and graphs. In the latter test, a graph may be printed in the test booklet which you are asked to use as the basis for answering questions.

4) Observation

A popular test for law-enforcement positions is the observation test. A picture is shown to you for several minutes, then taken away. Questions about the picture test your ability to observe both details and larger elements.

5) Following directions

In many positions in the public service, the employee must be able to carry out written instructions dependably and accurately. You may be given a chart with several columns, each column listing a variety of information. The questions require you to carry out directions involving the information given in the chart.

6) Skills and aptitudes

Performance tests effectively measure some manual skills and aptitudes. When the skill is one in which you are trained, such as typing or shorthand, you can practice. These tests are often very much like those given in business school or high school courses. For many of the other skills and aptitudes, however, no short-time preparation can be made. Skills and abilities natural to you or that you have developed throughout your lifetime are being tested.

Many of the general questions just described provide all the data needed to answer the questions and ask you to use your reasoning ability to find the answers. Your best preparation for these tests, as well as for tests of facts and ideas, is to be at your physical and mental best. You, no doubt, have your own methods of getting into an exam-taking mood and keeping "in shape." The next section lists some ideas on this subject.

IV. KINDS OF QUESTIONS

Only rarely is the "essay" question, which you answer in narrative form, used in civil service tests. Civil service tests are usually of the short-answer type. Full instructions for answering these questions will be given to you at the examination. But in case this is your first experience with short-answer questions and separate answer sheets, here is what you need to know:

1) Multiple-choice Questions

Most popular of the short-answer questions is the "multiple choice" or "best answer" question. It can be used, for example, to test for factual knowledge, ability to solve problems or judgment in meeting situations found at work.

A multiple-choice question is normally one of three types—
- It can begin with an incomplete statement followed by several possible endings. You are to find the one ending which *best* completes the statement, although some of the others may not be entirely wrong.
- It can also be a complete statement in the form of a question which is answered by choosing one of the statements listed.

- It can be in the form of a problem – again you select the best answer.

Here is an example of a multiple-choice question with a discussion which should give you some clues as to the method for choosing the right answer:

When an employee has a complaint about his assignment, the action which will *best* help him overcome his difficulty is to
- A. discuss his difficulty with his coworkers
- B. take the problem to the head of the organization
- C. take the problem to the person who gave him the assignment
- D. say nothing to anyone about his complaint

In answering this question, you should study each of the choices to find which is best. Consider choice "A" – Certainly an employee may discuss his complaint with fellow employees, but no change or improvement can result, and the complaint remains unresolved. Choice "B" is a poor choice since the head of the organization probably does not know what assignment you have been given, and taking your problem to him is known as "going over the head" of the supervisor. The supervisor, or person who made the assignment, is the person who can clarify it or correct any injustice. Choice "C" is, therefore, correct. To say nothing, as in choice "D," is unwise. Supervisors have and interest in knowing the problems employees are facing, and the employee is seeking a solution to his problem.

2) True/False Questions

The "true/false" or "right/wrong" form of question is sometimes used. Here a complete statement is given. Your job is to decide whether the statement is right or wrong.

SAMPLE: A roaming cell-phone call to a nearby city costs less than a non-roaming call to a distant city.

This statement is wrong, or false, since roaming calls are more expensive.

This is not a complete list of all possible question forms, although most of the others are variations of these common types. You will always get complete directions for answering questions. Be sure you understand *how* to mark your answers – ask questions until you do.

V. RECORDING YOUR ANSWERS

Computer terminals are used more and more today for many different kinds of exams.

For an examination with very few applicants, you may be told to record your answers in the test booklet itself. Separate answer sheets are much more common. If this separate answer sheet is to be scored by machine – and this is often the case – it is highly important that you mark your answers correctly in order to get credit.

An electronic scoring machine is often used in civil service offices because of the speed with which papers can be scored. Machine-scored answer sheets must be marked with a pencil, which will be given to you. This pencil has a high graphite content which responds to the electronic scoring machine. As a matter of fact, stray dots may register as answers, so do not let your pencil rest on the answer sheet while you are pondering the correct answer. Also, if your pencil lead breaks or is otherwise defective, ask for another.

Since the answer sheet will be dropped in a slot in the scoring machine, be careful not to bend the corners or get the paper crumpled.

The answer sheet normally has five vertical columns of numbers, with 30 numbers to a column. These numbers correspond to the question numbers in your test booklet. After each number, going across the page are four or five pairs of dotted lines. These short dotted lines have small letters or numbers above them. The first two pairs may also have a "T" or "F" above the letters. This indicates that the first two pairs only are to be used if the questions are of the true-false type. If the questions are multiple choice, disregard the "T" and "F" and pay attention only to the small letters or numbers.

Answer your questions in the manner of the sample that follows:

32. The largest city in the United States is
    A. Washington, D.C.
    B. New York City
    C. Chicago
    D. Detroit
    E. San Francisco

1) Choose the answer you think is best. (New York City is the largest, so "B" is correct.)
2) Find the row of dotted lines numbered the same as the question you are answering. (Find row number 32)
3) Find the pair of dotted lines corresponding to the answer. (Find the pair of lines under the mark "B.")
4) Make a solid black mark between the dotted lines.

VI. BEFORE THE TEST

Common sense will help you find procedures to follow to get ready for an examination. Too many of us, however, overlook these sensible measures. Indeed, nervousness and fatigue have been found to be the most serious reasons why applicants fail to do their best on civil service tests. Here is a list of reminders:

- Begin your preparation early – Don't wait until the last minute to go scurrying around for books and materials or to find out what the position is all about.
- Prepare continuously – An hour a night for a week is better than an all-night cram session. This has been definitely established. What is more, a night a week for a month will return better dividends than crowding your study into a shorter period of time.
- Locate the place of the exam – You have been sent a notice telling you when and where to report for the examination. If the location is in a different town or otherwise unfamiliar to you, it would be well to inquire the best route and learn something about the building.
- Relax the night before the test – Allow your mind to rest. Do not study at all that night. Plan some mild recreation or diversion; then go to bed early and get a good night's sleep.
- Get up early enough to make a leisurely trip to the place for the test – This way unforeseen events, traffic snarls, unfamiliar buildings, etc. will not upset you.
- Dress comfortably – A written test is not a fashion show. You will be known by number and not by name, so wear something comfortable.

- Leave excess paraphernalia at home – Shopping bags and odd bundles will get in your way. You need bring only the items mentioned in the official notice you received; usually everything you need is provided. Do not bring reference books to the exam. They will only confuse those last minutes and be taken away from you when in the test room.
- Arrive somewhat ahead of time – If because of transportation schedules you must get there very early, bring a newspaper or magazine to take your mind off yourself while waiting.
- Locate the examination room – When you have found the proper room, you will be directed to the seat or part of the room where you will sit. Sometimes you are given a sheet of instructions to read while you are waiting. Do not fill out any forms until you are told to do so; just read them and be prepared.
- Relax and prepare to listen to the instructions
- If you have any physical problem that may keep you from doing your best, be sure to tell the test administrator. If you are sick or in poor health, you really cannot do your best on the exam. You can come back and take the test some other time.

VII. AT THE TEST

The day of the test is here and you have the test booklet in your hand. The temptation to get going is very strong. Caution! There is more to success than knowing the right answers. You must know how to identify your papers and understand variations in the type of short-answer question used in this particular examination. Follow these suggestions for maximum results from your efforts:

1) Cooperate with the monitor

The test administrator has a duty to create a situation in which you can be as much at ease as possible. He will give instructions, tell you when to begin, check to see that you are marking your answer sheet correctly, and so on. He is not there to guard you, although he will see that your competitors do not take unfair advantage. He wants to help you do your best.

2) Listen to all instructions

Don't jump the gun! Wait until you understand all directions. In most civil service tests you get more time than you need to answer the questions. So don't be in a hurry. Read each word of instructions until you clearly understand the meaning. Study the examples, listen to all announcements and follow directions. Ask questions if you do not understand what to do.

3) Identify your papers

Civil service exams are usually identified by number only. You will be assigned a number; you must not put your name on your test papers. Be sure to copy your number correctly. Since more than one exam may be given, copy your exact examination title.

4) Plan your time

Unless you are told that a test is a "speed" or "rate of work" test, speed itself is usually not important. Time enough to answer all the questions will be provided, but this does not mean that you have all day. An overall time limit has been set. Divide the total time (in minutes) by the number of questions to determine the approximate time you have for each question.

5) Do not linger over difficult questions

If you come across a difficult question, mark it with a paper clip (useful to have along) and come back to it when you have been through the booklet. One caution if you do this – be sure to skip a number on your answer sheet as well. Check often to be sure that you have not lost your place and that you are marking in the row numbered the same as the question you are answering.

6) Read the questions

Be sure you know what the question asks! Many capable people are unsuccessful because they failed to *read* the questions correctly.

7) Answer all questions

Unless you have been instructed that a penalty will be deducted for incorrect answers, it is better to guess than to omit a question.

8) Speed tests

It is often better NOT to guess on speed tests. It has been found that on timed tests people are tempted to spend the last few seconds before time is called in marking answers at random – without even reading them – in the hope of picking up a few extra points. To discourage this practice, the instructions may warn you that your score will be "corrected" for guessing. That is, a penalty will be applied. The incorrect answers will be deducted from the correct ones, or some other penalty formula will be used.

9) Review your answers

If you finish before time is called, go back to the questions you guessed or omitted to give them further thought. Review other answers if you have time.

10) Return your test materials

If you are ready to leave before others have finished or time is called, take ALL your materials to the monitor and leave quietly. Never take any test material with you. The monitor can discover whose papers are not complete, and taking a test booklet may be grounds for disqualification.

VIII. EXAMINATION TECHNIQUES

1) Read the general instructions carefully. These are usually printed on the first page of the exam booklet. As a rule, these instructions refer to the timing of the examination; the fact that you should not start work until the signal and must stop work at a signal, etc. If there are any *special* instructions, such as a choice of questions to be answered, make sure that you note this instruction carefully.

2) When you are ready to start work on the examination, that is as soon as the signal has been given, read the instructions to each question booklet, underline any key words or phrases, such as *least, best, outline, describe* and the like. In this way you will tend to answer as requested rather than discover on reviewing your paper that you *listed without describing*, that you selected the *worst* choice rather than the *best* choice, etc.

3) If the examination is of the objective or multiple-choice type – that is, each question will also give a series of possible answers: A, B, C or D, and you are called upon to select the best answer and write the letter next to that answer on your answer paper – it is advisable to start answering each question in turn. There may be anywhere from 50 to 100 such questions in the three or four hours allotted and you can see how much time would be taken if you read through all the questions before beginning to answer any. Furthermore, if you come across a question or group of questions which you know would be difficult to answer, it would undoubtedly affect your handling of all the other questions.

4) If the examination is of the essay type and contains but a few questions, it is a moot point as to whether you should read all the questions before starting to answer any one. Of course, if you are given a choice – say five out of seven and the like – then it is essential to read all the questions so you can eliminate the two that are most difficult. If, however, you are asked to answer all the questions, there may be danger in trying to answer the easiest one first because you may find that you will spend too much time on it. The best technique is to answer the first question, then proceed to the second, etc.

5) Time your answers. Before the exam begins, write down the time it started, then add the time allowed for the examination and write down the time it must be completed, then divide the time available somewhat as follows:
    - If 3-1/2 hours are allowed, that would be 210 minutes. If you have 80 objective-type questions, that would be an average of 2-1/2 minutes per question. Allow yourself no more than 2 minutes per question, or a total of 160 minutes, which will permit about 50 minutes to review.
    - If for the time allotment of 210 minutes there are 7 essay questions to answer, that would average about 30 minutes a question. Give yourself only 25 minutes per question so that you have about 35 minutes to review.

6) The most important instruction is to *read each question* and make sure you know what is wanted. The second most important instruction is to *time yourself properly* so that you answer every question. The third most important instruction is to *answer every question*. Guess if you have to but include something for each question. Remember that you will receive no credit for a blank and will probably receive some credit if you write something in answer to an essay question. If you guess a letter – say "B" for a multiple-choice question – you may have guessed right. If you leave a blank as an answer to a multiple-choice question, the examiners may respect your feelings but it will not add a point to your score. Some exams may penalize you for wrong answers, so in such cases *only*, you may not want to guess unless you have some basis for your answer.

7) Suggestions
    a. Objective-type questions
        1. Examine the question booklet for proper sequence of pages and questions
        2. Read all instructions carefully
        3. Skip any question which seems too difficult; return to it after all other questions have been answered
        4. Apportion your time properly; do not spend too much time on any single question or group of questions

5. Note and underline key words – *all, most, fewest, least, best, worst, same, opposite,* etc.
6. Pay particular attention to negatives
7. Note unusual option, e.g., unduly long, short, complex, different or similar in content to the body of the question
8. Observe the use of "hedging" words – *probably, may, most likely,* etc.
9. Make sure that your answer is put next to the same number as the question
10. Do not second-guess unless you have good reason to believe the second answer is definitely more correct
11. Cross out original answer if you decide another answer is more accurate; do not erase until you are ready to hand your paper in
12. Answer all questions; guess unless instructed otherwise
13. Leave time for review

   b. Essay questions
     1. Read each question carefully
     2. Determine exactly what is wanted. Underline key words or phrases.
     3. Decide on outline or paragraph answer
     4. Include many different points and elements unless asked to develop any one or two points or elements
     5. Show impartiality by giving pros and cons unless directed to select one side only
     6. Make and write down any assumptions you find necessary to answer the questions
     7. Watch your English, grammar, punctuation and choice of words
     8. Time your answers; don't crowd material

8) Answering the essay question

Most essay questions can be answered by framing the specific response around several key words or ideas. Here are a few such key words or ideas:

M's: manpower, materials, methods, money, management
P's: purpose, program, policy, plan, procedure, practice, problems, pitfalls, personnel, public relations

   a. Six basic steps in handling problems:
     1. Preliminary plan and background development
     2. Collect information, data and facts
     3. Analyze and interpret information, data and facts
     4. Analyze and develop solutions as well as make recommendations
     5. Prepare report and sell recommendations
     6. Install recommendations and follow up effectiveness

   b. Pitfalls to avoid
     1. *Taking things for granted* – A statement of the situation does not necessarily imply that each of the elements is necessarily true; for example, a complaint may be invalid and biased so that all that can be taken for granted is that a complaint has been registered

2. *Considering only one side of a situation* – Wherever possible, indicate several alternatives and then point out the reasons you selected the best one
3. *Failing to indicate follow up* – Whenever your answer indicates action on your part, make certain that you will take proper follow-up action to see how successful your recommendations, procedures or actions turn out to be
4. *Taking too long in answering any single question* – Remember to time your answers properly

IX. AFTER THE TEST

Scoring procedures differ in detail among civil service jurisdictions although the general principles are the same. Whether the papers are hand-scored or graded by machine we have described, they are nearly always graded by number. That is, the person who marks the paper knows only the number – never the name – of the applicant. Not until all the papers have been graded will they be matched with names. If other tests, such as training and experience or oral interview ratings have been given, scores will be combined. Different parts of the examination usually have different weights. For example, the written test might count 60 percent of the final grade, and a rating of training and experience 40 percent. In many jurisdictions, veterans will have a certain number of points added to their grades.

After the final grade has been determined, the names are placed in grade order and an eligible list is established. There are various methods for resolving ties between those who get the same final grade – probably the most common is to place first the name of the person whose application was received first. Job offers are made from the eligible list in the order the names appear on it. You will be notified of your grade and your rank as soon as all these computations have been made. This will be done as rapidly as possible.

People who are found to meet the requirements in the announcement are called "eligibles." Their names are put on a list of eligible candidates. An eligible's chances of getting a job depend on how high he stands on this list and how fast agencies are filling jobs from the list.

When a job is to be filled from a list of eligibles, the agency asks for the names of people on the list of eligibles for that job. When the civil service commission receives this request, it sends to the agency the names of the three people highest on this list. Or, if the job to be filled has specialized requirements, the office sends the agency the names of the top three persons who meet these requirements from the general list.

The appointing officer makes a choice from among the three people whose names were sent to him. If the selected person accepts the appointment, the names of the others are put back on the list to be considered for future openings.

That is the rule in hiring from all kinds of eligible lists, whether they are for typist, carpenter, chemist, or something else. For every vacancy, the appointing officer has his choice of any one of the top three eligibles on the list. This explains why the person whose name is on top of the list sometimes does not get an appointment when some of the persons lower on the list do. If the appointing officer chooses the second or third eligible, the No. 1 eligible does not get a job at once, but stays on the list until he is appointed or the list is terminated.

X. HOW TO PASS THE INTERVIEW TEST

The examination for which you applied requires an oral interview test. You have already taken the written test and you are now being called for the interview test – the final part of the formal examination.

You may think that it is not possible to prepare for an interview test and that there are no procedures to follow during an interview. Our purpose is to point out some things you can do in advance that will help you and some good rules to follow and pitfalls to avoid while you are being interviewed.

What is an interview supposed to test?

The written examination is designed to test the technical knowledge and competence of the candidate; the oral is designed to evaluate intangible qualities, not readily measured otherwise, and to establish a list showing the relative fitness of each candidate – as measured against his competitors – for the position sought. Scoring is not on the basis of "right" and "wrong," but on a sliding scale of values ranging from "not passable" to "outstanding." As a matter of fact, it is possible to achieve a relatively low score without a single "incorrect" answer because of evident weakness in the qualities being measured.

Occasionally, an examination may consist entirely of an oral test – either an individual or a group oral. In such cases, information is sought concerning the technical knowledges and abilities of the candidate, since there has been no written examination for this purpose. More commonly, however, an oral test is used to supplement a written examination.

Who conducts interviews?

The composition of oral boards varies among different jurisdictions. In nearly all, a representative of the personnel department serves as chairman. One of the members of the board may be a representative of the department in which the candidate would work. In some cases, "outside experts" are used, and, frequently, a businessman or some other representative of the general public is asked to serve. Labor and management or other special groups may be represented. The aim is to secure the services of experts in the appropriate field.

However the board is composed, it is a good idea (and not at all improper or unethical) to ascertain in advance of the interview who the members are and what groups they represent. When you are introduced to them, you will have some idea of their backgrounds and interests, and at least you will not stutter and stammer over their names.

What should be done before the interview?

While knowledge about the board members is useful and takes some of the surprise element out of the interview, there is other preparation which is more substantive. It *is* possible to prepare for an oral interview – in several ways:

1) Keep a copy of your application and review it carefully before the interview

This may be the only document before the oral board, and the starting point of the interview. Know what education and experience you have listed there, and the sequence and dates of all of it. Sometimes the board will ask you to review the highlights of your experience for them; you should not have to hem and haw doing it.

2) Study the class specification and the examination announcement

Usually, the oral board has one or both of these to guide them. The qualities, characteristics or knowledges required by the position sought are stated in these documents. They offer valuable clues as to the nature of the oral interview. For example, if the job involves supervisory responsibilities, the announcement will usually indicate that knowledge of modern supervisory methods and the qualifications of the candidate as a supervisor will be tested. If so, you can expect such questions, frequently in the form of a hypothetical situation which you are expected to solve. NEVER go into an oral without knowledge of the duties and responsibilities of the job you seek.

3) Think through each qualification required

Try to visualize the kind of questions you would ask if you were a board member. How well could you answer them? Try especially to appraise your own knowledge and background in each area, *measured against the job sought*, and identify any areas in which you are weak. Be critical and realistic – do not flatter yourself.

4) Do some general reading in areas in which you feel you may be weak

For example, if the job involves supervision and your past experience has NOT, some general reading in supervisory methods and practices, particularly in the field of human relations, might be useful. Do NOT study agency procedures or detailed manuals. The oral board will be testing your understanding and capacity, not your memory.

5) Get a good night's sleep and watch your general health and mental attitude

You will want a clear head at the interview. Take care of a cold or any other minor ailment, and of course, no hangovers.

What should be done on the day of the interview?

Now comes the day of the interview itself. Give yourself plenty of time to get there. Plan to arrive somewhat ahead of the scheduled time, particularly if your appointment is in the fore part of the day. If a previous candidate fails to appear, the board might be ready for you a bit early. By early afternoon an oral board is almost invariably behind schedule if there are many candidates, and you may have to wait. Take along a book or magazine to read, or your application to review, but leave any extraneous material in the waiting room when you go in for your interview. In any event, relax and compose yourself.

The matter of dress is important. The board is forming impressions about you – from your experience, your manners, your attitude, and your appearance. Give your personal appearance careful attention. Dress your best, but not your flashiest. Choose conservative, appropriate clothing, and be sure it is immaculate. This is a business interview, and your appearance should indicate that you regard it as such. Besides, being well groomed and properly dressed will help boost your confidence.

Sooner or later, someone will call your name and escort you into the interview room. *This is it.* From here on you are on your own. It is too late for any more preparation. But remember, you asked for this opportunity to prove your fitness, and you are here because your request was granted.

What happens when you go in?

The usual sequence of events will be as follows: The clerk (who is often the board stenographer) will introduce you to the chairman of the oral board, who will introduce you to the other members of the board. Acknowledge the introductions before you sit down. Do not be surprised if you find a microphone facing you or a stenotypist sitting by. Oral interviews are usually recorded in the event of an appeal or other review.

Usually the chairman of the board will open the interview by reviewing the highlights of your education and work experience from your application – primarily for the benefit of the other members of the board, as well as to get the material into the record. Do not interrupt or comment unless there is an error or significant misinterpretation; if that is the case, do not hesitate. But do not quibble about insignificant matters. Also, he will usually ask you some question about your education, experience or your present job – partly to get you to start talking and to establish the interviewing "rapport." He may start the actual questioning, or turn it over to one of the other members. Frequently, each member undertakes the questioning on a particular area, one in which he is perhaps most competent, so you can expect each member to participate in the examination. Because time is limited, you may also expect some rather abrupt switches in the direction the questioning takes, so do not be upset by it. Normally, a board member will not pursue a single line of questioning unless he discovers a particular strength or weakness.

After each member has participated, the chairman will usually ask whether any member has any further questions, then will ask you if you have anything you wish to add. Unless you are expecting this question, it may floor you. Worse, it may start you off on an extended, extemporaneous speech. The board is not usually seeking more information. The question is principally to offer you a last opportunity to present further qualifications or to indicate that you have nothing to add. So, if you feel that a significant qualification or characteristic has been overlooked, it is proper to point it out in a sentence or so. Do not compliment the board on the thoroughness of their examination – they have been sketchy, and you know it. If you wish, merely say, "No thank you, I have nothing further to add." This is a point where you can "talk yourself out" of a good impression or fail to present an important bit of information. Remember, *you close the interview yourself*.

The chairman will then say, "That is all, Mr. _____, thank you." Do not be startled; the interview is over, and quicker than you think. Thank him, gather your belongings and take your leave. Save your sigh of relief for the other side of the door.

How to put your best foot forward

Throughout this entire process, you may feel that the board individually and collectively is trying to pierce your defenses, seek out your hidden weaknesses and embarrass and confuse you. Actually, this is not true. They are obliged to make an appraisal of your qualifications for the job you are seeking, and they want to see you in your best light. Remember, they must interview all candidates and a non-cooperative candidate may become a failure in spite of their best efforts to bring out his qualifications. Here are 15 suggestions that will help you:

1) Be natural – Keep your attitude confident, not cocky

If you are not confident that you can do the job, do not expect the board to be. Do not apologize for your weaknesses, try to bring out your strong points. The board is interested in a positive, not negative, presentation. Cockiness will antagonize any board member and make him wonder if you are covering up a weakness by a false show of strength.

2) Get comfortable, but don't lounge or sprawl

Sit erectly but not stiffly. A careless posture may lead the board to conclude that you are careless in other things, or at least that you are not impressed by the importance of the occasion. Either conclusion is natural, even if incorrect. Do not fuss with your clothing, a pencil or an ashtray. Your hands may occasionally be useful to emphasize a point; do not let them become a point of distraction.

3) Do not wisecrack or make small talk

This is a serious situation, and your attitude should show that you consider it as such. Further, the time of the board is limited – they do not want to waste it, and neither should you.

4) Do not exaggerate your experience or abilities

In the first place, from information in the application or other interviews and sources, the board may know more about you than you think. Secondly, you probably will not get away with it. An experienced board is rather adept at spotting such a situation, so do not take the chance.

5) If you know a board member, do not make a point of it, yet do not hide it

Certainly you are not fooling him, and probably not the other members of the board. Do not try to take advantage of your acquaintanceship – it will probably do you little good.

6) Do not dominate the interview

Let the board do that. They will give you the clues – do not assume that you have to do all the talking. Realize that the board has a number of questions to ask you, and do not try to take up all the interview time by showing off your extensive knowledge of the answer to the first one.

7) Be attentive

You only have 20 minutes or so, and you should keep your attention at its sharpest throughout. When a member is addressing a problem or question to you, give him your undivided attention. Address your reply principally to him, but do not exclude the other board members.

8) Do not interrupt

A board member may be stating a problem for you to analyze. He will ask you a question when the time comes. Let him state the problem, and wait for the question.

9) Make sure you understand the question

Do not try to answer until you are sure what the question is. If it is not clear, restate it in your own words or ask the board member to clarify it for you. However, do not haggle about minor elements.

10) Reply promptly but not hastily

A common entry on oral board rating sheets is "candidate responded readily," or "candidate hesitated in replies." Respond as promptly and quickly as you can, but do not jump to a hasty, ill-considered answer.

11) Do not be peremptory in your answers

A brief answer is proper – but do not fire your answer back. That is a losing game from your point of view. The board member can probably ask questions much faster than you can answer them.

12) Do not try to create the answer you think the board member wants

He is interested in what kind of mind you have and how it works – not in playing games. Furthermore, he can usually spot this practice and will actually grade you down on it.

13) Do not switch sides in your reply merely to agree with a board member

Frequently, a member will take a contrary position merely to draw you out and to see if you are willing and able to defend your point of view. Do not start a debate, yet do not surrender a good position. If a position is worth taking, it is worth defending.

14) Do not be afraid to admit an error in judgment if you are shown to be wrong

The board knows that you are forced to reply without any opportunity for careful consideration. Your answer may be demonstrably wrong. If so, admit it and get on with the interview.

15) Do not dwell at length on your present job

The opening question may relate to your present assignment. Answer the question but do not go into an extended discussion. You are being examined for a *new* job, not your present one. As a matter of fact, try to phrase ALL your answers in terms of the job for which you are being examined.

Basis of Rating

Probably you will forget most of these "do's" and "don'ts" when you walk into the oral interview room. Even remembering them all will not ensure you a passing grade. Perhaps you did not have the qualifications in the first place. But remembering them will help you to put your best foot forward, without treading on the toes of the board members.

Rumor and popular opinion to the contrary notwithstanding, an oral board wants you to make the best appearance possible. They know you are under pressure – but they also want to see how you respond to it as a guide to what your reaction would be under the pressures of the job you seek. They will be influenced by the degree of poise you display, the personal traits you show and the manner in which you respond.

ABOUT THIS BOOK

This book contains tests divided into Examination Sections. Go through each test, answering every question in the margin. We have also attached a sample answer sheet at the back of the book that can be removed and used. At the end of each test look at the answer key and check your answers. On the ones you got wrong, look at the right answer choice and learn. Do not fill in the answers first. Do not memorize the questions and answers, but understand the answer and principles involved. On your test, the questions will likely be different from the samples. Questions are changed and new ones added. If you understand these past questions you should have success with any changes that arise. Tests may consist of several types of questions. We have additional books on each subject should more study be advisable or necessary for you. Finally, the more you study, the better prepared you will be. This book is intended to be the last thing you study before you walk into the examination room. Prior study of relevant texts is also recommended. NLC publishes some of these in our Fundamental Series. Knowledge and good sense are important factors in passing your exam. Good luck also helps. So now study this Passbook, absorb the material contained within and take that knowledge into the examination. Then do your best to pass that exam.

EXAMINATION SECTION

EXAMINATION SECTION
TEST 1

DIRECTIONS: Each question or incomplete statement is followed by several suggested answers or completions. Select the one that BEST answers the question or completes the statement. *PRINT THE LETTER OF THE CORRECT ANSWER IN THE SPACE AT THE RIGHT.*

1. _____ refers to a ranger's power or right to give commands, enforce obedience, take action and make decisions.

    A. Jurisdiction
    B. License
    C. Authority
    D. Sanction

2. The primary objective of most of a park ranger's enforcement actions is

    A. correction and punishment
    B. establishing authority and control
    C. education and information
    D. decreasing liability

3. Which of the following ranger services is LEAST likely to be provided through visitor contact?

    A. Interpretive
    B. Resource management
    C. Safety
    D. Search, rescue and recovery

4. A ranger comes upon a location that she believes to be a crime scene, but she has no training in criminal investigation. As the first park official on the scene, she should

    A. disperse everyone in the area
    B. record existing and relevant data in a notebook
    C. straighten or clean up the scene
    D. interview available witnesses

5. In most automobiles, the VIN plate is on the

    A. driver's side doorjamb
    B. driver's side windshield post
    C. driver's side dashboard
    D. passenger's side dashboard

6. A park's "situation map" should be marked on a surface of

    A. wood or plywood
    B. paper
    C. enamel or clear acetate
    D. canvas

1

7. The Rhomberg test is a field test most useful for indicating _____ intoxication.

   A. alcohol
   B. marijuana
   C. cocaine
   D. methamphetamine

8. A ranger on patrol should imagine his/her key responsibility to be

   A. conservation
   B. prevention
   C. surveillance
   D. observation

9. The form of federal jurisdiction that a park ranger will encounter most rarely is _____ jurisdiction, which means the federal government has been granted the right by a state to exercise certain state authorities.

   A. partial
   B. proprietary
   C. multiple
   D. concurrent

10. One of the actions within a park ranger's continuum of enforcement levels is the verbal warning. The key to issuing a verbal warning is for a park ranger to

    A. maintain a stern and authoritative tone of voice
    B. convince the offender of the seriousness of the offense
    C. convince the offender that the warning is really just a friendly chat
    D. be certain he has the authority to implement the consequences if it becomes necessary

11. For most park agencies, the most appropriate training vehicle for providing training to rangers who will have law enforcement authority includes a
    I. basic agency-wide course of 40 to 80 hours
    II. 20- to 40-hour orientation course at the assigned park
    III. 3- to 6-month on-the-job training program at the assigned park
    IV. participation in special training courses as opportunities arise.

    A. I and II
    B. II and III
    C. II, III and IV
    D. I, II, III and IV

12. Generally, the use of vehicles for park patrol
    I. greatly increases a ranger's ability to respond quickly to emergencies
    II. is the optimal method for increasing personal contact with visitors
    III. affords the ranger a degree of protection
    IV. offers the most efficient method of patrol with limited man power

    A. I, II and III
    B. I, III and IV
    C. II and III
    D. I, II, III and IV

13. Whenever a suitable wall surface isn't available for conducting a search of an offender, a kneeling search may be appropriate. In a standard kneeling search, the

    A. offender's knees should be together
    B. offender's feet should be spread apart
    C. offender's hand should be raised high above his head
    D. ranger should search from behind the offender

13.____

14. When initiating communication with visitors in an enforcement situation, the ranger's most immediate responsibility is to

    A. help the visitor understand the seriousness of the offense
    B. create a supportive rather than defensive climate
    C. make sure the visitor is aware of the ranger's authority to enforce
    D. ensure that the visitor is physically incapable of mounting an attack

14.____

15. Which of the following types of knots is used to attach a rope to the middle of another rope?

    A. Prusik
    B. Clove hitch
    C. Square lashing
    D. Shear lashing

15.____

16. Listening is usually thought of as being accomplished on four levels. The highest level involves

    A. listening with understanding of the speaker's point of view
    B. making sense out of sound
    C. critically evaluating what is said
    D. understanding the literal meaning of what is said

16.____

17. Which of the following structures may generally be entered unconditionally by a ranger in an enforcement situation?
    I. Park administrative building
    II. Public restrooms
    III. Visitor abodes
    IV. Concessionaire's leased building

    A. I and II
    B. I, II and III
    C. II and III
    D. I, II, III and IV

17.____

18. Which of the following is most likely to be a standard item for a mounted patrol?

    A. Animal noose
    B. Survival kit
    C. Flares
    D. Hydraulic jack

18.____

19. "Thumbnail" descriptions of persons include each of the following, EXCEPT

    A. Hair color
    B. Eyes
    C. Clothing
    D. Race

20. A ranger is reading a park map grid reference. On such maps, a four-digit grid reference number refers to the grid square located to the _____ the point of intersection of the lines relating to the grid numbers.

    A. right and above
    B. right and below
    C. left and above
    D. left and below

21. It is usually permissible to search an offender incidental to an arrest. Which of the following statements about such searches is TRUE?

    A. During a legal search, a ranger may seize items that are not only in actual possession, but within reach of the person at the time of the search.
    B. Evidence of a crime other than the one for which the ranger has an arrest warrant is generally not seizable.
    C. Stop-and-frisk searches are permitted under most situations.
    D. A legal search may usually be conducted by any ranger who has arrest powers.

22. A ranger is helping to compose the interpretive text for visitor center exhibits. The best text-on-background color combination in terms of legibility would be

    A. black on white
    B. green on white
    C. green on red
    D. blue on white

23. Before conducting a search, a park ranger should always obtain a search warrant if there is time, or whenever there is doubt as to whether one is necessary. Generally, a search warrant is required if

    A. exceptional circumstances create probable cause that contraband or other evidence will soon be destroyed
    B. the search is of a motor vehicle that is capable of being moved out of the ranger's control and there is probable cause to believe that someone in the vehicle has been involved in the commission of a crime
    C. the search is of a habitable dwelling on park grounds that is owned by the park, but occupied by the suspect as a camping abode
    D. the search is incidental to a lawful arrest and confined to the offender's person

24. A ranger should consider the primary objective of a park agency's interpretive services to be

    A. informing
    B. dispelling commonly held assumptions
    C. furthering an agenda
    D. inciting the visitor to some action or feeling

25. In certain circumstances, search of a person or premises may be appropriate even though legal grounds are weak or absent. Such searches may be conducted with consent. Which of the following statements concerning consent searches is TRUE?

   A. The person granting consent does not necessarily have to be aware of the right to refuse consent.
   B. A consent to enter premises implies a consent to search.
   C. A statement welcoming a search implies that a warrant is not demanded.
   D. Consent may be revoked at any time, but the revocation does not invalidate any evidence seized prior to the revocation.

KEY (CORRECT ANSWERS)

1. C
2. C
3. B
4. B
5. C

6. C
7. A
8. D
9. A
10. D

11. C
12. B
13. D
14. B
15. A

16. A
17. A
18. C
19. B
20. A

21. A
22. D
23. C
24. D
25. D

TEST 2

DIRECTIONS: Each question or incomplete statement is followed by several suggested answers or completions. Select the one that BEST answers the question or completes the statement. *PRINT THE LETTER OF THE CORRECT ANSWER IN THE SPACE AT THE RIGHT.*

1. In most cases it is appropriate for a park ranger to think of visitors as
    I. not dependent on the ranger; it is the ranger who is dependent on them
    II. the most important people the ranger will come into contact with
    III. not an interruption of the ranger's work, but the main reason for it
    IV. outsiders who will alter the park, rather than an integral part of the environment

    A. I and II
    B. I, II and III
    C. II, III and IV
    D. I, II, III and IV

2. Which of following legal terms is used to denote the proof that a crime has occurred?

    A. *Corpus delicti*
    B. *Habeus corpus*
    C. *Respondent superior*
    D. Probable cause

3. In the continuum of a park ranger's enforcement priorities, "Priority 1" situations deal with

    A. the protection of visitors from each other
    B. situations in which neither the park nor its visitors are in any immediate danger
    C. the protection of the park's resources from the visitor
    D. the protection of visitors from hazardous conditions created by park resources

4. The strongest ropes are generally made of

    A. polypropylene
    B. nylon
    C. manila
    D. Dacron

5. A ranger is helping to compose the interpretive text for visitor center exhibits. For one exhibit, visitors will be about 15 feet from the text. The letters for this text should be at least _____ high.

    A. a half-inch
    B. an inch
    C. an inch-and-a-half
    D. two inches

6. The primary purposes of patrol include
    I. providing resource protection
    II. making assistance available to visitors
    III. providing a deterrent for destructive behavior
    IV. observing the park and visitor behavior

    A. I and II
    B. II and IV
    C. II, III and IV
    D. I, II, III and IV

7. A ranger is one of the first officials to arrive at the scene of a crime. Preliminary procedures that will ordinarily be undertaken by the investigating ranger include each of the following, EXCEPT

   A. safeguarding the area
   B. conducting a methodic crime scene search
   C. separating witnesses from bystanders and obtaining statements
   D. rendering assistance to the injured

8. In areas of _____ jurisdiction, only state law is considered to be in effect, meaning that federal officers may enforce rules and regulations only such as Title 36, CFR and other federal laws allow regardless of jurisdiction.

   A. partial
   B. proprietary
   C. concurrent
   D. exclusive

9. To be legal, a search warrant should specifically identify the
   I. property to be seized
   II. place to be searched
   III. limits of the search
   IV. probable cause upon which the search is based

   A. I and II
   B. II, III and IV
   C. III and IV
   D. I, II, III and IV

10. Which of the following is a guideline that should be followed in handling a domestic dispute on park property?

    A. If the situation seems to justify the intervention of a professional counselor, recommend counseling in a general way.
    B. Offer legal advice if either of the parties is considering legal action.
    C. Ask questions that will determine who is at fault or who began the altercation.
    D. Try to stay out of such disputes unless it becomes clear that someone is in danger of imminent physical harm.

11. Rangers are often brought into contact with groups who represent "subcultures"-groups of a similar age, race, occupation or other grouping characteristics that may lead to the development of a kind of dialect or language system all their own. In communicating with these groups—especially in enforcement situations—it is important for the ranger to

    A. acknowledge only standard grammatical English
    B. understand the "language" of the subculture, but not to use it
    C. try to communicate with these groups using their own dialect or jargon
    D. try to speak as little as possible

12. Rangers without law enforcement authority are empowered, in some situations, to
    I. issue citations
    II. detain visitors
    III. search visitors
    IV. seize property

    A. I only
    B. I and II
    C. I, II and III
    D. I, II, III and IV

13. Which of the following is a disadvantage associated with foot patrol?

    A. Ranger's presence is suggested, rather than seen or heard
    B. Restricted to extensive-use areas
    C. Direct contact with visitors is inhibited
    D. Limited ability to respond to situations outside the immediate area

14. Guidelines for search-and-rescue operations within a park include
    I. Radio-equipped searchers should be sent to danger or vantage points.
    II. If dogs are used, they should be on a leash.
    III. Searches should generally not be continued after dark unless a life-or-death situation exists.
    IV. Each searcher should periodically call out the name(s) of the lost person(s).

    A. I and II
    B. I, II and III
    C. IV only
    D. I, II, III and IV

15. The ability of park rangers to implement enforcement services is dependent upon a number of factors. Which of the following is LEAST likely to be one of these factors?

    A. The park agency's policies
    B. The ranger's level of certainty about the appropriateness of enforcement
    C. The individual ranger's level of training and expertise
    D. The authority and jurisdiction authorized by law

16. Good listening skills for rangers include
    I. Forming judgements before listening to the speaker, based on appearance and demeanor
    II. Considering listening to be an active process
    III. Always taking notes while listening
    IV. Listening to how something is being said before concentrating on the actual content of the message

    A. I and II
    B. II only
    C. II, III and IV
    D. I, II, III and IV

17. Which of the following is NOT generally considered part of the standard frisk procedure? 17.____

    A. Offender's feet spread about two feet apart.
    B. Offender's hands extended above the head, with fingers spread.
    C. Ranger moves fingertips over all searchable areas, crushing clothing to locate concealed weapons.
    D. Offenders considered dangerous should be handcuffed prior to the frisk.

18. One of the signs that a person has overdosed on a stimulant is 18.____

    A. cold, clammy skin
    B. fatigue
    C. slurred speech
    D. convulsions

19. Which of the following is NOT a guideline that should usually be followed in conducting patrols? 19.____

    A. Patrols should always follow the same method, route, and schedule.
    B. Patrol rangers should periodically stop at "overview" points.
    C. Open patrol is, in most situations, preferred to hidden patrol.
    D. Whenever possible, patrols should be conducted by a team of two.

20. In relaying a description of an individual, the first detail given is usually 20.____

    A. sex   B. age   C. race   D. height

21. Normally, searches of vehicles by a park ranger require a search warrant. Exceptions include 21.____

    I. whenever probable cause to search exists
    II. the search is incidental to an arrest
    III. items are in open view through the vehicle's window
    IV. the vehicle has stopped at an authorized roadblock

    A. I only
    B. I and II
    C. I, II and III
    D. I, II, III and IV

22. Which of the following is LEAST likely to be a standard item for a cycle patrol? 22.____

    A. Portable spotlight
    B. First aid kit
    C. Maps and brochures
    D. Folding shovel

23. A ranger must attempt to stop a moving vehicle to implement an enforcement action. While in motion, the ranger should stay within _____ feet of the vehicle. 23.____

    A. 15 and 20   B. 25 and 40   C. 50 and 75   D. 100 and 200

24. Research demonstrates that _____ percent of a ranger's duty time involves some form of communication. 24.____

    A. 55-65
    B. 65-75
    C. 75-85
    D. 85-95

25. A ranger is called on to approach an offender who is belligerent. Guidelines to follow during such an encounter include 25.____
    I. making sure that a weapon is visible and at the ready
    II. trying to bargain with the offender for better behavior
    III. if you do not have the authority to make an arrest, trying to give the impression that you do
    IV. regardless of the provocation, never exhibiting anger or impatience

    A. I only
    B. I and II
    C. IV only
    D. II, III and IV

KEY (CORRECT ANSWERS)

1.	B	11.	B
2.	A	12.	A
3.	A	13.	D
4.	B	14.	D
5.	B	15.	B
6.	D	16.	B
7.	B	17.	C
8.	B	18.	D
9.	D	19.	A
10.	A	20.	A

21. C
22. D
23. C
24. C
25. C

TEST 3

DIRECTIONS: Each question or incomplete statement is followed by several suggested answers or completions. Select the one that BEST answers the question or completes the statement. *PRINT THE LETTER OF THE CORRECT ANSWER IN THE SPACE AT THE RIGHT.*

1. A ranger is composing a sketch of an accident scene. He will need to discriminate between temporary, short-lived, and long-lived evidence. Which of the following would be considered short-lived evidence?

   A. Gasoline puddles
   B. Vehicle debris
   C. Skid marks
   D. Gouges in the pavement

2. In most situations, the best attitude for the park ranger to adopt is one that is _____ oriented.

   A. service
   B. enterprise
   C. task
   D. staff

3. In the park setting, courts have ruled that search-and-seizure laws apply to visitor abodes (motor homes, trailers, screen canopies, rented cabins), as well as the area surrounding the abode and normally considered a part thereof (campsite, trash can, storage shed, etc.). The legal term for this surrounding area is

   A. environs
   B. curtilage
   C. quadrangle
   D. milieu

4. Which of the following is NOT a guideline that a park ranger should use in handling a complaint?

   A. Remember that some complaints should be taken more seriously than others
   B. Focus initially on the facts surrounding the situation or problem
   C. Always thank the complainant for his or her interest
   D. Notify the complainant when corrective action has been taken

5. Guidelines for a park ranger's enforcement actions include
   I. the use of physical force should be limited to the minimum necessary to implement the action
   II. the vigor or severity of enforcement actions should be dependent on the attitude of the offender
   III. whenever a ranger is unable to secure cooperation, he should withdraw from the immediate area and seek appropriate assistance
   IV. whenever doubt exists as to whether a situation actually constitutes a violation, or whether the suspect is in fact the perpetrator, the ranger should rule in favor of the visitor and try to resolve the doubt

   A. I and II
   B. I, III and IV
   C. I and IV
   D. I, II, III and IV

6. A park ranger should usually think of her primary duty as

   A. assuring each park visitor a quality experience
   B. enforcing the existing rules within park boundaries
   C. observing visitor behaviors and being prepared for any problems that might arise
   D. protecting the park's most important resources

7. Which of the following is NOT a principle that should guide the composition and delivery of interpretive services in a park?

   A. Interpretation should tell the whole story, rather than just a part of it.
   B. Interpretation should arouse curiosity in addition to giving facts.
   C. The best interpretation sticks to information within the "comfort zone" of visitors.
   D. The best interpretation occurs through person-to-person communication.

8. _____ patrol is the method that provides the greatest amount of visitor access, but usually prohibits extensive observation of visitor behavior and park conditions.

   A. Cycle
   B. Mounted
   C. Foot
   D. Vehicle

9. One of the signs that a person has overdosed on a depressant is

   A. hallucinations
   B. slow pulse
   C. cold, clammy skin
   D. constricted pupils

10. A ranger is conducting a field interview to determine the cause of an incident. The ranger should know that of all the behaviors that suggest an untruthful response, the one most commonly demonstrated by deceitful people is

    A. bringing the hand to the head
    B. interrupting the questioner
    C. hesitation
    D. crossing the arms over the chest

11. A ranger is conducting a field interview to record a visitor's perceptions of an event. In recording the visitor's account, the ranger should remember each of the following general truths about human perception EXCEPT that

    A. people tend to overestimate the length of verticals while underestimating the width of horizontals
    B. danger and stress cause people to underestimate duration and distance
    C. light-colored objects tend to be seen as heavier and nearer than dark objects of the same size and distance away
    D. people usually recall actions and events better than objects

12. If a DWI suspect refuses to submit to a chemical test, many jurisdictions accept this as an admission of intoxication resulting in the revocation of driving privileges for a period of time. This result, however, is predicated on several criteria. Which of the following is NOT one of these criteria?   12._____

    A. The ranger has probable cause to believe the suspect is DWI.
    B. The suspect has already completed a standard' field sobriety test.
    C. The ranger placed the suspect under arrest.
    D. The ranger specifically requested the suspect to submit to a chemical test.

13. A ranger is reading a park map grid reference. On this map, the numbers are read from   13._____

    A. left to right and top to bottom
    B. left to right and bottom to top
    C. right to left and top to bottom
    D. right to left and bottom to top

14. Defensive measures consist of several levels of defense. The level known as "defensive opposition" involves   14._____

    A. warding off blows with limbs or a baton
    B. the use of a firearm
    C. the use of chemical irritants
    D. simply ignoring verbal and visual abuse

15. Which of the following is NOT an element of the "legal scope" of a park ranger's jurisdiction?   15._____

    A. The park's physical boundaries
    B. Traffic codes
    C. Fish and game laws
    D. Criminal statutes

16. Which of the following is an example of a "transitional" interpretive experience?   16._____

    A. Slide presentation
    B. Visitor center exhibit
    C. Outdoor interpretive stations
    D. Automobile tour

17. A ranger is designing an interpretive activity for a group of elementary school children who are all about eight years old. For children at this age,   17._____

    A. ideas, rather than objects, are very important
    B. relations with others are based primarily on self-interest
    C. there is a strong desire for independence from adults
    D. peer relationships are very important

18. Which of the following is most likely to be a standard item for a foot patrol?   18._____

    A. Jumper cables
    B. Tranquilizer gun
    C. Folding stretcher
    D. Transceiver

19. In the continuum of a park ranger's enforcement priorities, "Priority 3" situations deal with

   A. the protection of visitors from hazardous conditions created by park resources
   B. the protection of the park's resources from the visitor
   C. the protection of visitors from each other
   D. situations in which neither the park nor its visitors are in any immediate danger

20. Recreational resources may be managed under the guidance of several viewpoints. The _____ viewpoint holds that resources should be used in an essentially "as is" manner, and that visitor use should blend with the resource base.

   A. preservationist
   B. landscape maintenance
   C. conservationist
   D. recreation activity

21. Which of the following is NOT a guideline that should be used for the conduct of station duty?

   A. Whenever rangers are in conversation with visitors, they should stand.
   B. Each question should be answered as if it were the first time the ranger has heard it.
   C. Rangers should remain sitting or standing behind a counter.
   D. Rangers should attempt to serve all visitors who need assistance.

22. Which of the following statements about search warrants is typically FALSE?

   A. Searchers may remain only a sufficient length of time as is "reasonably" necessary to search for and seize the property described in the search warrant.
   B. Generally, searchers may not seize items relating to criminal activity that are not specifically identified in the search warrant
   C. Search warrants for the premises do not permit a search of all persons present in the premises
   D. In most situations, real estate can be seized under a search warrant

23. A ranger's boundary maintenance responsibilities typically include each of the following functions EXCEPT

   A. physically locating the boundary line, either by previous marks or survey
   B. identifying trespass and/or encroachment
   C. marking and signing the boundary
   D. preventing erosion of coastal/shoreline boundaries

24. The park's public relations program must
   I. emphasize specific stages in a process, rather than ultimate goals
   II. solve the problems of others while solving the problems of the park
   III. focus on challenges and shortcomings that are in need of assistance or support
   IV. consist of actions that are coordinated and integrated

   A. I only
   B. I, II and III
   C. II and IV
   D. I, II, III and IV

25. Arrests can normally be made by park rangers
    I. on an arrest warrant
    II. on view of a felony being committed
    III. on reasonable suspicion of a felony
    IV. on reasonable suspicion of a misdemeanor

    A. I only
    B. I and II
    C. I, II and III
    D. I, II, III and IV

KEY (CORRECT ANSWERS)

1.	C	11.	B
2.	A	12.	B
3.	B	13.	B
4.	A	14.	A
5.	B	15.	A
6.	A	16.	D
7.	C	17.	D
8.	C	18.	D
9.	C	19.	B
10.	A	20.	C

21. C
22. D
23. D
24. C
25. C

EXAMINATION SECTION
TEST 1

DIRECTIONS: Each question or incomplete statement is followed by several suggested answers or completions. Select the one that BEST answers the question or completes the statement. *PRINT THE LETTER OF THE CORRECT ANSWER IN THE SPACE AT THE RIGHT.*

1. Which of the following natural resources is classified as inexhaustible/immutable, or incapable of much change or alteration through human activity? 1____

   A. Agricultural products
   B. Atomic energy
   C. Waterpower of flowing streams
   D. Mineral resources

2. Each of the following practices is a current method for maintaining the utility of cattle grazing rangeland EXCEPT 2____

   A. manipulating stock herds
   B. reseeding
   C. firing
   D. maintaining constant grazing pressure

3. The one of the following considered to be an ADVANTAGE of monocultural forest harvesting is 3____

   A. superior wood quality
   B. makes use of built-in ecological balancing mechanisms
   C. allows nurturing of shade-intolerant species
   D. decreased susceptibility to fires

4. The type of soil that is BEST able to hold water is 4____

   A. silt   B. sandy clay
   C. silty clay   D. loam

5. The practice of *chipping, or* breaking the forest harvest down into smaller particles that can be compressed into useful products, can INCREASE the forest yield by _____ %. 5____

   A. 25   B. 50   C. 100   D. 200

6. The _____ industry generates the MOST revenue in the United States. 6____

   A. steel   B. cattle
   C. textiles   D. automobile

7. Which of the following is NOT considered to be a guiding principle in the current model for conserving natural resources? 7____

   A. Balancing individual privilege with individual responsibility
   B. Ultimate government control of conservation efforts
   C. Concentrated, singular use of particular resources
   D. Frequent inventory and projection of resource use

8. One of soil's macronutrients is

   A. cobalt   B. calcium   C. zinc   D. copper

9. Food production in the United States is currently hindered by all of the following factors EXCEPT the

   A. loss of farmland to land development
   B. gradually increasing average temperatures
   C. huge fossil fuel input requirement for production
   D. transfer of water to urban populations

10. The bark of trees, long discarded as useless by loggers, has proven to be a useful resource for all of the following purposes EXCEPT

    A. medical uses
    B. construction of building frames
    C. production of chemicals for tanning leather
    D. oil-well drilling compounds

11. Of the following, the one that is NOT generally considered to be an advantage associated with the use of organic fertilizers is

    A. increased rate of water release
    B. prevention of leaching
    C. improved soil structure
    D. maximum aeration of root zone

12. APPROXIMATELY _____ percent of the earth's freshwater supply is underground.

    A. 30   B. 50   C. 75   D. 95

13. Which of the following is NOT generally considered to be part of the ocean's contribution as a natural resource?
    A

    A. highway for international transport
    B. replenisher of oxygen supply through algeal photosynthesis
    C. major source of important vitamins in the human diet
    D. major source of important proteins in the human diet

14. The natural resource GENERALLY considered to be inexhaustible, but whose quality can be impaired by misuse, is

    A. rangeland   B. marine fish and mammals
    C. static mineral resources   D. solar energy

15. The one of the following resources that can be converted into methane gas by high-pressure steam heating is

    A. high-sulfur coal
    B. solid animal wastes
    C. petroleum
    D. human garbage and solid wastes

16. Given the current methods of using fossil fuels, the LEAST defensible (most wasteful), according to scientists, is

    A. synthetic or bacterial food production
    B. heating
    C. petrochemicals
    D. synthetic polymers

17. The BEST way to restore soil fertility is by

    A. organic fertilizers B. inorganic fertilizers
    C. crop rotation   D. strip cropping

18. The MINIMUM amount of time that toxic material will remain in a given groundwater supply is generally considered to be _____ years.

    A. 10   B. 30   C. 200   D. 1,000

19. What is considered to be the MOST influential factor governing the occurrence and behavior of aquatic life?

    A. Availability of food   B. Availability of sunlight
    C. Availability of oxygen   D. Temperature

20. Which of the following has NOT proven to be a consequence involved in the use of solar energy?

    A. Toxicity of working fluids
    B. Decrease in photosynthetic rates of surrounding flora
    C. Climatic change
    D. Marine pollution

21. More than 50% of the coal that has ever been mined from the earth has been extracted in the last years.

    A. 100   B. 50   C. 25   D. 10

22. The natural resource classified as exhaustible but renewable, meaning that its permanence is dependent on how it is used by humans, is

    A. fossil fuels   B. wildlife species
    C. solar energy   D. soil

23. The one of the following that is NOT a limiting power held by the International Whaling Commission over commercial whalers is

    A. protecting certain species
    B. deciding minimum length for permissible kill
    C. protecting breeding grounds
    D. protecting calves and nursing cows

24. Which of the following is generally accepted as the MOST promising solution to the increasing worldwide food shortage?

   A. Development of more effective fertilizers
   B. Vigorous human population control
   C. More efficient pest control
   D. Decreased reliance on meat as a food source

24_____

25. The contaminants PRIMARILY responsible for the depletion of the earth's atmospheric ozone are

   A. carbon monoxide
   C. dioxins
   B. chlorinated fluorocarbons
   D. steam

25_____

KEY (CORRECT ANSWERS)

1.	B	11.	A
2.	D	12.	D
3.	C	13.	C
4.	B	14.	D
5.	D	15.	A
6.	B	16.	B
7.	C	17.	A
8.	B	18.	C
9.	B	19.	D
10.	B	20.	B

21. C
22. D
23. C
24. B
25. B

TEST 2

DIRECTIONS: Each question or incomplete statement is followed by several suggested answers or completions. Select the one that BEST answers the question or completes the statement. *PRINT THE LETTER OF THE CORRECT ANSWER IN THE SPACE AT THE RIGHT.*

1. Which of the following is currently the MOST promising method for the management of the earth's wildlife resources?   1_____

   A. Introduction of exotics
   B. B. Habitat development
   C. Predator control
   D. Game laws

2. The element of American society that is MOST responsible for consuming the largest share of energy resources is   2_____

   A. industry
   B. home construction
   C. transportation
   D. recreation

3. Of all the water drawn and transported for irrigation purposes in the United States, APPROXIMATELY _____ percent is eventually absorbed by the root systems of crops.   3_____

   A. 10   B. 25   C. 50   D. 75

4. The APPROXIMATE rate at which the Mississippi River currently carries topsoil into the Gulf of Mexico is _____ tons per _____.   4_____

   A. thirty; minute
   B. one hundred; minute
   C. fifteen; second
   D. fifty; hour

5. According to current projections, it will be approximately _____ years before the world's fossil fuel resources are completely exhausted, given current methods of use.   5_____

   A. thirty-five
   B. fifty
   C. seventy-five
   D. one hundred

6. Each of the following is considered to be a disadvantage to monocultural systems for forest harvesting EXCEPT   6_____

   A. long harvesting rotations
   B. inefficiency in growing and harvesting large crops
   C. runoff from intensive chemical use
   D. creation of oversimplified ecosystems

7. _____ is considered to be among soil's micronutrients.   7_____

   A. Manganese
   B. Nitrate
   C. Potassium
   D. Calcium

8. In relation to the population growth of the United States, what is the increase in per capita rate energy consumption? It is increasing at about _____ rate of population growth.   8_____

   A. half the
   B. the same
   C. twice the
   D. five times the

21

9. Which of the following is NOT considered to be a disadvantage associated with the damming of flowing streams and rivers?

    A. Decreased energy potential
    B. Increased flooding
    C. Sedimentation of reservoirs
    D. Complications with the irrigating process

10. Given the topography of most United States farmland, the one of the following which has NOT proven an efficient method for the control of soil erosion by water is

    A. contour farming
    B. gully reclamation
    C. terracing
    D. planting shelterbelts

11. Of the following natural resources, the one classified as a consumptively used resource, or one whose eventual exhaustion is CERTAIN given current use patterns, is

    A. gem minerals
    B. freshwater fish
    C. stationary water sources
    D. natural gas

12. In forestry, a sustained-yield harvest program, one that produces a moderate crop that can be harvested year after year, is called

    A. silvicultural
    B. clear-cutting
    C. agricultural
    D. monocultural

13. Approximately _____ tons of soil are washed away ANNUALLY from the United States.

    A. fourteen million
    B. fifty-five million
    C. one billion
    D. three billion

14. Each of the following is considered to be a disadvantage associated with *channelization*, or the artificial widening of rivers and streams, EXCEPT

    A. loss of hardwood timber
    B. loss of wildlife habitat
    C. lowering of water table
    D. increased flood risk

15. The MOST defensible (least wasteful) use of aquifer water, according to most current scientists, is to

    A. irrigate monocultural crop systems
    B. relieve drought
    C. provide for industrial cleaning processes
    D. fill existing reservoirs

16. Given the current methods of using fossil fuels, the MOST defensible (least wasteful) one, according to scientists, is

    A. essential liquid fuels
    B. heating
    C. industrial purposes
    D. electricity

17. The annual allotment of acres of _____ rangeland per head is considered to be universally standard for a single cattle animal's grazing.

   A. two   B. four   C. eight   D. twelve

18. APPROXIMATELY _____ percent of the extracted forest product in the United States is used for lumber.

   A. 30   B. 50   C. 70   D. 95

19. _____ is NOT considered to be an influential factor in the depletion of American soil nutrients.

   A. Cropping
   B. Erosion
   C. Pesticide use
   D. Fertilization

20. Which of the following is NOT considered to be a factor contributing to the decline of our freshwater fish resources?

   A. Decreasing habitat temperatures
   B. Toxic industrial waste
   C. Oxygen depletion
   D. Siltation

21. Of the following uses of a metallic natural resource, the one which is NOT generally considered to be consumptive or exhausting is

   A. zinc in galvanized iron
   B. tin in toothpaste tubes
   C. aluminum in cans and containers
   D. lead in gasoline

22. Each of the following is an effect of oil pollution on marine ecosystems EXCEPT

   A. introduction of carcinogens into food chain
   B. acceleration of photosynthetic rates
   C. concentration of chlorinated hydrocarbons
   D. immediate mortality of marine animals

23. The forestry practice of *clear-cutting* is defensively used in the

   A. old-growth firs of the Pacific Northwest
   B. oak groves throughout the Midwest
   C. sequoia groves of Northern California
   D. pine barrens of New Jersey

24. Each of the following is a factor that affects the erosion of soil by water EXCEPT

   A. volume of precipitation
   B. wind patterns
   C. topography of land
   D. type of vegetational cover

25. Which of the following is classified as an inorganic soil fertilizer?

   A. Legumes   B. Manure   C. Sewage   D. Nitrates

KEY (CORRECT ANSWERS)

1. B
2. A
3. B
4. C
5. A

6. B
7. A
8. D
9. C
10. C

11. D
12. A
13. C
14. D
15. B

16. A
17. C
18. A
19. D
20. A

21. C
22. B
23. A
24. B
25. D

EXAMINATION SECTION
TEST 1

DIRECTIONS: Each question or incomplete statement is followed by several suggested answers or completions. Select the one that BEST answers the question or completes the statement. *PRINT THE LETTER OF THE CORRECT ANSWER IN THE SPACE AT THE RIGHT.*

1. The current trend among MOST ecologists is to consider the coastal zones of America

    A. a group of diverse, stable ecosystems whose respective managements require a variety of individual approaches
    B. systems that are unique to this continent and require an entirely different set of management techniques from other continental coast zones
    C. a group of unstable ecosystems whose already fragile balance has been destroyed by modern industrial practices
    D. a single natural ecosystem requiring integration of management techniques

2. Of the following methods for controlling industrial particulate discharge into the air, the one which has the GREATEST potential efficiency is

    A. wet scrubbing
    B. fabric filter bag house
    C. electrostatic precipitation
    D. cyclone filter

3. The process by which objects or solid materials are removed from a water supply is called

    A. straining   B. treatment
    C. screening   D. precipitating

4. All of the following are generally considered obstacles to United States air quality control operations EXCEPT

    A. high number of uncertain cause-effect relationships
    B. resistance from industrial operations
    C. little danger perceived by the public
    D. relatively small number of particulate contaminants that have been identified

5. The MOST critical step in any given industrial waste management program is the

    A. phase separation   B. preliminary investigation
    C. process modification   D. contaminant removal

6. The one of the following that is NOT an option for the control of coastal management offered by the Federal Coastal Management Program is

    A. direct state control
    B. local control subject to state review
    C. local control consistent with state standards
    D. regional control based upon state collaboration

7. The process through which gaseous contaminants are removed from the air is called 7.____

   A. desorption
   B. adsorption
   C. distillation
   D. precipitation

8. An automobile's catalytic converter is designed to keep all of the following contaminants from being discharged into the air EXCEPT 8.____

   A. lead
   B. carbon monoxide
   C. hydrocarbons
   D. nitrogen oxides

9. Which of the following is a chemical process of waste-water treatment? 9.____

   A. Screening
   B. Distillation
   C. Sedimentation
   D. Coagulation

10. The stage that occurs LAST in the treatment process of sanitary sewage is 10.____

    A. sedimentation
    B. screening out solids
    C. biological oxidation
    D. filtering through grit chambers

11. The element of air quality control that can be monitored but NOT managed is 11.____

    A. regulatory standards
    B. emissions
    C. meteorology and dispersion
    D. air quality

12. Currently, the rationale behind MOST water quality control operations is 12.____

    A. public health
    B. aesthetic qualities of water resource
    C. protection of aquatic life
    D. preserving recreational capabilities of water resource

13. In the process of air quality improvement, the practice used as a precleaning process before more efficient methods are applied is called 13.____

    A. electrostatic precipitation
    B. mechanical cleaning
    C. gas conditioning
    D. process modifications

14. Which of the following practiced methods for desaliniza-tion of water makes use of a salt-filtering membrane? 14.____

    A. Freezing
    B. Distillation
    C. Reverse osmosis
    D. Electrodialysis

15. The FUNDAMENTAL criterion for managing coastal basins is the 15.____

    A. geological configuration of the basin
    B. depth of the basin
    C. ecological vitality of the system
    D. degree of water exchange or flushing rate

16. The LEAST desirable method for heating gases that are intended to be released from an air cleaning unit is by

    A. direct combustion
    B. heat exchangers
    C. indirect heating of ambient air
    D. cooling entering gases

17. Of the following stages of conventional wastewater treatment, the one that occurs FIRST is

    A. chlorination
    B. sedimentation
    C. oxidation
    D. discharge

18. The air quality control devices capable of removing BOTH particulate and gaseous contaminants from the air are

    A. cyclone filters
    B. wet scrubbers
    C. adsorbers
    D. filter baghouses

19. The process of restoration is considered acceptable by MOST ecologists if it is implemented to

    A. compensate for an operation that has been projected as being harmful
    B. correct inadvertent harm or past problems
    C. mitigate the damage in advance of a harmful practice
    D. improve the aesthetics of an environment that is near development

20. Turbidity, or ultrafine particle solids in a water supply, are PRIMARILY removed through the process of

    A. screening
    B. distillation
    C. coagulation
    D. oxidation

21. The object of chemical removal processes in air quality control is to

    A. convert gases to particulate matter
    B. increase the water saturation point of the air medium
    C. convert gases into innocuous chemical compounds
    D. vaporize particulate matter

22. Which of the following is NOT a practice associated with the restoration of silt-polluted coastal basins?

    A. Limiting dredging to active vegetative periods
    B. Construction of bulkheads along the shore
    C. Implementation of soil conservation practices in adjacent farmlands
    D. Diversion of runoff waters from basin

23. _____ standards are applied to municipal water control operations to specify the MAXIMUM concentration of certain constituents of a given water supply.

    A. Procedural
    B. Performance
    C. Investigation
    D. Design

24. Which of the following is NOT among the most effective methods for the prevention of aquifer contamination? 24._____

    A. Industrial zoning
    B. Strict chemical storage rules
    C. Trenching
    D. Watershed protection

25. Of the following, the chemical process that is NOT considered a control mechanism for air quality is 25._____

    A. masking
    B. particulate conversion
    C. reduction
    D. oxidation

KEY (CORRECT ANSWERS)

1. D
2. C
3. C
4. C
5. B

6. D
7. B
8. A
9. D
10. C

11. C
12. C
13. B
14. C
15. D

16. A
17. B
18. B
19. B
20. C

21. A
22. A
23. B
24. C
25. A

TEST 2

DIRECTIONS: Each question or incomplete statement is followed by several suggested answers or completions. Select the one that BEST answers the question or completes the statement. *PRINT THE LETTER OF THE CORRECT ANSWER IN THE SPACE AT THE RIGHT.*

1. The term for the process that removes algae or turbidity from a water supply during the water treatment process is

    A. screening
    B. straining
    C. treatment
    D. discharge

    1.____

2. The method for treating groundwater contamination MOST often used for drinking water supplies is _____ treatment.

    A. chemical
    B. carbon
    C. aerobic biological
    D. ozonation/radiation

    2.____

3. Which of the following is NOT one of the primary factors determining the operation of coastal basin management?

    A. Circulation type
    B. Climate
    C. Geology
    D. Depth

    3.____

4. All of the following are practical methods for limiting the discharge of sulfur oxides into the air EXCEPT

    A. desulfurization of oil
    B. limiting coal use to low-sulfur varieties
    C. removal of sulfur from industrial water supplies
    D. removal of sulfur from coal

    4.____

5. The one of the following that is NOT a practice associated with the construction of spoil islands that will protect marina sites in coastal waters is

    A. vegetation with both upland plants and marsh grasses
    B. avoidance of existing vital areas
    C. constructing elliptical islands parallel to water flow
    D. use of fine soil materials in construction

    5.____

6. The FIRST step in any water quality control procedure is

    A. determination of the plant site
    B. compilation of data needed to reach sound decisions about objectives
    C. imposing immediate short-term controls on water quality
    D. establishment of design standards for plant operations

    6.____

7. Of the following methods for controlling industrial particulate discharge into the air, the one that makes use of gravitational forces is

    A. wet scrubbing
    B. fabric filter bag house
    C. electrostatic precipitation
    D. cyclone filter

    7.____

8. An example of a physical process of wastewater treatment is

   A. coagulation
   B. distillation
   C. ion exchange
   D. pH adjustment

9. The type of marine environment that is considered to be MOST in need of management is the

   A. lagoon
   B. bay
   C. ocean
   D. tidal river

10. Of the practiced methods for desalinization of water, the MOST widely used in the United States is

    A. freezing
    B. distillation
    C. reverse osmosis
    D. electrodialysis

11. Each of the following is a noncrystalline adsorbent used to remove contaminants from the air EXCEPT

    A. metallic oxides
    B. activated carbon
    C. silica gel
    D. D, activated alumina

12. The guiding practice of a shorelands management operation is

    A. excavating drainage canals
    B. clearing vegetation
    C. maintaining natural drainage and stream flow
    D. covering land with impervious surfaces

13. In water treatment, the mixing process during which particles form into aggregate masses that settle out is called

    A. osmosis
    B. flocculation
    C. straining
    D. oxidation

14. The type of standards applied to municipal water control operations that specify the required characteristics of a given water supply are _____ standards.

    A. design
    B. performance
    C. procedural
    D. investigation

15. _____ standards are applied to municipal water control operations that define the approaches and methods followed in water quality control activities.

    A. Procedural
    B. Design
    C. Investigation
    D. Performance

16. Marsh-grass plantings are widely used near coastal waters for all of the following purposes EXCEPT

    A. stabilizing dredge spoil
    B. creation of marshes
    C. revitalization of microorganisms
    D. creation of alternative bulkheads

17. Which of the following has NOT been widely attempted as a method for the control of automotive emissions?   17.____

    A. Reduction of automobile traffic in urban areas
    B. Altering the composition of motor fuels
    C. Filtering or converting devices for emissions
    D. Modification of the conventional engine

18. The guiding factor for what is an acceptable MINIMUM flow into coastal ecosystems is the   18.____

    A. sedimentation of inlet basin
    B. strength of tidal backflow
    C. critical survival point for microorganisms
    D. dry-season low flows under natural conditions

19. In preparing water that is to be considered drinkable, the PRIMARY method for odor prevention is   19.____

    A. chlorine-ammonia treatment
    B. fluoridation
    C. flocculation
    D. filtration

20. The MOST effective method for containing a contaminant leakage plume that has deeply penetrated an underground water source is   20.____

    A. trenching
    B. installing a clay barrier
    C. well pumping
    D. chemical or biological treatment

21. The ULTIMATE goal of the 1972 Amendment to the Water Pollution Control Act was   21.____

    A. enforceable standards limiting industrial waste disposal practices in United States waters
    B. total elimination of the discharge of pollutants into navigable United States waters
    C. banning of the production and marketing of harmful water pollutants
    D. elimination of water pollutants categorized as *most dangerous* by the Environmental Protection Agency

22. The process by which contaminant chemicals are removed during the water treatment process is called   22.____

    A. screening   B. sedimentation
    C. straining   D. treatment

23. All of the following are aspects of major concern in the protection of coastal basins EXCEPT   23.____

    A. changes in circulation caused by alteration of basin configuration
    B. degradation of ecological condition of basin and its margins
    C. loss of ecologically vital areas
    D. salinity of basin waters

24. The process of lime coagulation is used to remove _____ from a water supply. 24._____
   A. phosphates
   B. lead
   C. nitrates
   D. iron

25. Of the following, the LEAST effective method for controlling the effect of automotive emissions has been 25._____
   A. parking restrictions in urban areas
   B. carpooling incentives
   C. modification of liquid fuels
   D. toll bridges and highways

KEY (CORRECT ANSWERS)

1. B		11. A	
2. B		12. C	
3. B		13. B	
4. C		14. A	
5. D		15. A	
6. B		16. C	
7. D		17. D	
8. B		18. D	
9. A		19. A	
10. B		20. C	

21. B
22. D
23. D
24. A
25. C

EXAMINATION SECTION
TEST 1

DIRECTIONS: Each question or incomplete statement is followed by several suggested answers or completions. Select the one that BEST answers the question or completes the statement. *PRINT THE LETTER OF THE CORRECT ANSWER IN THE SPACE AT THE RIGHT.*

1. Which one of the following is NOT responsible for wetland formation? 1.____

   A. Glaciation
   B. Vegetation
   C. Erosion
   D. Beaver dams

2. Wetlands which are created adjacent to lakes will result by the deposition of various elements. 2.____
   Which of the following is one of those elements?

   A. Coal B. Wind C. Rain D. Gravel

3. How are wetlands created in the Arctic region? The sun melts the 3.____

   A. underlying soil, while organic soils at the surface remain frozen
   B. surface of frozen river beds, while underlying sediment remains frozen
   C. surface of frozen organic soils, while the underlying soil remains frozen
   D. underlying sediment of river beds, while the surface area remains frozen

4. For a twenty-year period beginning in 1951, which of the following was a MAJOR cause in the increase of wetland acreage in Massachusetts? 4.____

   A. Erosion
   B. Sedimentation
   C. Beaver dams
   D. Thawing

5. The two hydrologic characteristics which have the GREATEST influence in determining the habitat values of a wetland are the_____ and the_____ 5.____

   A. salt content of the water; erosion of soil
   B. depth of the water; fluctuation of water depth
   C. fluctuation of water depth; concentration of plant life
   D. erosion of soil; existence of nearby basins

6. Which type of wetland occurs MOSTLY in shallow lake basins? 6.____

   A. Bog B. Tundra C. Swamp D. Marsh

7. The MAXIMUM depth of inland freshwater marshes is 7.____

   A. 6 inches B. 1 foot C. 2 feet D. 3 feet

8. Inland saline wetlands occur PRIMARILY in which section of the United States? 8.____

   A. Eastern B. Southern C. Western D. Northern

9. Pocosins are a type of 9.____

   A. tundra B. marsh C. swamp D. bog

33

10. Which description would BEST fit the type of vegetation found in tundras? 10.____

    A. Spongy, undecayed, saturated with water
    B. Woody undecayed, unsaturated
    C. Willows, button bush, and dogwoods exist
    D. Plant include water lilies and reeds

11. Riparian habitats describe areas adjacent to 11.____

    A. forests   B. lakes   C. streams   D. mountains

12. In the United States, mangroves are found PRIMARILY along the coastal regions of what state? 12.____

    A. Florida   B. Maine
    C. Georgia   D. Mississippi

13. Which of the following CORRECTLY identifies two states in which tidal freshwater wetlands are found? 13.____

    A. Texas and Maine   B. Delaware and Alabama
    C. New York and Maryland   D. Virginia and New Jersey

14. Which of the following states would NOT be a location for wooded swamps? 14.____

    A. Georgia   B. Ohio   C. Michigan   D. Wisconsin

15. Wetlands provide several ecological services.
    Which one of the following is NOT an ecological service? 15.____

    A. Groundwater recharge   B. Prime development location
    C. Floodpeak reduction   D. Shoreline erosion control

16. Four characteristics of vegetated wetlands are responsible for reducing shoreline erosion.
    Which one of the following is NOT one of these characteristics? 16.____

    A. Absorption of wave energy by the plants
    B. The low gradient of the shore that dissipates wave energy
    C. The deposition of suspended sediment
    D. The occurrence of tidal currents

17. Two nutrients which are necessary for the growth of algae are nitrogen and 17.____

    A. carbon   B. phosphorus   C. hydrogen   D. calcium

18. Wetlands comprise APPROXIMATELY _____% of the area of Alaska. 18.____

    A. 20   B. 40   C. 60   D. 80

19. Wetlands comprise APPROXIMATELY _____% of the area of the contiguous United States (excluding Alaska and Hawaii). 19.____

    A. 5   B. 15   C. 25   D. 35

20. The red-bellied turtle is considered an endangered species whose territory is 20.____

    A. Maine
    B. Massachusetts
    C. Rhode Island
    D. Vermont

21. One of the Federal agencies empowered to protect wetlands is the NMFS, whose initials stand for 21.____

    A. Natural Maritime Fisheries Service
    B. National Maritime Forestry Service
    C. Natural Marine Forestry Service
    D. National Marine Fisheries Service

22. Federal income tax write-offs are provided as incentives for farmers to drain wetlands for agricultural use. 22.____
    A tax deduction up to _____ percent of gross farm income is allowed in a single year.

    A. 10   B. 20   C. 25   D. 30

23. Which one of the following development activities is considered to be the MAJOR source of Alaskan wetland losses? 23.____

    A. Filling
    B. Excavating
    C. Draining
    D. Flooding

24. Present nationwide rates of wetland conversion are only half of those measured during the 1950's and 1960's. This reduction is PRIMARILY due to 24.____

    A. government programs
    B. agricultural drainage
    C. urbanization
    D. mining

25. The average annual net-loss rate for vegetated wetlands in the lower 48 states from the mid-1950's to the mid-1970's was about _____ acres. 25.____

    A. 250,000   B. 1,000,000   C. 500,000   D. 750,000

KEY (CORRECT ANSWERS)

1. B
2. D
3. C
4. C
5. B

6. A
7. D
8. C
9. D
10. A

11. C
12. A
13. D
14. B
15. B

16. D
17. B
18. C
19. A
20. B

21. D
22. C
23. A
24. B
25. C

EXAMINATION SECTION
TEST 1

DIRECTIONS: Each question or incomplete statement is followed by several suggested answers or completions. Select the one that BEST answers the question or completes the statement. *PRINT THE LETTER OF THE CORRECT ANSWER IN THE SPACE AT THE RIGHT.*

1. Each of the following is an example of a biome EXCEPT the   1.____

    A. North American prairie
    B. Grand Canyon
    C. tropical rain forest
    D. grasslands of the sub-Sahara

2. When an aquatic environment experiences an explosion in the population of microorganisms, the organisms later die and decompose, causing a chain reaction of death and decay until the body of water becomes marshy.   2.____
    This process is called

    A. eutrophication   B. putrefaction
    C. aerobiosis   D. biodegradation

3. The total weight of all the living organisms in any given system is called   3.____

    A. ecotone   B. biomass
    C. demography   D. census

4. What is the name for an organism, usually a mold or fungus, that consumes the tissue of dead plants or animals?   4.____

    A. Parasite   B. Epiphyte
    C. Saprophyte   D. Autotroph

5. The term for an arctic or mountainous area that is too cold to support trees and is vegetated with low mosses and grasses is   5.____

    A. savanna   B. taiga   C. steppe   D. tundra

6. In a body of water, microscopic free-floating organisms that photosynthesize their own food are called   6.____

    A. krill   B. zooplankton
    C. phytoplankton   D. plasma

7. Animals that receive their energy from direct consumption of plant matter are called _____ consumers.   7.____

    A. primary   B. secondary
    C. tertiary   D. quaternary

8. Each of the following is one of the principal reasons, imposed by humans, for the extinction of modern species EXCEPT   8.____

    A. imposed breeding combinations
    B. destruction of habitat

C. introduction of foreign species
D. extermination of predators

9. When an ecosystem has reached a final stage of development in which it can only be changed by some outside agent, such as the introduction of another species, this is called a

   A. critical level
   B. climax community
   C. saturation
   D. plateau

10. Which of the following animals are MOST likely to exhibit territorial behaviors?

    A. Large grazing mammals
    B. Small predatory mammals
    C. Fishes
    D. Birds

11. Which of the types of associations below does NOT result in a positive effect for both species involved in the relationship?

    A. Symbiosis
    B. Commensalism
    C. Parasitism
    D. Mutualism

12. A plant (such as moss) that grows on another plant but does not use the host plant for food is called a(n)

    A. osmotroph
    B. epiphyte
    C. fungus
    D. phagocyte

13. What is the term for organic matter that is in the soil and is characterized by slow decomposition?

    A. Topsoil
    B. Substrate
    C. Subsoil
    D. Humus

14. Evolution involves changing gene frequencies resulting from each of the following EXCEPT

    A. genetic drift
    B. selection pressure from the environment and interacting species
    C. learned survival behaviors
    D. recurrent mutations

15. What is the name for a partially enclosed coastal body of shallow water that has a free connection with the open sea?

    A. Delta
    B. Estuary
    C. Bay
    D. Aquifer

16. Autotrophs are organisms that obtain their energy

    A. directly from the sun
    B. through the consumption of plant matter
    C. through predation of other animals
    D. from decomposing plant and animal tissues

17. When the common gene pool's genetic flow is interrupted by an isolating mechanism, resulting in species diversity or the formation of a new species, what natural selection process has occurred?

    A. Mutation
    B. Speciation
    C. Character displacement
    D. Gestation

17.____

18. The surface volume of water in the ocean or a large lake that receives enough light to support photosynthesis is called the _____ zone.

    A. benthic
    B. eukaryotic
    C. littoral
    D. euphotic

18.____

19. Which of the following is NOT capable of transforming molecular nitrogen into forms that are usable by living organisms?

    A. Photochemical reactions
    B. Lightning
    C. Specialized bacteria and algae
    D. Atmospheric pressure

19.____

20. What kind of ecosystems GENERALLY characterize temperate areas with low rainfall?

    A. Desert
    B. Prairie
    C. Deciduous forest
    D. Tundra

20.____

21. All the non-living organic matter in an ecosystem is known collectively as

    A. ore   B. plankton   C. detritus   D. particulate

21.____

22. In regions where chemical air pollutants have darkened the surrounding trees, some species of moths adapt by shifting their population's coloring from light to dark. This adaptation is known as

    A. industrial melanism
    B. homeostasis
    C. genetic osmosis
    D. natural succession

22.____

23. In the United States, which of the following species has made the most successful adaptation to the growth and expansion of human populations?

    A. Mountain lion
    B. Bighorn sheep
    C. Deer
    D. Bison

23.____

24. The vertebrate animals that appear FIRST on the evolutionary record are

    A. birds   B. fish   C. reptiles   D. mammals

24.____

25. All organisms that obtain their energy from sources other than sunlight are known collectively as

    A. autotrophs
    B. primary consumers
    C. heterotrophs
    D. omnivores

25.____

KEY (CORRECT ANSWERS)

1.	B	11.	C
2.	A	12.	B
3.	B	13.	D
4.	C	14.	C
5.	D	15.	B
6.	C	16.	A
7.	A	17.	B
8.	A	18.	D
9.	B	19.	D
10.	D	20.	B

21. C
22. A
23. C
24. B
25. C

TEST 2

DIRECTIONS: Each question or incomplete statement is followed by several suggested answers or completions. Select the one that BEST answers the question or completes the statement. *PRINT THE LETTER OF THE CORRECT ANSWER IN THE SPACE AT THE RIGHT.*

1. Dystrophic lakes are characterized by which of the following conditions?　　1.____

    A. High concentrations of calcium and oxygen
    B. Inadequate decomposition of matter
    C. Lack of photosynthetic organisms
    D. Large number and variety of organisms

2. Which of the animals below is generally considered to have the LEAST complex social order among members of its species?　　2.____

    A. African lion
    B. Honeybee
    C. North American alligator
    D. Canada goose

3. The taiga is the　　3.____

    A. coniferous forest of the northern latitudes of North America
    B. scrub desert of Southwestern North America
    C. temperate deciduous forest of Eurasia
    D. subtropical grasslands of Africa

4. The uppermost trees on a mountain slope inhabit an area known as the　　4.____

    A. Longren   B. tundra   C. humus   D. Krummholz

5. Which of the following organisms is likely to be MORE abundant in a swiftly-moving stream than in a slow stream?　　5.____

    A. Phytoplankton   B. Fish
    C. Crayfish   D. Zooplankton

6. A wheat field has an inherent ability to support more locusts than a short-grass prairie. Therefore, it is said to have a _____ for locusts.　　6.____

    A. commensal requirement
    B. greater environmental resistance
    C. more limiting habitat
    D. larger carrying capacity

7. The place where wildlife lives is called　　7.____

    A. habitat   B. pasture   C. home   D. tundra

8. The unique function of a particular species, along with its habitat, are known together as its　　8.____

    A. home range   B. critical level
    C. ecotone   D. ecological niche

41

9. Which of the types of wild species below probably has the LOWEST risk of extinction in the modern world?   9.____

    A. Highly specialized or immobile organisms
    B. Animals that aggregate and migrate in large groups
    C. Large grazing animals
    D. Large carnivorous predators

10. With what kind of species association do wild rose bushes and mountain lions interact?   10.____

    A. Competition   B. Parasitism
    C. Neutralism   D. Mutualism

11. Which of the bird species below is currently the LEAST endangered in the United States?   11.____

    A. Bald eagle   B. Ivory-billed woodpecker
    C. California condor   D. Whooping crane

12. When populations of differing species become dependent on each other for survival, the relationship is described as   12.____

    A. neutralism   B. mutualism
    C. unibiosis   D. parasitism

13. Which of the organisms below is an example of an ungulate?   13.____

    A. Rhesus monkey   B. Kodiak bear
    C. Tule elk   D. Cheetah

14. Large North American carnivores such as the timber wolf and the black bear generally prey upon the same types of animal species.
    Therefore, they are said to share the same   14.____

    A. habitat   B. food chain
    C. ecological niche   D. trophic level

15. Which is the LIKELIEST result of overcrowding on a species population?   15.____

    A. Immediate adaptation
    B. Forced migration
    C. An explosion in predation
    D. Reduced reproductive yield

16. Respiration that takes place without the presence of oxygen is described as   16.____

    A. antibiotic   B. carbonic
    C. anaerobic   D. unsaturated

17. Environmental resistance is the   17.____

    A. natural resilience of the environment to disturbances from outside sources
    B. tendency of ecosystems to remain the same over a period of time
    C. environmental interactions which collectively inhibit the growth of a species
    D. worldwide industrial practices that repeatedly damage the natural environment

18. Which of the animals below is characterized by a matriarchal social order?   18.____

    A. African elephant   B. Mountain gorilla
    C. Caribou   D. American bald eagle

19. In the months after lava flow has cooled and settle on a Hawaiian island, the area is gradually populated by ferns and lichens.   19.____
    Which successional stage does this represent?

    A. Primary   B. Secondary   C. Tertiary   D. Quaternary

20. With what kind of species association do intertidal barnacles and mussels interact?   20.____

    A. Competition   B. Parasitism
    C. Neutralism   D. Mutualism

21. Which of the following ecosystems below is an example of a climax system?   21.____
    A(n)

    A. woodland meadow   B. old-growth redwood forest
    C. inland marsh   D. small wooded pond

22. In a climate that is milder than that of the coniferous forest, where rainfall is abundant relative to evaporation, what kind of ecological community would be MOST likely?   22.____

    A. Tundra   B. Tallgrass prairie
    C. Short-grass prairie   D. Deciduous forest

23. The middle waters of a lake, where oxygen content falls off rapidly with depth, are the   23.____

    A. hypolimnion   B. benthic zone
    C. thermocline   D. euphotic zone

24. The control mechanisms within an ecosystem that maintain constancy by resisting external stresses are known collectively as   24.____

    A. homeostasis   B. contrapuntal mechanisms
    C. environmental resistance D. heterotrophic modulation

25. Biotic potential is the   25.____

    A. largest possible size of an individual organism
    B. range of adaptive flexibility for an organism in a given environment
    C. maximum rate of growth for a species population
    D. range of possibilities for an evolving ecosystem

KEY (CORRECT ANSWERS)

1.	B	11.	A
2.	C	12.	B
3.	A	13.	C
4.	D	14.	B
5.	C	15.	D
6.	D	16.	C
7.	A	17.	C
8.	D	18.	A
9.	B	19.	A
10.	C	20.	A

21. B
22. D
23. C
24. A
25. C

EXAMINATION SECTION
TEST 1

DIRECTIONS: Each question or incomplete statement is followed by several suggested answers or completions. Select the one that BEST answers the question or completes the statement. *PRINT THE LETTER OF THE CORRECT ANSWER IN THE SPACE AT THE RIGHT.*

1. Which of the following is NOT a factor contributing to slower evaporation rates in areas sheltered by trees?

    A. The reduced capacity of cool, moist forest air to absorb evaporated water
    B. The prevention of evaporation by layers of leaf mold on forest soil
    C. The slightly higher rainfall in forested areas
    D. Tree foliage acting as a windbreak to block the introduction of drier air

1.____

2. Which of the following is NOT an effect of a tree's competition with other trees in a forest community?

    A. Outward spreading of crowns
    B. Natural pruning of lower branches
    C. Rapid upward growth of crowns
    D. Overlap of side-branching leaves

2.____

3. The part of a tree's trunk that is no longer living is called

    A. sapwood
    B. heartwood
    C. cambium
    D. inner bark

3.____

4. Which of the following is NOT a silvicultural system for harvesting lumber?

    A. Localized selection
    B. The strip system
    C. Two-storied seed
    D. Clear-cutting

4.____

5. Solid organic products of a tree's photosynthesis USUALLY end up

    A. in the center of the tree
    B. in the leaves
    C. stored in the roots
    D. in the thin layer between wood and bark

5.____

6. A tree in a forest community serves the well-being of its neighbors in each of the following ways EXCEPT

    A. protection from wind
    B. shielding leaves from direct sunlight
    C. enriching the earth through fallen twigs and foliage
    D. keeping the surrounding air cooler in warm weather

6.____

7. Unforested watersheds are different in appearance from forested watersheds. The PRIMARY difference is that unforested watersheds

    A. are marked by furrows and canyons
    B. are less abundant in wildlife
    C. erode more slowly
    D. are more likely to contain large bodies of water

7.____

8. Which of the following is NOT one of the main requirements for a forest to be of the best service to humans who practice conservative forestry?

    A. Protection from elements such as fire and overgrazing
    B. Wide expanses of space between each tree
    C. Strong and abundant reproduction
    D. A regular supply of harvestable trees

9. Which of the following elements is NOT one of the chief components of wood?

    A. Nitrogen   B. Oxygen   C. Carbon   D. Hydrogen

10. The release of water vapor into the air from a tree's leaves is called

    A. photosynthesis   B. osmosis
    C. transpiration   D. ossification

11. In forestry terminology, which of the following represents the more advanced stage of growth for a tree?

    A. Small pole   B. Standard
    C. Veteran   D. Large sapling

12. Trees in a forest community compete for each of the following EXCEPT

    A. growing space   B. sunlight
    C. cooler air   D. water

13. The inner side of a tree's cambium layer forms

    A. wood   B. bark   C. pith   D. leaves

14. The tallest trees of any species are USUALLY found in

    A. gently sloping hillsides
    B. low-lying valley land
    C. the upper slopes of high mountains
    D. far northern latitudes

15. Which of the following negative environmental side effects is made possible by preserving sections of forest as national park land?

    A. Decrease in nationwide lumber revenue
    B. Trampling of potential germinating ground by visitors
    C. Severe pollution of forest air by visiting automobiles
    D. Contamination of forest water supply

16. In contrast to conservative forestry, ordinary or destructive forestry

    A. is practiced according to a working plan for harvesting a crop
    B. does not usually affect trees that are left standing during the harvest
    C. regards the forest as working capital that will provide successive crops
    D. produces higher short-term yields

17. Winged seeds are successful PRIMARILY because

    A. their whirl simulates a drilling motion that will help plant the seed
    B. their slow downward motion increases the possibility of lateral dispersion
    C. their roots are more likely to penetrate dense needle or leaf cover on the ground
    D. they are usually heavy enough to remain planted

18. In comparison to wood harvested from dense forest growth, wood from trees that are spaced widely apart tends to be

    A. harder   B. less combustible
    C. knottier   D. softer

19. The MAIN reason that forest temperatures are generally cooler than surrounding environments is that

    A. water contained in leaves is more difficult to warm than solid organic matter
    B. forests generally grow in more northern latitudes
    C. forests receive less light
    D. trees do not generate as much heat as other living creatures

20. The outer side of a tree's cambium layer forms

    A. leaves   B. bark   C. twigs   D. wood

21. Which of the following is NOT an element of most conservative foresting systems?

    A. Rules for the selection and marking of trees
    B. Ensuring future reproduction of forest trees
    C. Planting saplings in harvested areas
    D. Estimating the revenue of future yields

22. In addition to respiration through leaves, trees breathe through openings in the bark called

    A. ventricles   B. lenticels   C. spiracles   D. organelles

23. If the amount of wood that grows in a healthy forest repeatedly exceeds the amount harvested, the EVENTUAL result will be

    A. a continual increase in the harvestable forest crop
    B. a supply of healthy wood that is greater than the current demand
    C. a dramatic change in the forest ecosystem
    D. overmature, decaying trees that are not useful to human purposes

24. Mineral constituents of a tree's organic matter

    A. are released through the leaves during photosynthesis
    B. are the primary ingredient of wood
    C. reappear as ashes when any part of the tree is burned
    D. are what give chlorophyll its green color

25. The act of lighting a fire that is designed to move against the wind toward a forest fire and compete with it for fuel is called

    A. creating a fire line   B. back-firing
    C. dousing   D. brush-firing

KEY (CORRECT ANSWERS)

1.	C	11.	C
2.	C	12.	C
3.	B	13.	A
4.	D	14.	B
5.	D	15.	B
6.	B	16.	D
7.	A	17.	B
8.	B	18.	C
9.	A	19.	A
10.	C	20.	B

21.	C
22.	B
23.	D
24.	C
25.	B

EXAMINATION SECTION
TEST 1

DIRECTIONS: Each question or incomplete statement is followed by several suggested answers or completions. Select the one that BEST answers the question or completes the statement. *PRINT THE LETTER OF THE CORRECT ANSWER IN THE SPACE AT THE RIGHT.*

1. On the average, which months of the year present the GREATEST wildfire hazard due to low relative humidity? 1.____
    A. April-May
    B. June-July
    C. August-September
    D. October-November

2. To cut vegetation just above ground level, the tool MOST often used by firefighters is the 2.____
    A. round-point shovel
    B. barron tool
    C. axe
    D. brush hook

3. Using fire engines rather than aircraft would NOT be an advantage because they 3.____
    A. have less restricted access to fire sites
    B. can be used at night
    C. can carry water in varying capacities
    D. are not greatly restricted by visibility

4. On any sizable wildland fire, the LARGEST portion of suppression personnel is *usually* made up of 4.____
    A. logistics personnel
    B. hand crews
    C. air attack personnel
    D. demobilization units

5. Each of the following stages in the fire-fighting process requires sizing-up EXCEPT 5.____
    A. reception of the first call for a fire
    B. traveling to the fire site
    C. arrival at the fire site
    D. after mopping up the fire

6. The recommended MINIMUM width of a fire line constructed in brush fuels of medium density is _____ feet. 6.____
    A. 3   B. 6   C. 9   D. 12

7. Each of the following conditions is likely to *increase* the effectiveness of firefighting air-tankers EXCEPT 7.____
    A. predomination of grass or light brush fuel
    B. fire incidence extending past mid-afternoon
    C. increased steepness of site topography
    D. decrease in wind movement

8. The pincer action is employed when crews attack a fire 8.____
    A. along both flanks of a fire, pushing them gradually toward the head, or front
    B. from both the front and the heel of a fire

49

C. along one flank of a fire to protect exposed area
D. from many points, in different directions

9. In firefighting terms, a fire's spread is considered moderate if its rate is

    A. of no consequence
    B. less than one mile per hour
    C. less than three miles per hour
    D. less than five miles per hour

10. During the hottest part of the day, _____ exposures of a given area will USUALLY contain the highest fuel temperatures.

    A. north and south
    B. east and west
    C. south and west
    D. north and east

11. Which of the following is NOT a danger created by late spring rains on grazing land?

    A. Matting of grasses close to the ground
    B. Removal of protective dust cover
    C. Leaching action in curing grasses that make them less palatable to livestock
    D. Increase in short-term fire risk

12. During the day, winds on a slope will GENERALLY

    A. blow uphill
    B. blow downhill
    C. blow across the slope in one direction
    D. gust in varying directions across the slope

13. The temperature at any given altitude at which the air becomes completely saturated with moisture is referred to as the

    A. relative humidity
    B. aspect
    C. apex
    D. dew point

14. In order to adequately serve the needs of a fire crew, the water pump on a wildland engine should have a capacity of AT LEAST _____ gallons per minute.

    A. 75   B. 250   C. 500   D. 1000

15. Usually, the MOST dangerous point from which to attack a wildfire directly is from

    A. uphill
    B. the heel
    C. a leeward flank
    D. an anchor point

16. A *convection column* is a term referring to

    A. an inversion in the normal pattern of heat distribution in the air
    B. a direct assault upon the head of an advancing fire
    C. a current of air rising through a fire
    D. the landward course of marine wind currents

17. Which type of cloud formation usually indicates the MOST adverse atmospheric conditions for firefighting?

    A. Stratus
    B. Cirrus
    C. Cirrostratus
    D. Cumulus

18. The effect of wildfire on soils is USUALLY

    A. a lowering of the water repellent layer
    B. combustion of mineral elements
    C. a scorched, watertight seal at ground level
    D. extraction of important soil nutrients

19. A wildfire's point of origin is referred to as its

    A. heel
    B. anchor point
    C. green
    D. hot spot

20. When an airtanker drops its retardant from one tank at a time, at widely spread intervals on the same site, which pattern of release is it using?

    A. Vortex   B. Burst   C. Split   D. Salvo

21. The firefighter's hand tool that is shaped like a hoe on one side and a rake on the other is the

    A. pulaski
    B. barron tool
    C. axe
    D. brush hook

22. Which of the following is NOT a disadvantage in attacking a wildfire directly?

    A. It exposes firefighters to flame and smoke.
    B. It results in the construction of an irregular and longer fire line.
    C. Normally, it does not take advantage of natural or manmade fire barriers.
    D. It does not eliminate fuels at the fire's edge.

23. Which of the following is NOT an advantage in clearing potential fire fuels by hand?

    A. Selective pruning of trees and brush
    B. Minimum disturbance of fuel break site
    C. Relatively rapid progress
    D. Leaves soil layer intact

24. In order to control a fire that is burning in an area of medium brush fuel, what is the APPROXIMATE guideline rate, in feet per hour, for the deployment of a fire line?

    A. 225   B. 300   C. 450   D. 900

25. The expansion of a fire's smoke column at higher altitudes is due to a widening of air currents, or

    A. convection
    B. entraining
    C. subduction
    D. trailing

KEY (CORRECT ANSWERS)

1.	B	11.	D
2.	D	12.	A
3.	A	13.	D
4.	B	14.	B
5.	D	15.	A
6.	B	16.	C
7.	C	17.	D
8.	A	18.	A
9.	B	19.	C
10.	C	20.	C

21. B
22. D
23. C
24. C
25. B

TEST 2

DIRECTIONS: Each question or incomplete statement is followed by several suggested answers or completions. Select the one that BEST answers the question or completes the statement. *PRINT THE LETTER OF THE CORRECT ANSWER IN THE SPACE AT THE RIGHT.*

1. In timber fires, an upward-spreading burn that creates enough heat to advance horizontally through treetops without regard to the surface fire is called a(n) _____ crown fire.

    A. passive
    B. active
    C. independent
    D. lateral

    1._____

2. According to the National Wildfire Coordinating Group, a wildland fire is categorized as *large* if it consumes more than

    A. 30 acres of timber
    B. 100 acres of brush
    C. 400 acres of woodland
    D. 700 acres of grass

    2._____

3. When fuel moisture is uniformly below five percent,

    A. fine fuels (grasses and brush) and heavy fuels (logs) burn at the same rate
    B. fine fuels burn more quickly than heavy fuels
    C. heavy fuels burn more quickly than fine fuels
    D. heavy fuels burn and spread while fine fuels extinguish themselves

    3._____

4. Of the following ecosystem types, which one averages the HIGHEST frequency of naturally-occurring wildfires?

    A. Prairie
    B. Dry temperate forest
    C. Desert scrub
    D. Boreal forest

    4._____

5. Which of the following animals is MOST likely to increase the likelihood of fire in a forested area?

    A. Tree-dwelling birds
    B. Beaver
    C. Squirrels
    D. Grazing animals

    5._____

6. Generally, the SAFEST spot from which to engage in a direct attack on a fire site is

    A. a good distance upslope from the fire
    B. right on the fire's edge
    C. behind the fire, in already burned areas
    D. a few feet from the head of the fire

    6._____

7. What is usually recommended as the MINIMUM length of hose, in feet, for the reels on a wildland engine?

    A. 50   B. 150   C. 300   D. 500

    7._____

8. In general, the condition which is responsible for MOST firefighting injuries and emergencies is

    A. sudden wind shift
    B. fire running upslope
    C. equipment failure
    D. sudden wind shift

    8._____

53

9. _____ action is the term for an indirect attack in which high fire intensity requires control lines to be established well in advance of the fire perimeter.

   A. Confinement B. Flanking
   C. Protective D. Area control

10. A scratch line is

    A. an unfinished, preliminary control line designed to check the fire's spread
    B. the line marking a fire's origin, usually located downslope from the head
    C. the systematic firebreak dug out by hand crews along the fire's perimeter
    D. the border between burned-out land and green vegetation

11. The direction in which the slope of a hill or mountain faces is known as its

    A. berm B. aspect
    C. inversion D. azimuth

12. All forest fires are classified by type under the category Class

    A. A B. B C. C D. D

13. What is cold trailing?

    A. Setting a fire in the center of a fire site to create a strong indraft
    B. Fighting a fire from inside the burned-out area
    C. Controlling a partly-dead fire edge to dig out and trench live spots
    D. Dropping an aircraft regardant payload in a continuous line over the fire site

14. What is the recommended MINIMUM width, in feet, of a fire line constructed in grass fuels?

    A. 3 B. 6 C. 9 D. 12

15. In order to safely set a prescribed fire, what level of humidity is considered to be ACCEPTABLE?

    A. 10-20% B. 25-35% C. 40-50% D. 65-75%

16. In a wildfire's column, the area between the combustion zone and the convection zone is known as the _____ zone.

    A. smoke fallout B. condensation convection
    C. transition D. fuel

17. What is the firefighting term for the layer of partly decomposed organic material of the forest floor that lies beneath the litter of freshly fallen leaves, needles, and twigs?

    A. Slash B. Duff C. Eddy D. Snag

18. The directional device used to locate fires, consisting of a straightedge fixed with sights, is called a(n)

    A. sextant B. sight line
    C. alidade D. azimuth

19. The burning pattern of an extremely violent fire, caused by many spot fires interacting on each other, is known as a(n) _____ pattern.

    A. time
    B. spotty
    C. burnout
    D. area ignition

20. A hand tool with an axe blade at one end and a hoe-type cutting edge at the other, used by firefighters to scrape and grub out roots, is the

    A. round-point shovel
    B. Mcleod tool
    C. pulaski
    D. brush hook

21. Which of the following is NOT an advantage associated with the use of portable pumps by firefighters?

    A. High efficiency in application of water
    B. Ability to draft water from a number of static sources
    C. Lightweight and easy to carry for long periods of time
    D. Provides access to all areas of the fire perimeter

22. When an airtanker releases its payload in an overlapping series from 2 to 8 tanks, a _____ pattern is being employed.

    A. salvo
    B. trail
    C. vortex
    D. split

23. What is the APPROXIMATE temperature, in degrees F., at which woody fuels will burst into flame?

    A. 212
    B. 320
    C. 540
    D. 920

24. The MAIN cause of irregular spread patterns in fires that burn in deeply sloped sites is

    A. erratic wind movements
    B. numerous natural fire barriers
    C. roll of burning debris
    D. uneven distribution of moisture

25. A break or change in the natural vegetation which might impede the progress of future fires is, in firefighting terms, called a

    A. fuel break
    B. fire line
    C. firebreak
    D. backfire

KEY (CORRECT ANSWERS)

1.	C	11.	B
2.	A	12.	A
3.	A	13.	C
4.	A	14.	A
5.	C	15.	B
6.	B	16.	C
7.	B	17.	B
8.	B	18.	C
9.	D	19.	D
10.	A	20.	C

21. C
22. B
23. C
24. C
25. A

———

EXAMINATION SECTION
TEST 1

DIRECTIONS: Each question or incomplete statement is followed by several suggested answers or completions. Select the one that BEST answers the question or completes the statement. *PRINT THE LETTER OF THE CORRECT ANSWER IN THE SPACE AT THE RIGHT.*

1. In order to control a fire that is burning in an area of grassy fuel, what is the APPROXIMATE guideline rate, in feet per hour, for the deployment of a fire line?   1.____

    A. 225　　　　　B. 300　　　　　C. 450　　　　　D. 900

2. In comparison to fine fuels such as grass and brush, heavy fuels, such as logs, are USUALLY   2.____

    A. wetter on the surface
    B. lower in temperature during the day
    C. drier at any given time of day
    D. lower in temperature at night

3. The burning pattern of a fast-moving fire with a well-defined perimeter is known as a(n) _____ pattern.   3.____

    A. time　　　　　　　　　　B. spotty
    C. burnout　　　　　　　　D. area ignition

4. For small point fires, the vehicle used MOST often by firefighters is the   4.____

    A. pickup pumper　　　　　B. engine
    C. aircraft　　　　　　　　　D. water tender

5. Which of the following is NOT an advantage of an indirect attack on a wildfire?   5.____

    A. The amount of total fire line is limited
    B. The burned area is decided beforehand according to a plan
    C. Reduction in the loss of resources, compared to other methods
    D. Mopping-up exercises are reduced

6. If the slope of a fire site doubles, the corresponding result in the rate of the fire's spread   6.____

    A. is cut in half
    B. remains about the same
    C. is also doubled
    D. becomes four times greater

7. In general, the TALLEST flames in any wildfire can be found   7.____

    A. at the heel　　　　　　　B. at the head
    C. on the leeward flank　　D. on the windward flank

8. The transfer of heat energy from particle to particle of matter, by contact, is   8.____

    A. conduction　　　　　　　B. conflagration
    C. convection　　　　　　　D. envelopment

57

9. In firefighting terms, *report time* is the time elapsed from the

   A. start of the fire until its discovery
   B. discovery of the fire to the notification of the first person to perform work on it
   C. first work on the fire until a holding control line is established
   D. completion of organized mop-up until a fire is declared out

10. What is the term for a free-flowing prevailing wind that moves at an elevation where it is not influenced by topography?

   A. Gradient   B. Chinook   C. Gale   D. Foehn

11. A trench dug in front of a hand line is PRIMARILY used for

   A. a static water source for portable pumps
   B. prevention of leeward spot fires
   C. interception of downward-rolling burning materials
   D. emergency shelter for hand crews

12. _____ feet of 1 1/2" hose is usually recommended as a MINIMUM complement to the wildland engine's equipment.

   A. 200-500
   B. 500-800
   C. 800-1,000
   D. 1,000-1,500

13. During situations of possible danger, the pilot of an airtanker can reduce risks to the ground crew by doing each of the following EXCEPT

   A. flying parallel with the fire line
   B. communicating the moment of drop to the ground crew
   C. remaining high until the moment of actual drop
   D. making protective drops near the crew before moving upslope

14. The device that gives a helicopter its widest area of retardant coverage is a

   A. dump tank
   B. blower
   C. helitorch
   D. spray boom

15. The progressive hose lay, a configuration that makes the most use of *tees* and *laterals*, is more likely than others to be used to

   A. knock down flare-ups along the fire's flanks
   B. attack the head directly
   C. control hot spots
   D. construct parallel fire lines

16. How far into the soil does the heat from an average wildfire penetrate?

   A. A few centimeters
   B. 6-12 inches
   C. 1-3 feet
   D. 6-12 feet

17. The firefighting term for the forest debris left by logging, pruning, thinning, or brush cutting is

   A. duff   B. snag   C. scratch   D. slash

18. *Burning out* is a term referring to

    A. removal, by intentional burning, of unburned fuels inside the fire line
    B. the full suppression of a wildfire
    C. setting fires in the center of a broad fire site in order to create indrafts
    D. the gradual, natural process of a fire's decline that is not affected by firefighting efforts

19. The term for the method of determining a fire's location by using intersecting lines of sight from two different points is

    A. convection   B. indexing
    C. cross-shooting   D. inversion

20. A *holdover fire* is a type of fire

    A. caused by windblown burning material from a main fire
    B. extending beyond the predicted range of spread
    C. requiring the use of personnel from all available units
    D. remaining dormant for a considerable time by smoldering through undergrowth and vegetable soil

21. In firefighting terms, the time elapsed from the report of a fire to the first effective worker until the worker responds to the report is called _____ time.

    A. getaway   B. report   C. control   D. travel

22. To initially knock down flare-ups that occur in front of a hose line, the nozzle operator should apply water in a _____ the flare-up.

    A. stream aimed directly at
    B. narrow-angled fog aimed directly at
    C. wide-angled fog aimed directly at
    D. stream aimed slightly uphill from

23. When fuel moisture is uniformly above fifteen percent,

    A. fine fuels (grasses and brush) and heavy fuels (logs) burn at the same rate
    B. fine fuels burn more quickly than heavy fuels
    C. heavy fuels burn more quickly than fine fuels
    D. heavy fuels burn and spread while fine fuels extinguish themselves

24. A swirl of air that is situated within the main current is a(n)

    A. column   B. finger   C. eddy   D. whirlwind

25. To scrape the fire line down to the level of mineral soils that will not burn, a firefighter MOST often uses the

    A. round-point shovel   B. barron tool
    C. axe   D. brush hook

KEY (CORRECT ANSWERS)

1.	D	11.	C
2.	B	12.	D
3.	A	13.	A
4.	A	14.	D
5.	C	15.	C
6.	D	16.	A
7.	B	17.	D
8.	A	18.	A
9.	B	19.	C
10.	A	20.	D

21. A
22. A
23. D
24. C
25. A

TEST 2

DIRECTIONS: Each question or incomplete statement is followed by several suggested answers or completions. Select the one that BEST answers the question or completes the statement. *PRINT THE LETTER OF THE CORRECT ANSWER IN THE SPACE AT THE RIGHT.*

1. The firefighting term for a standing dead tree from which the leaves and smaller branches have fallen is

    A. snag   B. slash   C. stump   D. duff

    1._____

2. An undercut line is

    A. the level beneath a fire to which heat will penetrate
    B. a line marking the minimum estimated range of a fire's spread
    C. a special type of hose used to penetrate into the bottom-most layer of fuel
    D. a fire line constructed below a fire on a slope

    2._____

3. The act of throwing mineral soil around the base of an unlighted tree stalk in order to prevent ignition is

    A. backfiring   B. banking
    C. basing   D. buildup

    3._____

4. Heavily loaded aircraft are more likely to pose a danger to hand crews than lighter ones because

    A. stronger vortex currents from their wings could cause sudden changes in fire behavior
    B. increased operating noise makes ground communication difficult
    C. the heavier craft are more likely to crash
    D. larger retardant payloads can injure hand crews if dropped directly on them

    4._____

5. When crews attack together along the line of a given flank of a fire, they are employing the method of direct assault called _____ action.

    A. flanking   B. anchor point
    C. tandem   D. envelopment

    5._____

6. Temperature inversions increase the danger of spreading fires by

    A. providing stable air at lower altitudes
    B. feeding downward-flowing air currents
    C. accelerating the rate of spread at higher altitudes
    D. drying most fuels at lower altitudes

    6._____

7. An extended, landscaped fuel break designed to protect an entire community from fire is referred to as

    A. limbed-up zone   B. greenbelt
    C. cul-de-sac   D. staging area

    7._____

8. In order to control a fire that is burning in an area of woodland or industry debris fuel, the APPROXIMATE guideline, in feet per hour, for the deployment of a fire line is

    A. 225   B. 300   C. 450   D. 900

    8._____

9. When all potential fuels in a given area are exposed to direct sunlight, which of the following conditions is USUAL?

    A. Ground fuels are warmer than aerial fuels.
    B. Ground fuels are cooler than aerial fuels.
    C. Heavy fuels are warmer than fine fuels.
    D. All fuels are nearly the same temperature.

10. Which type of cloud characteristic generally indicates the MOST favorable conditions for fighting wildfires?

    A. Cumulus
    B. Cumulonimbus
    C. Virga
    D. Stratus

11. In timber fires, an upward-spreading burn that does not create enough heat to advance horizontally through tree-tops along with the surface fire is called a(n) _____ crown fire.

    A. passive
    B. active
    C. independent
    D. lateral

12. In a wildfire's column, the area that divides the convection zone and the condensation zone is called the _____ zone.

    A. fuel
    B. transition
    C. smoke fallout
    D. combustion

13. The recommended MINIMUM width of a fire line constructed in heavy brush that is approximately six feet in height is _____ feet.

    A. 3   B. 6   C. 9   D. 12

14. In order to insure mobility and safety, the water tank on a wildland engine should NOT hold much more than _____ gallons.

    A. 300   B. 500   C. 700   D. 1200

15. By constructing a continuous line from five to thirty feet along the edge of an advancing fire, either by clearing or firing, crews employ the _____ method of indirect attack.

    A. spot firing
    B. parallel
    C. burning-out
    D. backfiring

16. Fire whirls, or violent, tornado-like movements of fire that can pick up debris and put crews in immediate danger, are MOST likely to occur

    A. on flat ground
    B. near the bottom of furrows and canyons
    C. on the leeward side of ridges
    D. on the windward side of ridges

17. In firefighting terms, the spread of a fire is considered dangerous if its rate _____ per hour.

    A. exceeds five hundred yards
    B. is at least one mile
    C. is between one and three miles
    D. exceeds three miles

18. Of the following ecosystem types, which averages the LOWEST frequency of naturally-burning wildfires? 18.____

    A. Alpine tundra
    B. Subalpine forest
    C. Annual grassland
    D. Boreal forest

19. Which of the following devices has proven to be MOST effective in clearing heavy fuels such as slash and timber? 19.____

    A. Crosscut saw
    B. Chain saw
    C. Bulldozer
    D. Adze

20. When an airtanker opens all its tanks to release its total payload at one time and place, it is using the _____ pattern. 20.____

    A. salvo   B. pulaski   C. trail   D. split

21. During airtanker drops, which of the following does NOT usually create the potential for trouble on the ground? The 21.____

    A. aircraft is flying high and quickly
    B. air is still and calm
    C. fire is burning in open brush or scattered timber
    D. airtanker is large or heavily loaded

22. During the night, winds on a slope will GENERALLY 22.____

    A. blow uphill
    B. blow downhill
    C. blow across the slope in one direction
    D. gust in varying directions across the slope

23. A _____ mile per hour wind velocity is considered to be acceptable in order to safely set a prescribed fire. 23.____

    A. 0-4   B. 4-10   C. 10-17   D. 17-22

24. Grass is the fuel in wildland fires that creates the 24.____

    A. greatest danger to ground personnel
    B. most irregular burn patterns
    C. most dramatic loss of wildlife habitat
    D. greatest spread speed for fires

25. Because of the clockwise corkscrewing of slope fire updrafts, the GREATEST danger of advance spot fires is *usually* 25.____

    A. in advance of the fire's head
    B. far downhill from the fire
    C. along the right flank of the fire
    D. along the left flank of the fire

KEY (CORRECT ANSWERS)

1. A
2. D
3. B
4. A
5. C

6. C
7. B
8. A
9. A
10. D

11. A
12. C
13. C
14. C
15. B

16. C
17. C
18. A
19. B
20. A

21. A
22. B
23. B
24. D
25. C

ABILITY TO APPLY STATED LAWS, RULES AND REGULATIONS

EXAMINATION SECTION

TEST 1

DIRECTIONS: Each question or incomplete statement is followed by several suggested answers or completions. Select the one that BEST answers the question or completes the statement. *PRINT THE LETTER OF THE CORRECT ANSWER IN THE SPACE AT THE RIGHT.*

Questions 1-2.

DIRECTIONS: Questions 1 and 2 are to be answered on the basis of the following passage.

Effective January 1, 2022, employees who are entitled to be paid at an overtime minimum wage rate according to the terms of a state minimum wage order must be paid for overtime at a rate at least time and one-half of the appropriate regular minimum wage rate for non-overtime work. For the purpose of this policy statement, the term *appropriate regular minimum* wage rate means $10.05 per hour or a lower minimum wage rate established in accordance with the provisions of a state minimum wage order. OVERTIME MINIMUM WAGES MAY NOT BE OFFSET BY PAYMENTS IN EXCESS OF THE REGULAR MINIMUM RATE OR NON-OVERTIME WORK.

1. A worker who ordinarily works forty hours a week at an agreed wage of $12.00 an hour is required to work ten hours in excess of forty during a payroll week and is paid for the extra ten hours at his $12.00 per hour rate.
Using the information contained in the above passage, it is BEST to conclude
   A. this was a correct application of the regulation
   B. this was an incorrect application of the regulation
   C. the employee was not underpaid because he or she agreed upon the wage rate
   D. the employee did not perform his job well

1.____

2. According to the information in the above passage, the employee in Question 1 was MOST likely underpaid at least
   A. $180.00   B. $30.75
   C. $60.00   D. not underpaid at all

2.____

Question 3.

DIRECTIONS: Question 3 is to be answered on the basis of the following passage.

The following guidelines establish a range of monetary assessments for various types of child labor violations. They are general in nature and may not cover every specific situation. In determining the appropriate monetary amount within the range shown, consideration will be given to the criteria enumerated in the statute, namely *the size of the employer's business, the good faith of the employer, the gravity of the violation, the history of previous violations, and the failure to comply with record keeping or other requirements.* For example, the penalty for a larger firm (25 or more employees) would tend to be in the higher range since such firms should have knowledge of the laws. The gravity of the violation would depend on such factors as the age of the minor, whether required to be in school, and the degree of exposure to the hazards of prohibited occupations. Failure to keep records of the hours of work of the minors would also have a bearing on the size of the penalty.

1.
   a. No employment certificate—child of employer (Sec. 131 or 132)
   b. No posted hours of work (Sect. 178)

   1st Violation - $0-$100
   2nd Violation - $100-$250
   3rd Violation - $250-$500

2.
   a. Invalid employment certificate, e.g., student non-factory rather than general for a 16 year old in non-factory work (Sec. 132)
   b. Maximum or prohibited hours—less than one half hour beyond limit on any day, occasional, no pattern. (Sec. 130. 2e, 131.3f, 170.1, 171.1, 170l2, 172.1, 173.1; Ed. L. 3227, 3228)

   1st Violation - $0-$100
   2nd Violation - $150-$250
   3rd Violation - $250-$500

3.
   a. No employment certificate. (Sec. 130.2e, 131.3f, 131, 132, 138; Ed. L. 3227, 3228; ACAL 35.01, 35.05)
   b. Maximum of prohibited hours – (1) less than one half hour beyond limit on regular basis, (2) more than one half hour beyond limit either occasional or on a regular basis (Sec. 130.2e, 131.3f, 170.1, 170.2, 172.1, 173.1;Ed. L. 3227, 3228)

   1st Violation - $100-$250
   2nd Violation - $250-$500
   3rd Violation - $400-$500

4. Prohibited Occupations—Hazardous Employment (Sec. 130.1, 131.3f, 131.2, 133)

   1st Violation - $300-$500
   2nd Violation - $400-$500
   3rd Violation - $400-$500

<u>COMPLIANCE CONFERENCE PRIOR TO ASSESSMENT OF PENALTY</u>
After a child labor violation is reported, a compliance conference will be scheduled affording the employer the opportunity to be heard on the reported violation. A determination regarding the assessment of a civil penalty will be made following the conference.

<u>RIGHT TO APPEAL</u>
If the employer is aggrieved by the determination following such conference, the employer has the right to appeal such determination within 60 days of the date of issuance to the Industrial Board of Appeals, 194 Washington Avenue, Albany, New York 12210 as prescribed by its Rules of Procedure.

3. According to the above passage, a firm with its third violation of child labor laws regarding no posted hours of work (Sec. 178) and prohibited occupations- hazardous employment would be fined 3.____
   A. $600$1,000
   B. $650
   C. $1,000
   D. cannot be determined from the information given

Question 4.

DIRECTIONS: Question 4 is to be answered on the basis of the following passage.

Section 198c.   Benefits or Wage Supplements

1. In addition to any other penalty or punishment otherwise prescribed by law, any employer who is party to an agreement to pay or provide benefits or wage supplements to employees or to a third party or fund for the benefit of employees and who fails, neglects, or refuses to pay the amount or amounts necessary to provide such benefits or furnish such supplements within thirty days after such payments are required to be made, shall be guilty of a misdemeanor, and upon conviction shall be punished as provided in Section One Hundred Ninety-Eight-a of this article. Where such employer is a corporation, the president, secretary treasurer, or officers exercising corresponding functions shall each be guilty of a misdemeanor.

2. As used in this section, the term *benefits* or *wage supplements* includes, but is not limited to, reimbursement for expenses; health, welfare, and retirement benefits; and vacation, separation or holiday pay.

4. According to the above passage, an employer who had agreed to furnish an employee with a car and then failed to provide a car is 4.____
   A. not guilty of a misdemeanor
   B. most likely guilty of a misdemeanor
   C. not affected by the above regulation
   D. guilty of a felony

Question 5.

DIRECTIONS: Question 5 is to be answered on the basis of the following passage.

Manual workers must be paid weekly and not later than seven calendar days after the end of the week in which the wages are earned. However, a manual worker employed by a non-profitmaking organization must be paid in accordance with the agreed terms of employment, but not less frequently than semi-monthly. A manual worker means a mechanic, workingman, or laborer. Railroad workers, other than executives, must be paid on or before Thursday of each week the wages earned during the seven day period ending on Tuesday of the preceding week. Commission sales personnel must be paid in accordance with the agreed terms of employment but not less frequently than once in each month and not later than the last day of the month following the month in which the money is earned. If the monthly payment of wages, salary, drawing account or commissions is substantial, then additional compensation such as incentive earnings may be paid less frequently than once in each month, but in no event later than the time provided in the employment agreement.

5. A non-executive railroad worker has not been paid for the previous week's work. It is Wednesday.
   According to the above passage, which of the following is TRUE?
   The above regulation
   A. was not violated since the ending period is the following Tuesday
   B. was violated
   C. was not violated since the employee could be paid on Thursday
   D. does not apply in this case

5.____

Questions 6.

DIRECTIONS: Question 6 is to be answered on the basis of the following passage.

No deductions may be made from wages except deductions authorized by law, or which are authorized in writing by the employee and are for the employee's benefit. Authorized deductions include payments for insurance premiums, pensions, U.S. bonds, and union dues, as well as similar payments for the benefit of the employee. An employer may not make any payment by separate transaction unless such charge or payment is permitted as a deduction from wages. Examples of illegal deductions or charges include payments by the employee for spoilage, breakage, cash shortages or losses, and cost and maintenance of required uniforms.

6. An employee working on a cash register is short $40 at the end of his shift. The $40 is deducted from his wages.
   According to the above passage, the deduction is
   A. legal because it is legal to deduct cash losses
   B. legal because the employee is at fault
   C. illegal because the employee was not told of the deduction in advance
   D. illegal

6.____

Questions 7-8.

DIRECTIONS: Questions 7 and 8 are to be answered on the basis of the following passage.

No employee shall be paid a wage at a rate less than the rate at which an employee of the opposite sex in the same establishment is paid for equal work on a job, the performance of which requires equal skill, effort, and responsibility, and which is performed under similar working conditions, except where payment is made pursuant to a differential based on:
   a. A system which measures earnings by quantity or quality of production
   b. A merit system
   c. A seniority system; or
   d. Any other factor other than sex.

Any violation of the above is illegal.

7. A woman working in a factory on a piece-rate system as a sewing machine operator received less pay than a male sewing machine operator who finished more items.
   According to the above regulation, this is
   A. legal
   B. illegal
   C. legal, but not ethical
   D. no conclusion can be made from the information given

8. A male worker is in the same job title as a female worker. The male worker has been employed by the firm for three years, the female for two.
   Using the regulation stated above, if the male worker is paid more than the female worker, the action is
   A. legal
   B. illegal
   C. legal, but not ethical
   D. no conclusion can be made from the information given

Question 9.

DIRECTIONS: Question 9 is to be answered on the basis of the following passage.

Section 162. <u>Time Allowed for Meals</u>

1. Every person employed in or in connection with a factory shall be allowed at least sixty minutes for the noon day meal.

2. Every person employed in or in connection with a mercantile or other establishment or occupation coming under the provisions of this chapter shall be allowed at least forty-five minutes for the noon day meal, except as in this chapter otherwise provided.

3. Every person employed for a period or shift starting before noon and continuing later than seven o'clock in the evening shall be allowed an additional meal period of at least twenty minutes between five and seven o'clock in the evening.

4. Every person employed for a period or shift of more than six hours starting between the hours of one o'clock in the afternoon and six o'clock in the morning, shall be allowed at least sixty minutes for a meal period when employed in or in connection with a factory, and forty-five minutes for a meal period when employed in or in connection with a mercantile or other establishment or occupation coming under the provision of this chapter, at a time midway between the beginning and end of such employment.

5. The commissioner may permit a shorter time to be fixed for meal periods than hereinbefore provided. The permit therefore shall be in writing and shall be kept conspicuously posted in the main entrance of the establishment. Such permit may be revoked at any time.

In administering this statute, the Department applies the following interpretations and guidelines:

<u>Employee Coverage</u>: Section 162 applies to every person in any establishment or occupation covered by the Labor Law. Accordingly, all categories of workers are covered, including white collar management staff.

<u>Shorter Meal Periods</u>: The Department will permit a shorter meal period of not less than 30 minutes as a matter of course, without application by the employer, so long as there is no indication of hardship to employees. A meal period of not less than 20 minutes will be permitted only in special or unusual cases after investigation and issuance of a special permit.

9. An employee is given twenty minutes for lunch 9.____
According to the information given in the above passage, the employer
    A. is in violation
    B. is not in violation
    C. should be fined $250
    D. no conclusion can be made from the information given

Question 10.

DIRECTIONS: Question 10 is to be answered on the basis of the following passage.

An employee shall not be obliged to incur expenses in the arrangement whereby the employee's wages or salary are directly deposited in a bank or financial institution or in the withdrawal of such wages or salary from the bank or financial institution. Some examples of expenses are as follows:

    1. A service charge, per check charge, or administrative or processing charge.
    2. Carfare in order to get to the bank or financial institution to withdraw wages.

An employee shall not be obliged to lose a substantial amount of uncompensated time in order to withdraw wages from a bank or financial institution. Although the employer is not required to provide employees with paid time in which to withdraw such monies, the Department has held that the employer should provide for the loss of time when the employee requires more than 15 minutes to withdraw wages. Such time includes travel time to and from, as well as actual time spent at the bank or financial institution in withdrawing such monies. The loss of such time without compensation constitutes a difficulty.

The withdrawal of wages may not interfere with an employee's meal period to the extent that it decreases the meal period to less than 30 minutes. Thus, although the time required for withdrawal of wages may be 15 minutes or less, the loss of even 8 or 9 minutes from a thirty minute meal period creates a difficulty.

10. An employee is unable to withdraw wages at any time other than her lunch break. She needs twenty minutes to withdraw wages and has a forty-five minute lunch break.
    According to the information contained in the above passage, the employer
    A. is in violation
    B. is not in violation
    C. should be fined $250
    D. no conclusion can be made from the information given

KEY (CORRECT ANSWERS)

1.	B	6.	D
2.	B	7.	A
3.	D	8.	A
4.	B	9.	D
5.	C	10.	A

SOLUTIONS

1. The answer is choice B. According to the passage, the employee should have been paid "at a rate at least time and one half of the appropriate regular <u>minimum wage rate</u> for non-overtime work." Remember, it's important to consider only what has been given in the reading passage. Choice C is incorrect because it is illegal in this case to agree on something other than the law. Minimum standards are set by law so that employers cannot coerce, or otherwise persuade, employees to work at less than what is deemed fair. It could be argued that this is outside knowledge, but if you think about it, it's only common sense. Why bother having a minimum wage law, or minimum rates for overtime, or child labor laws if someone can just sign away his or her rights when an employer asks him or her to? If you didn't know this, you could still have eliminated this choice because the passage says, "ordinarily works 40 hours at an agreed wage of $12.00 per hour." The wording implies that this was agreed on for the <u>normal</u> work week.

2. The answer is choice B. The employee needs to be paid at a rate of time and a half. The employee has worked an extra ten hours at the hourly rate of $12.00 an hour. The passage states that the employee must be paid "at least time and one half of the appropriate regular minimum wage rate for non-overtime work." Minimum wage is given as $10.05 per hour. Time and a half of that would be $10.05 times 1.5, or $15.075 per hour. This employee is paid only $12.00 per hour for each hour of overtime. That's $3.075 less for each of the ten hours over forty hours, or a total of $30.75 less than he should have been paid. (10 × $3.075 = $30.75) You may have read the passage incorrectly, and thought the employee should have been paid time and a half on the $12.00 wage, but the passage does not state this. It states that the minimum payment is time and a half on <u>minimum hourly wage</u>, not on the employee's current wage rate. If you assumed the employee should have been paid $18.00 an hour, you probably would have picked choice C. Very tricky question. NOTE: The employee could have been paid less than half the minimum wage under special circumstances. Since there is nothing to indicate that the special circumstances apply, and since the question stem says "most likely," choice B is still considered the best choice.

3. The answer is choice D. This is another tricky question. The passage states, "The following guidelines establish a range of monetary assessments for various types of violations. They are general in nature and <u>may not cover every specific situation</u>. In determining the appropriate monetary amount within the range shown, considered will be given to the criteria enumerated in the statute...." The passage then goes on to list all of the various possibilities. We don't know the circumstances, so choice D is the safest choice. If the question stem had been phrased "would most likely be fined," a case might possibly have been made for a different answer. The way it stands, choice D is the best choice because we can't say what, the fine <u>definitely</u> <u>would be</u>.

4. The answer is choice B. The last sentence states that "the term benefits or wage supplements includes <u>but is not limited to</u>...." This, coupled with the wording of the first paragraph, would mean that there is a good possibility the broken agreement would be judged a misdemeanor.

5. The answer is choice C. This is directly supported by the fourth sentence.

6. The answer is choice D. The last sentence states that "examples of <u>illegal deductions</u> or charges include payments by the employee for spoilage, breakage, <u>cash shortages</u> or losses...."

7. The answer is choice A. The key here is the phrase <u>piece-rate system</u>. The passage states that one of the exceptions is "a system which measures earnings by quantity or quality of production." That's piecework where extra pay may be given for extra production or effort. It's logical—and not too much—to assume that the man was paid more because he finished more items.

8. The answer is choice A. The passage states that one of the exceptions is a seniority system. The question stem says that the man had worked there for three years while the woman had only worked there for two years.

9. The answer is choice D. The last sentence of the passage states that "a meal period of not less than twenty minutes will be permitted only in special or unusual cases after investigation and issuance of the special permit." Since we don't know the circumstances, we can't <u>definitely</u> say the employer is or is not in violation.

10. The answer is choice A. The next to last sentence of the passage states that "the withdrawal of wages may not interfere with an employee's meal period to the extent that it decreases the meal period to less than twenty minutes." The employee can only withdraw wages during her meal period. If the employee has a forty-five minute lunch break, and needs twenty minutes to withdraw funds, then she only has twenty-five minutes for lunch, which the passage states is not sufficient.

EXAMINATION SECTION
TEST 1

DIRECTIONS: Each question or incomplete statement is followed by several suggested answers or completions. Select the one that BEST answers the question or completes the statement. *PRINT THE LETTER OF THE CORRECT ANSWER IN THE SPACE AT THE RIGHT.*

Questions 1-10.   MEMORY

DIRECTIONS: Questions 1 through 10 are to be answered SOLELY on the basis of the following passage, which contains a story about an incident involving police officers. You will have ten minutes to read and study the story. You may not write or make any notes while studying it. After ten minutes, close the memory booklet and do not look at it again. Then, answer the questions that follow.

You are one of a number of police officers who have been assigned to help control a demonstration inside Baldwin Square, a major square in the city. The demonstration is to protest the U.S. involvement in Iraq. As was expected, the demonstration has become nasty. You and nine other officers have been assigned to keep the demonstrators from going up Bell Street which enters the Square from the northwest. During the time you have been assigned to Bell Street, you have observed a number of things.

Before the demonstration began, three vans and a wagon entered the Square from the North on Howard Avenue. The first van was a 1989 blue Ford, plate number 897-JLK. The second van was a 1995 red Ford, plate number 899-LKK. The third van was a 1997 green Dodge step-van, plate number 997-KJL. The wagon was a blue 1998 Volvo with a luggage rack on the roof, plate number 989-LKK. The Dodge had a large dent in the left-hand rear door and was missing its radiator grill. The Ford that was painted red had markings under the paint which made you believe that it had once been a telephone company truck. Equipment for the speakers' platform was unloaded from the van, along with a number of demonstration signs. As soon as the vans and wagon were unloaded, a number of demonstrators picked up the signs and started marching around the square. A sign reading *U.S. Out Now* was carried by a woman wearing red jeans, a black tee shirt, and blue sneakers. A man with a beard, a blue shirt, and Army pants began carrying a poster reading *To Hell With Davis.* A tall, Black male and a Hispanic male had been carrying a large sign with *This Is How Vietnam Started* in big black letters with red dripping off the bottom of each letter.

A number of the demonstrators are wearing black armbands and green tee shirts with the peace symbol on the front. A woman with very short hair who was dressed in green and yellow fatigues is carrying a triangular-shaped blue sign with white letters. The sign says *Out Of Iraq*.

A group of 12 demonstrators have been carrying six fake coffins back and forth across the Square between Apple Street on the West and Webb Street on the East. They are shouting *Death to Hollis and his Henchmen*. Over where Victor Avenue enters the Square from the South, a small group of demonstrators (two men and three women) just started painting slogans on the walls surrounding the construction of the First National Union Bank and Trust.

2 (#1)

1. Which street is on the opposite side of the Square from Victor Avenue?
   A. Bell   B. Howard   C. Apple   D. Webb

2. How many officers are assigned with you?
   A. 8   B. 6   C. 9   D. 5

3. Howard Avenue enters the Square from which direction?
   A. Northwest   B. North   C. East   D. Southwest

4. The van that had PROBABLY been a telephone truck had plate number
   A. 899-LKK   B. 989-LKK   C. 897-JKL   D. 997-KJL

5. What is the color of the sign carried by the woman with very short hair?
   A. Blue   B. White   C. Black   D. Red

6. The man wearing the army pants has a(n)
   A. Afro   B. beard
   C. triangular-shaped sign   D. black armband

7. Which vehicle had plate number 989-LKK? The
   A. red Ford   B. blue Ford   C. Volvo   D. Dodge

8. The bank under construction is located _____ of the Square.
   A. north   B. south   C. east   D. west

9. How many people are painting slogans on the walls surrounding the construction site?
   A. 4   B. 5   C. 6   D. 7

10. What is the name of the bank under construction?
    A. National Union Bank and Trust
    B. First National Bank and Trust
    C. First Union National Bank and Trust
    D. First National Union Bank and Trust

KEY (CORRECT ANSWERS)

1. B
2. C
3. B
4. A
5. A
6. B
7. C
8. B
9. B
10. D

TEST 2

DIRECTIONS: Each question or incomplete statement is followed by several suggested answers or completions. Select the one that BEST answers the question or completes the statement. *PRINT THE LETTER OF THE CORRECT ANSWER IN THE SPACE AT THE RIGHT.*

Questions 1-15.

DIRECTIONS: Questions 1 through 15 are to be answered SOLELY on the basis of the Memory Booklet given below.

MEMORY BOOKLET

The following passage contains a story about an incident involving police officers. You will have ten minutes to read and study the story. You may not write or make any notes while studying it. The first questions in the examination will be based on the passage. After ten minutes, close the memory booklet, and do not look at it again. Then, answer the questions that follow.

Police Officers Boggs and Thomas are patrolling in a radio squad car on a late Saturday afternoon in the spring. They are told by radio that a burglary is taking place on the top floor of a six-story building on the corner of 5th Street and Essex and that they should deal with the incident.

The police officers know the location and know that the Gold Jewelry Company occupies the entire sixth floor. They also know that, over the weekends, the owner has gold bricks in his office safe worth $500,000.

When the officers arrive at the location, they lock their radio car. They then find the superintendent of the building who opens the front door for them. He indicates he has neither seen nor heard anything suspicious in the building. However, he had just returned from a long lunch hour. The officers take the elevator to the sixth floor. As the door of the elevator with the officers opens on the sixth floor, the officers hear the door of the freight elevator in the rear of the building closing and the freight elevator beginning to move. They leave the elevator and proceed quickly through the open door of the office of the Gold Jewelry Company. They see that the office safe is open and empty. The officers quickly proceed to the rear staircase. They run down six flights of stairs, and they see four suspects leaving through the rear entrance of the building.

They run through the rear door and out of the building after the suspects. The four suspects are running quickly through the parking lot at the back of the building. The suspects then make a right-hand turn onto 5th Street and are clearly seen by the officers. The officers see one white male, one Hispanic male, one Black male, and one white female.

77

The white male has a beard and sunglasses. He is wearing blue jeans, a dark red and blue jacket, and white jogging shoes. He is carrying a large green duffel bag over his shoulder.

The Hispanic male limps slightly and has a dark moustache. He is wearing dark brown slacks, a dark green sweat shirt, and brown shoes. He is carrying a large blue duffel bag.

The Black male is clean-shaven, wearing black corduroy pants, a multi-colored shirt, a green beret, and black boots. He is carrying a tool box.

The white female has long dark hair and is wear-ing light-colored blue jeans, a white blouse, sneakers, and a red kerchief around her neck. She is carrying a shotgun.

The officers chase the suspects for three long blocks without getting any closer to them. At the intersection of 5th Street and Pennsylvania Avenue, the suspects separate. The white male and the Black male rapidly get into a 1992 brown Ford stationwagon. The stationwagon has a roof rack on top and a Connecticut license plate with the letters *JEAN* on it. The stationwagon departs even before the occupants close the door completely.

The Hispanic male and the white female get into an old blue Dodge van. The van has a CB antenna on top, a picture of a cougar on the back doors, a dented right rear fender, and a New Jersey license plate. The officers are not able to read the plate numbers on the van.

The officers then observe the stationwagon turn left and enter an expressway going to Connecticut. The van turns right onto Illinois Avenue and proceeds toward the tunnel to New Jersey.

The officers immediately run back to their radio car to radio in what happened.

1. Which one of the following suspects had sunglasses on?   1._____

    A. White male   B. Hispanic male
    C. Black male   D. White female

2. Which one of the following suspects was carrying a shotgun?   2._____

    A. White male   B. Hispanic male
    C. Black male   D. White female

3. Which one of the following suspects was wearing a green beret?   3._____

    A. White male   B. Hispanic male
    C. Black male   D. White femal

4. Which one of the following suspects limped slightly?   4._____

    A. White male   B. Hispanic male
    C. Black male   D. White female

5. Which one of the following BEST describes the stationwagon used?   5._____
    A

    A. 1992 brown Ford   B. 1992 blue Dodge
    C. 1979 brown Ford   D. 1979 blue Dodge

6. Which one of the following BEST describes the suspect or suspects who used the sta-   6.____
tionwagon?
A

    A. Black male and a Hispanic male
    B. white male and a Hispanic male
    C. Black male and a white male
    D. Black male and a white female

7. The van had a license plate from which of the following states?   7.____

    A. Connecticut   B. New Jersey
    C. New York   D. Pennsylvania

8. The license plate on the stationwagon read as follows: 8.____

    A. JANE   B. JOAN   C. JEAN   D. JUNE

9. The van used had a dented _____ fender.   9.____

    A. left rear   B. right rear
    C. right front   D. left front

10. When last seen by the officers, the van was headed toward   10.____

    A. Connecticut   B. New Jersey
    C. Pennsylvania   D. Long Island

11. The female suspect's hair can BEST be described as   11.____

    A. long and dark-colored   B. short and dark-colored
    C. long and light-colored   D. short and light-colored

12. Which one of the following suspects was wearing a multicolored shirt?   12.____

    A. White male   B. Hispanic male
    C. Black male   D. White female

13. Blue jeans were worn by the _____ male suspect and the _____ suspect.   13.____

    A. Hispanic; white female   B. Black; Hispanic male
    C. white; white female   D. Black; white male

14. The color of the duffel bag carried by the Hispanic male suspect was   14.____

    A. blue   B. green   C. brown   D. red

15. The Hispanic male suspect was wearing   15.____

    A. brown shoes   B. black shoes
    C. black boots   D. jogging shoes

KEY (CORRECT ANSWERS)

1. A
2. D
3. C
4. B
5. A

6. C
7. B
8. C
9. B
10. B

11. A
12. C
13. C
14. A
15. A

READING COMPREHENSION
UNDERSTANDING AND INTERPRETING WRITTEN MATERIAL
COMMENTARY

The ability to read, understand, and interpret written materials texts, publications, newspapers, orders, directions, expositions, legal passages is a skill basic to a functioning democracy and to an efficient business or viable government.

That is why almost all examinations—for beginning, middle, and senior levels—test reading comprehension, directly or indirectly.

The reading test measures how well you understand what you read. This is how it is done: You read a paragraph and several statements based on a question. From the statements, you choose the one statement, or answer, that is BEST supported by, or BEST matches, what is said in the paragraph.

SAMPLE QUESTIONS

DIRECTIONS: Each question has five suggested answers, lettered A, B, C, D, and E. Decide which one is the BEST answer. *PRINT THE LETTER OF THE CORRECT ANSWER IN THE SPACE AT THE RIGHT.*

1. The prevention of accidents makes it necessary not only that safety devices be used to guard exposed machinery but also that mechanics be instructed in safety rules which they must follow for their own protection and that the light in the plant be adequate.
   The paragraph BEST supports the statement that industrial accidents
   A. are always avoidable
   B. may be due to ignorance
   C. usually result from inadequate machinery
   D. cannot be entirely overcome
   E. result in damage to machinery

1.____

ANALYSIS

Remember what you have to do:
- First: Read the paragraph.
- Second: Decide what the paragraph means.
- Third: Read the five suggested answers.
- Fourth: Select the one answer which BEST matches what the paragraph says or is BEST supported by something in the paragraph. (Sometimes you may have to read the paragraph again in order to be sure which suggested answer is best.)

This paragraph is talking about three steps that should be taken to prevent industrial accidents:
1. Use safety devices on machines
2. Instruct mechanics in safety rules
3. Provide adequate lighting

SELECTION

With this in mind, let's look at each suggested answer. Each one starts with "industrial accidents…"

SUGGESTED ANSWER A
Industrial accidents (A) are always avoidable
(The paragraph talks about how to avoid accidents but does not say that accidents are always avoidable.)

SUGGESTED ANSWER B
Industrial accidents (B) may be due to ignorance.
(One of the steps given in the paragraph to prevent accidents is to instruct mechanics on safety rules. This suggests that lack of knowledge or ignorance of safety rules causes accidents. This suggested answer sounds like a good possibility for being the right answer.)

SUGGESTED ANSWER C
Industrial accidents (C) usually result from inadequate machinery.
(The paragraph does suggest that exposed machines cause accidents, but it doesn't say that it is the usual cause of accidents. The word *usually* makes this a wrong answer.)

SUGGESTED ANSWER D
Industrial accidents (D) cannot be entirely overcome.
(You may know from your own experience that this is a true statement. But that is not what the paragraph is talking about. Therefore, it is NOT the correct answer.)

SUGGESTED ANSWER E
Industrial accidents (E) result in damage to machinery.
(This is a statement that may or may not be true, but, in any case, it is NOT covered by the paragraph.)

Looking back, you see that the one suggested answer of the five given that BEST matches what the paragraph says is:
Industrial accidents (B) may be due to ignorance.
The CORRECT answer then is B.
Be sure you read ALL the possible answers before you make your choice. You may think that none of the five answers is really good, but choose the BEST one of the five.

2. Probably few people realize, as they drive on a concrete road, that steel is used to keep the surface flat in spite of the weight of the busses and trucks. Steel bars, deeply embedded in the concrete, provide sinews to take the stresses so that the stresses cannot crack the slab or make it wavy.

   The paragraph BEST supports the statement that a concrete road
   - A. is expensive to build
   - B. usually cracks under heavy weights
   - C. looks like any other road
   - D. is used only for heavy traffic
   - E. is reinforced with other material

   2.____

ANALYSIS

This paragraph is commenting on the fact that
1. few people realize, as they drive on a concrete road, that steel is deeply embedded
2. steel keeps the surface flat
3. steel bars enable the road to take the stresses without cracking or becoming wavy

SELECTION

Now read and think about the possible answers:

A. A concrete road is expensive to build.
   (Maybe so, but that is not what the paragraph is about.)

B. A concrete road usually cracks under heavy weights.
   (The paragraph talks about using steel bars to prevent heavy weights from cracking concrete roads. It says nothing about how usual it is for the roads to crack. The word *usually* makes this suggested answer wrong.)

C. A concrete road looks like any other road.
   (This may or may not be true. The important thing to note is that it has nothing to do with what the paragraph is about.)

D. A concrete road is used only for heavy traffic.
   (This answer at least has something to do with the paragraph—concrete roads are used with heavy traffic but it does not say "used only.")

E. A concrete road is reinforced with other material.
   This choice seems to be the correct one on two counts. First, the paragraph does suggest that concrete roads are made stronger by embedding steel bars in them. This is another way of saying "concrete roads are reinforced with steel bars." Second, by the process of elimination, the other four choices are ruled out as correct answers simply because they do not apply.

You can be sure that not all the reading question will be so easy as these.

SUGGESTIONS FOR ANSWERING READING QUESTIONS

1. Read the paragraph carefully. Then read each suggested answer carefully. Read every word, because often one word can make the difference between a right or wrong answer.

2. Choose that answer which is supported in the paragraph itself. Do not choose an answer which is a correct statement unless it is based on information in the paragraph.

3. Even though a suggested answer has many of the words used in the paragraph, it may still be wrong.

4. Look out for words—such as *always*, *never*, *entirely*, or *only*—which tend to make a suggested answer wrong.

5. Answer first those questions which you can answer most easily. Then, work on the other questions.

6. If you can't figure out the answer to the question, guess.

READING COMPREHENSION
UNDERSTANDING AND INTERPRETING WRITTEN MATERIAL
EXAMINATION SECTION
TEST 1

DIRECTIONS: Each question or incomplete statement is followed by several suggested answers or completions. Select the one that BEST answers the question or completes the statement. *PRINT THE LETTER OF THE CORRECT ANSWER IN THE SPACE AT THE RIGHT.*

Questions 1-3.

DIRECTIONS: Questions 1 through 3 are to be answered SOLELY on the basis of the following paragraph.

    The final step in an accident investigation is the making out of the police report. In the case of a traffic accident, the officer should go right from the scene to his office to write up the report. However, if a person was injured in the accident and taken to a hospital, the officer should visit him there before going to his office to prepare his report. This personal visit to the injured person does not mean that the office must make a physical examination; but he should make an effort to obtain a statement from the injured person or persons. If this is not possible, information should be obtained from the attending physician as to the extent of the injury. In any event, without fail, the name of the physician should be secured and the report should state the name of the physician and the fact that he told the officer that, at a certain stated time on a certain stated date, the injuries were of such and such a nature. If the injured person dies before the officer arrives at the hospital, it may be necessary to take the responsible person into custody at once.

1. When a person has been injured in a traffic accident, the one of the following actions which it is necessary for a police officer to take in connection with the accident report is to
   A. prepare the police report immediately after the accident, and then go to the hospital to speak to the victim
   B. do his utmost to verify the victim's story prior to preparing the official police report of the incident
   C. be sure to include the victim's statement in the police report in every case
   D. try to get the victim's version of the accident prior to preparing the police report

1.____

2. When one of the persons injured in a motor vehicle accident dies, the above paragraph provides that the police officer
   A. must immediately take the responsible person into custody, if the injured person is already dead when the officer appears at the scene of the accident
   B. must either arrest the responsible person or get a statement from him, if the injured person dies after arrival at the hospital

2.____

C. may have to immediately arrest the responsible person, if the injured person dies in the hospital prior to the officer's arrival there
D. may refrain from arresting the responsible person, but only if the responsible person is also seriously injured

3. When someone has been injured in a collision between two automobiles and is given medical treatment shortly thereafter by a physician, the one of the following actions which the police officer MUST take with regard to the physician is to
   A. obtain his name and his diagnosis of the injuries, regardless of the place where treatment was given
   B. obtain his approval of the portion of the police report relating to the injured person and the treatment given him prior to and after his arrival at the hospital
   C. obtain his name, his opinion of the extent of the person's injuries, and his signed statement of the treatment he gave the injured person
   D. set a certain stated time on a certain stated date for interviewing him, unless he is an attending physician in a hospital

Questions 4-7.

DIRECTIONS: Questions 4 through 7 are to be answered SOLELY on the basis of the following paragraph.

Because of the importance of preserving physical evidence, the patrolman should not enter a scene of a crime if it can be examined visually from one position and if no other pressing duty requires his presence there. However, there are some responsibilities that take precedence over preservation of evidence. Some examples are: rescue work, disarming dangerous persons, quelling a disturbance. However, the patrolman should learn how to accomplish these more vital tasks, while at the same time preserving as much evidence as possible. If he finds it necessary to enter upon the scene, he should quickly study the place of entry to learn if any evidence will suffer by his contact; then he should determine the routes to be used in walking to the spot where his presence is required. Every place where a foot will fall or where a hand or other part of his body will touch, should be examined with the eye. Objects should not be touched or moved unless there is a definite and compelling reason. For identification of most items of physical evidence at the initial investigation, it is seldom necessary to touch or move them.

4. The one of the following titles which is the MOST appropriate for the above paragraph is:
   A. Determining the Priority of Tasks at the Scene of a Crime
   B. The Principal Reasons for Preserving Evidence at the Scene of a Crime
   C. Precautions to Take at the Scene of a Crime
   D. Evidence to be Examined at the Scene of a Crime

5. When a patrolman feels that it is essential for him to enter the immediate area where a crime has been committed, he should
   A. quickly but carefully glance around to determine whether his entering the area will damage any evidence present
   B. remove all objects of evidence from his predetermined route in order to avoid stepping on them
   C. carefully replace any object immediately if it is moved or touched by his hands or any other part of his body
   D. use only the usual place of entry to the scene in order to avoid disturbing any possible clues left on rear doors and windows by the criminal

6. The one of the following which is the LEAST urgent duty of a police officer who has just reported to the scene of a crime is to
   A. disarm the hysterical victim of the crime who is wildly waving a loaded gun in all directions
   B. give first aid to a possible suspect who has been injured while attempting to leave the scene of the crime
   C. prevent observers from attacking and injuring the persons suspected of having committed the crime
   D. preserve from damage or destruction any evidence necessary for the proper prosecution of the case against the criminals

7. A police officer has just reported to the scene of a crime in response to a phone call.
   The BEST of the following actions for him to take with respect to objects of physical evidence present at the scene is to
   A. make no attempt to enter the crime scene if his entry will disturb any vital physical evidence
   B. map out the shortest straight path to follow in walking to the spot where the physical evidence may be found
   C. move such objects of physical evidence as are necessary to enable him to assist the wounded victim of the crime
   D. quickly examine all objects of physical evidence in order to determine which objects may be touched and which may not

Questions 8-11.

DIRECTIONS: Questions 8 through 11 are to be answered SOLELY on the basis of the following paragraph.

After examining a document and comparing the characters with specimens of other specimens of other handwritings, the laboratory technician may conclude that a certain individual did write the questioned document. This opinion could be based on a large number of similar, as well as a small number of dissimilar but explainable characteristics. On the other hand, if the laboratory technician concludes that the person in question did not write the questioned document, such an opinion could be based on the large number of characteristics which are dissimilar, or even on a small number which are dissimilar provided that these are of overriding significance, and despite the presence of explainable similarities. The laboratory expert is not always able to give a positive opinion. He may state that a certain individual probably did or did not write the questioned document. Such an opinion is usually the result of insufficient material, either in the questioned document or in the specimens submitted for comparison. Finally, the expert may be unable to come to any conclusion at all because of insufficient material submitted for comparison or because of improper specimens.

8. The one of the following which is the MOST appropriate title for the above paragraph is: 8.____
   A. Similar and Dissimilar Characteristics in Handwriting
   B. The Limitations of Handwriting Analysis in Identifying the Writer
   C. The Positive Identification of Suspects Through Their Handwriting
   D. The Inability to Identify an Individual Through His Handwriting

9. When a handwriting expert compares the handwriting on two separate documents and decides that they were written by the same person, his conclusions are generally based on the fact that 9.____
   A. a large number of characteristics in both documents are dissimilar but the few similar characteristics are more important
   B. all the characteristics are alike in both documents
   C. similar characteristics need to be examined as to the cause for their similarity
   D. most of the characteristics in both documents are alike and their few differences are readily explainable

10. If a fingerprint technician carefully examines a handwritten threatening letter and compares it with specimens of handwriting made by a suspect, he would be MOST likely to decide that the suspect did NOT write the threatening letter when the handwriting specimens and the letter have 10.____
    A. a small number of dissimilarities
    B. a small number of dissimilar but explainable characteristics
    C. important dissimilarities despite the fact that these may be few
    D. some similar characteristics that are easily imitated or disguised

11. There are instances when even a trained handwriting expert cannot decide definitely whether or not a certain document and a set of handwriting specimens were written by the same person. 11.____
    This inability to make a positive decision generally arises in situations where
    A. only one document of considerable length is available for comparison with a sufficient supply of handwriting specimens
    B. the limited nature of the handwriting specimens submitted restricts their comparability with the questioned document
    C. the dissimilarities are not explainable
    D. the document submitted for comparison does not include all the characteristics included in the handwriting specimens

Questions 12-14.

DIRECTIONS: Questions 12 through 14 are to be answered SOLELY on the basis of the following paragraph.

In cases of drunken driving, or of disorderly conduct while intoxicated, too many times some person who had been completely under the influence of alcoholic liquor at the time of his arrest has walked out of court without any conviction just because an officer failed to make the proper observation. Many of the larger cities and counties make use of various scientific methods to determine the degree of intoxication of a person, such as breath, urine, and blood tests. Many of the smaller cities, however, do not have the facilities to make these various tests, and must, therefore, rely on the observation tests given at the scene. These consist, among other things, of noticing how the subject walked, talked, and acted. One test that is usually given at night is the eye reaction to light, which the officer gives by shining his flashlight into the eyes of the subject. The manner in which the pupils of the eyes react to the light helps to determine the sobriety of a person. If he is intoxicated, the pupils of his eyes are dilated more at night than the eyes of a sober person. Also, when a light is flashed into the eyes of a sober person, his pupils contract instantly, but in the case of a person under the influence of liquor, the pupils contract very slowly.

12. Many persons who have been arrested on a charge of driving while completely intoxicated have been acquitted by a judge because the arresting officer had neglected to
    A. bring the driver to court while he was still under the influence of alcohol
    B. make the required scientific tests to fully substantiate his careful personal observations of the driver's intoxicated condition
    C. submit to the court any test results showing the driver's condition or degree of drunkenness
    D. watch the driver closely for some pertinent facts which would support the officer's suspicions of the driver's intoxicated condition

13. When a person is arrested for acting in a disorderly and apparently intoxicated manner in public, the kind of test which would fit in BEST with the thought of the above statement is:
    A. In many smaller cities, a close watch on his behavior and of his reactions to various blood and body tests
    B. In many smaller cities, having him walk a straight line
    C. In most larger counties, close watch of the speed of his reactions to the flashlight test
    D. In most cities of all sizes, the application of the latest scientific techniques in the analysis of his breath

14. When a person suspected of driving a motor vehicle while intoxicated is being examined to determine whether or not he actually is intoxicated, one of the methods used is to shine the light of a flashlight into his eyes.

When this method is used, the NORMAL result is that the pupils of the suspect's eyes will
- A. expand instantly if he is fully intoxicated, and remain unchanged if he is completely sober
- B. expand very slowly if he has had only a small amount of alcohol, and very rapidly if he has had a considerable amount of alcohol
- C. grow smaller at once if he is sober, and grow smaller more slowly if he is intoxicated
- D. grow smaller very slowly if he is fully sober, and grow smaller instantaneously if he is fully intoxicated

Questions 15-17.

DIRECTIONS: Questions 15 through 17 are to be answered SOLELY on the basis of the following paragraph.

Where an officer has personal knowledge of facts, sufficient to constitute reasonable grounds to believe that a person has committed or is committing a felony, he may arrest him, and, after having lawfully placed him under arrest, may search and take into his possession any incriminating evidence. The right of an officer to make an arrest and search is not limited to cases where the officer has personal knowledge of the commission of a felony, because he may act upon information conveyed to him by third persons which he believes to be reliable. Where an officer, charged with the duty of enforcing the law, receives information from apparently reliable sources, which would induce in the mind of the prudent person a belief that a felony was being or had been committed, he may make an arrest and search the person of a defendant, but he is not justified in acting on anonymous information alone.

15. When a felony has been committed, an officer would be acting MOST properly if he arrested a man
    - A. when he, the officer, has a police report that the man is suspected of having been involved in several minor offenses
    - B. when he, the officer, has received information from a usually reliable source that the man was involved in the crime
    - C. only when he, the officer, has personal knowledge that the man has committed the felony
    - D. when he, the officer, knows for a fact that the man has associated in the past with several persons who had been seen near the scene of the felony

15.____

16. An officer would be acting MOST properly if he searched a suspect for incriminating evidence
    - A. when he has received detailed information concerning the fact that the suspect is going to commit a felony
    - B. only after having lawfully arrested the suspect and charged him with having committed a felony
    - C. when he has just received an anonymous tip that the suspect had just committed a felony and is in illegal possession of stolen goods

16.____

D. in order to find in his possession legally admissible evidence on the basis of which the officer could then proceed to arrest the suspect for having committed a felony

17. A police officer has received information from an informant that a crime has been committed. The informant has also named two persons who he says committed the crime.
The officer's decision to both arrest and search the two suspects would be
   A. *correct*, if it would not be unreasonable to assume that the crime committed is a felony, and if the informant has been trustworthy in the past
   B. *incorrect*, if the informant has no proof but his own word to offer that a felony has been committed, although he has always been trustworthy in the past
   C. *correct*, if it would be logical and prudent to assume that the information is accurate regardless of whether the offense committed is a felony or a less serious crime
   D. *incorrect*, even if the informant produces objective and seemingly convincing proof that a felony has been committed, but has a reputation of occasional past unreliability

17.____

Questions 18-20.

DIRECTIONS: Questions 18 through 20 are to be answered SOLELY on the basis of the following paragraph.

If there are many persons at the scene of a hit-and-run accident, it would be a waste of time to question all of them; the witness needed is the one who can best describe the missing auto. Usually the person most qualified to do this is a youth of fifteen or sixteen years of age. He is more likely to be able to tell the make and year of a car than most other persons. A woman may be a good witness as to how the accident occurred, but usually will be unable to tell the make of the car. As soon as any information with regard to the missing car or its description is obtained, the police officer should call or radio headquarters and have the information put on the air. This should be done without waiting for further details, for time is an important factor. If a good description of the wanted car is obtained, then the next task is to get a description of the driver. In this hunt, it is found that a woman is often a more accurate witness than a man. Usually she will be able to state the color of clothes worn by the driver. If the wanted driver is a woman, another woman will often be able to tell the color and sometimes even the material of the clothing worn.

18. A hit-and-run accident has occurred and a police officer is attempting to obtain information from persons who had witnessed the incident.
It would generally be BEST for him to question a
   A. boy in his late teens, when the officer is seeking an accurate description of the age, coloring, and physical build of the driver of the car
   B. man, when the officer is seeking an accurate description of the driver of the car and the color and material of his coat, suit, and hat

18.____

C. woman, when the officer is seeking an accurate description of the driver of the car
D. young teenage girl, when the officer is seeking an accurate description of the style and color of the clothes worn by the driver of the car

19. Time is an important factor when an attempt is being made to apprehend the guilty driver in a hit-and-run accident.
However, the EARLIEST moment when the police should broadcast a radio announcement of the crime is when a(n)
    A. description of the missing car or any facts concerning it have been obtained
    B. tentative identification of the driver of the missing car has been made
    C. detailed description of the missing car and its occupant has been obtained
    D. eyewitness account has been obtained of the accident, including the identity of the victim, the extent of injuries, and the make and license number of the car

19.____

20. The time when it would be MOST desirable to get a description of the driver of the hit-and-run car is
    A. after getting a description of the car itself
    B. before transmitting information concerning the car to headquarters for broadcasting
    C. as soon as the officer arrives at the scene of the accident
    D. as soon as the victim of the accident has been given needed medical assistance

20.____

KEY (CORRECT ANSWERS)

1.	D	11.	B
2.	C	12.	D
3.	A	13.	B
4.	C	14.	C
5.	A	15.	B
6.	D	16.	B
7.	C	17.	A
8.	B	18.	C
9.	D	19.	A
10.	C	20.	A

TEST 2

DIRECTIONS: Each question or incomplete statement is followed by several suggested answers or completions. Select the one that BEST answers the question or completes the statement. *PRINT THE LETTER OF THE CORRECT ANSWER IN THE SPACE AT THE RIGHT.*

Questions 1-4.

DIRECTIONS: Questions 1 through 4 are to be answered SOLELY on the basis of the following paragraph.

    Automobile tire tracks found at the scene of a crime constitute an important link in the chain of physical evidence. In many cases, these are the only clues available. In some areas, unpaved ground adjoins the highway or paved streets. A suspect will often park his car off the paved portion of the street when committing a crime, sometimes leaving excellent tire tracks. Comparison of the tire track impressions with the tires is possible only when the vehicle has been found. However, the initial problem facing the police is the task of determining what kind of car probably made the impressions found at the scene of the crime. If the make, model, and year of the car which made the impressions can be determined, it is obvious that the task of elimination is greatly lessened.

1. The one of the following which is the MOST appropriate title for the above paragraph is:
   A. The Use of Automobiles in the Commission of Crimes
   B. The Use of Tire Tracks in Police Work
   C. The Capture of Criminals by Scientific Police Work
   D. The Positive Identification of Criminals Through Their Cars

1.____

2. When searching for clear signs left by the car used in the commission of a crime, the MOST likely place for the police to look would be on the
   A. highway adjoining unpaved streets
   B. highway adjacent to paved street
   C. paved street adjacent to the highway
   D. unpaved ground adjacent to a highway

2.____

3. Automobile tire tracks found at the scene of a crime are of value as evidence in that they are
   A. generally sufficient to trap and convict a suspect
   B. the most important link in the chain of physical evidence
   C. often the only evidence at hand
   D. circumstantial rather than direct

3.____

4. The PRIMARY reason for the police to try to find out which make, model, and year of car was involved in the commission of a crime is to
   A. compare the tire tracks left at the scene of the crime with the type of tires used on cars of that make
   B. determine if the mud on the tires of the suspected car matches the mud in the unpaved road near the scene of the crime

4.____

C. reduce to a large extent the amount of work involved in determining the particular car used in the commission of a crime
D. alert the police patrol forces to question the occupants of all automobiles of this type

Questions 5-8.

DIRECTIONS: Questions 5 through 8 are to be answered SOLELY on the basis of the following paragraph.

When stopping vehicles on highways to check for suspects or fugitives, the police use an automobile roadblock whenever possible. This consists of three cars placed in prearranged positions. Car number one is parked across the left lane of the roadway with the front diagonally facing toward the center line. Car number two is parked across the right lane, with the front of the vehicle also toward the center line, in a position perpendicular to car number one and approximately twenty feet to the rear. Continuing another twenty feet to the rear along the highway, car number three is parked in an identical manner to car number one. The width of the highway determines the angle or position in which the autos should be placed. In addition to the regular roadblock signs and the uses of flares at night only, there is an officer located at both the entrance and exit to direct and control traffic from both directions. This type of roadblock forces all approaching autos to reduce speed and zigzag around the police cars. Officers standing behind the parked cars can most safely and carefully view all passing motorists. Once a suspect is inside the block, it becomes extremely difficult to crash out.

5. Of the following, the MOST appropriate title for this paragraph is: 5.____
   A. The Construction of an Escape-Proof Roadblock
   B. Regulation of Automobile Traffic Through a Police Roadblock
   C. Safety Precautions Necessary in Making an Automobile Roadblock
   D. Structure of a Roadblock to Detain Suspects or Fugitives

6. When setting up a three-car roadblock, the *relative* positions of the cars should be such that 6.____
   A. the front of car number one is placed diagonally to the center line and faces car number three
   B. car number three is placed parallel to the center line and its front faces the right side of the road
   C. car number two is placed about 20 feet from car number one and its front faces the left side of the road
   D. car number three is parallel to and about 20 feet away from car number one

7. Officers can observe occupants of all cars passing through the roadblock with GREATEST safety when 7.____
   A warning flares are lighted to illuminate the area sufficiently at night
   B. warning signs are put up at each end of the roadblock
   C. they are stationed at both the exit and the entrance of the roadblock
   D. they take up positions behind cars in the roadblock

8. The type of automobile roadblock described in the above paragraph is of value 8._____
   in police work because
   A. a suspect is unable to escape its confines by using force
   B. it is frequently used to capture suspects with no danger to the police
   C. it requires only two officers to set up and operate
   D. vehicular traffic within its confines is controlled as to speed and direction

Questions 9-11.

DIRECTIONS: Questions 9 through 11 are to be answered SOLELY on the basis of the following paragraph.

A problem facing the police department in one area of the city was to try to reduce the number of bicycle thefts which had been increasing at an alarming rate in the past three or four years. A new program was adopted to get at the root of the problem. Tags were printed, reminding youngsters that bicycles left unlocked can be easily stolen. The police concentrated on such places as theaters, a municipal swimming pool, an athletic field, and the local high school, and tied tags on all bicycles which were not locked. The majority of bicycle thefts took place at the swimming pool. In 2019, during the first two weeks the pool was open, an average of 10 bicycle was stolen there daily. During the same two-week period, 30 bicycles a week were stolen at the athletic field, 15 at the high school, and 11 at all theaters combined. In 2020, after tagging the unlocked bicycles, it was found that 20 bicycles a week were stolen at the pool and 5 at the high school. It was felt that the police tags had helped the most, although the school officials had helped to a great extent in this program by distributing "locking" notices to parents and children, and the use of the loudspeaker at the pool urging children to lock their bicycles had also been very helpful.

9. The one of the following which had the GREATEST effect in the campaign to 9._____
   reduce bicycle stealing was the
   A. distribution of "locking" notices by the school officials
   B. locking of all bicycles left in public places
   C. police tagging of bicycles left unlocked by youngsters
   D. use of the loudspeaker at the swimming pool

10. The tagging program was instituted by the police department CHIEFLY to 10._____
    A. determine the areas where most bicycle thieves operated
    B. instill in youngsters the importance of punishing bicycle thieves
    C. lessen the rising rate of bicycle thefts
    D. recover as many as possible of the stolen bicycles

11. The figures showing the number of bicycle thefts in the various areas surveyed 11._____
    indicate that in 2019
    A. almost as many thefts occurred at the swimming pool as at all theaters combined
    B. fewer thefts occurred at the athletic field than at both the high school and all theaters combined
    C. more than half the thefts occurred at the swimming pool
    D. twice as many thefts occurred at the high school as at the athletic field

Questions 12-13.

DIRECTIONS: Questions 12 and 13 are to be answered SOLELY on the basis of the following paragraph.

A survey has shown that crime prevention work is most successful if the officers are assigned on rotating shifts to provide for around-the-clock coverage. An officer may work days for a time and then be switched to nights. The prime object of the night work is to enable the officer to spot conditions inviting burglars. Complete lack of, or faulty locations of, night lights and other conditions that may invite burglars, which might go unnoticed during daylight hours, can be located and corrected more readily through night work. Night work also enables the officer to check local hangouts of juvenile, such as bus and railway depots, certain cafes or pool halls, the local roller rink, and the building where a juvenile dance is held every Friday night. Detectives also join patrolmen cruising in radio patrol cars to check on juveniles loitering late at night and to spot-check local bars for juveniles.

12. The MOST important purpose of assigning officers to night shifts is to make it possible for them to
    A. correct conditions which may not be readily noticed during the day
    B. discover the locations of, and replace, missing and faulty night lights
    C. locate criminal hangouts
    D. notice things at night which cannot be noticed during the daytime

13. The type of shifting of officers which BEST prevents crime is to have
    A. day-shift officers rotated to night work
    B. rotating shifts provide sufficient officers for coverage 24 hours daily
    C. an officer work around the clock on a 24-hour basis as police needs arise
    D. rotating shifts to give the officers varied experience

Questions 14-15.

DIRECTIONS: Questions 14 and 15 are to be answered SOLELY on the basis of the following paragraph.

Proper firearms training is one phase of law enforcement which cannot be ignored. No part of the training of a police officer is more important or more valuable. The officer's life and often the lives of his fellow officers depend directly upon his skill with the weapon he is carrying. Proficiency with the revolver is not attained exclusively by the volume of ammunition used and the number of hours spent on the firing line. Supervised practice and the use of training aids and techniques help make the shooter. It is essential to have a good firing range where new officers are trained and older personnel practice in scheduled firearms sessions. The fundamental points to be stressed are grip, stance, breathing, sight alignment and trigger squeeze. Coordination of thought, vision, and motion must be achieved before the officer gains confidence in his shooting ability. Attaining this ability will make the student a better officer and enhance his value to the force.

14. A police officer will gain confidence in his shooting ability only after he has
    A. spent the required number of hours on the firing line
    B. been given sufficient supervised practice
    C. learned the five fundamental points
    D. learned to coordinate revolver movement with his sight and thought

15. Proper training in the use of firearms is one aspect of law enforcement which must be given serious consideration CHIEFLY because it is the
    A. most useful and essential single factor in the training of a police officer
    B. one phase of police officer training which stresses mental and physical coordination
    C. costliest aspect of police officer training involving considerable expense for the ammunition used in target practice
    D. most difficult part of police officer training, involving the expenditure of many hour on the firing line

Questions 16-20.

DIRECTIONS: Questions 16 through 20 are to be answered SOLELY on the basis of the following paragraph.

Lifting consists of transferring a print that has been dusted with powder to a transfer medium in order to preserve the print. Chemically developed prints cannot be lifted. Proper lifting of fingerprints is difficult and should be undertaken only when other means of recording the print are neither available nor suitable. Lifting should not be attempted from a porous surface. There are two types of commercial lifting tape which are good transfer mediums: rubber adhesive lift, one side of which is gummed and covered with thin, transparent celluloid; and transparent lifting tape, made of cellophane, one side of which is gummed. A package of acetate covers, frosted on one side and used to cover and protect the lifted print, accompanies each roll. If commercial tape is not available, transparent scotch tape may be used. The investigator should remove the celluloid or acetate cover from the lifting tape; smooth the tape, gummy side down, firmly and evenly over the entire print; gently peel the tape off the surface; replace the cover; and attach pertinent identifying data to the tape. All parts of the print should come in contact with the tape; air pockets should be avoided. The print will adhere to the lifting tape. The cover permits the print to be viewed and protects it from damage. Transparent lifting tape does not reverse the print. If a rubber adhesive lift is utilized, the print is reversed. Before a direct comparison can be made, the lifted print must be photographed, the negative reversed and a positive made.

16. An investigator wishing to preserve a record of fingerprints on a highly porous surface should
    A. develop them chemically before attempting to lift them
    B. lift them with scotch tape only when no other means of recording the prints are available
    C. employ some method other than lifting
    D. dust them with powder before attempting to lift them with rubber adhesive lift

17. Disregarding all other considerations, the SIMPLEST process to use in lifting a fingerprint from a window pane is that involving the use of 17.____
    A. rubber adhesive lift, because it gives a positive print in one step
    B. dusting powder and a camera, because the photograph is less likely to break than the window pane
    C. a chemical process, because it both develops and preserves the print at the same time
    D. transparent lifting tape, because it does not reverse the print

18. When a piece of commercial lifting tape is being used by an investigator wishing to lift a clear fingerprint from a smoothly-finished metal safe-door, he should 18.____
    A. prevent the ends of the tape from getting stuck to the metal surface because of the danger of forming air-pockets and thus damaging the print
    B. make certain that the tape covers all parts of the print and no air-pocket are formed
    C. carefully roll the tape over the most significant parts of the print only to avoid forming air-pockets
    D. be especially cautious not to destroy the air-pockets since this would tend to blur the print

19. When fingerprints lifted from an object found at the scene of a crime are to be compared with the fingerprints of a suspect, the lifted print 19.____
    A. can be compared directly only if a rubber adhesive lift was used
    B. cannot be compared directly if transparent scotch tape was used
    C. can be compared directly if transparent scotch tape was used
    D. must be photographed first and a positive made if any commercial lifting tape was used

20. When a rubber adhesive lift is to be used to lift a fingerprint, the one of the following which must be gently peeled off FIRST is the 20.____
    A. acetate cover   B. celluloid strip
    C. dusted surface   D. tape off the print surface

KEY (CORRECT ANSWERS)

1.	B	11.	C
2.	D	12.	A
3.	C	13.	B
4.	C	14.	D
5.	D	15.	A
6.	C	16.	C
7.	D	17.	D
8.	D	18.	B
9.	C	19.	C
10.	C	20.	B

READING COMPREHENSION
UNDERSTANDING AND INTERPRETING WRITTEN MATERIAL

EXAMINATION SECTION
TEST 1

DIRECTIONS: Each question or incomplete statement is followed by several suggested answers or completions. Select the one that BEST answers the question or completes the statement. *PRINT THE LETTER OF THE COREECT ANSWER IN THE SPACE AT THE RIGHT.*

Questions 1-3.

DIRECTIONS: Questions 1 through 3 are to be answered SOLELY on the basis of the following paragraph.

When wood products are heated sufficiently under fire conditions, they undergo thermal decomposition and evolve various combustible gases or vapors which burn as the familiar flames. After these volatile decomposition products of the wood are driven off, the combustible residue is essentially carbon which on further heating undergoes surface combustion reactions with the oxygen of the air, producing considerable heat (glowing), but usually very little flame.

1. The one of the following explanations of thermal decomposition that is MOST accurate is that it is a process by which

    A. heat is transferred from solid substances to gaseous substances
    B. a substance is consumed during the course of a fire
    C. a substance is broken down into component parts when subjected to heat
    D. heat is generated until the ignition point of the substance is reached

2. The one of the following statements that is MOST accurate is that pure carbon has an ignition temperature which, compared to the combustible vapors of wood, is

    A. lower
    B. approximately the same
    C. higher
    D. higher or lower, depending upon the variety of wood involved

3. A substance which burns with a large amount of flames is one that

    A. contains a large amount of inorganic material
    B. produces during the burning process a large amount of pure carbon
    C. contains a large amount of calories per unit of combustibles
    D. produces during the burning process a large amount of combustible gases or vapors

Questions 4-7.

DIRECTIONS: Questions 4 through 7 are to be answered SOLELY on the basis of the following paragraph.

For the five year period 1996-2000, inclusive, the average annual fire loss in the United States amounted to approximately $2,709,760,000. Included in this estimate is $2,045,332,000 damage to buildings and contents, and $564,328,000 average annual loss in aircraft, motor vehicles, forest and other miscellaneous fires not involving buildings. Preliminary estimates indicate that the total United States fire loss in 1981 was $3,230,000,000. These are property damage fire losses only and do not include indirect losses resulting from fires which are just as real and sometimes far more serious than property damage losses. But because evaluation of indirect monetary losses is usually very difficult, their importance in the national fire waste picture is often overlooked.

4. According to the data in the above paragraph, the BEST of the following estimates of the total direct fire loss in the United States for the six year period 1996-2001, inclusive, is

    A. $2,800,000,000
    B. $5,400,000,000
    C. $14,000,000,000
    D. $16,800,000,000

5. The BEST example of an indirect fire loss, as that term is used in the above paragraph, is monetary loss due to

    A. smoke or water damage to exposures
    B. condemnation of foodstuffs following a fire
    C. interruption of business following a fire
    D. forcible entry by firemen operating at a fire

6. Suppose that during the period 2001-2005 the average annual fire loss to buildings and contents increases 10 percent and the average annual loss due to fires not involving buildings decreases 10 percent.
The MOST valid of the following conclusions is that the average annual fire loss for the 2001-2005 period, compared to the losses for the 1996-2000 period,

    A. will increase
    B. will decrease
    C. will be unchanged
    D. cannot be calculated from the information given

7. If a comparison is made between total annual direct and indirect fire losses on the basis of the information given in the above paragraph, the MOST valid of the following conclusions is that

    A. generally direct losses are higher
    B. generally indirect losses are higher
    C. generally direct and indirect losses are approximately equal
    D. there is not sufficient information to determine which is higher or if they are approximately equal

Questions 8-10.

DIRECTIONS: Questions 8 through 10 are to be answered SOLELY on the basis of the following paragraph.

The soda-acid fire extinguisher is the commonest type of water solution extinguisher in which pressure is used to expel the water. The chemicals used are sodium bicarbonate (baking soda) and sulfuric acid. The sodium bicarbonate is dissolved in water, and this solution is the extinguishing agent. The extinguishing value of the stream is that of an equal quantity of water.

8. According to the above paragraph, the soda-acid extinguisher, compared to others of the same type, is the

   A. most widely used
   B. most effective in putting out fire
   C. cheapest to operate
   D. easiest to operate

9. In the soda-acid extinguisher, the fire is put out by a solution of sodium bicarbonate and

   A. sulfuric acid
   B. baking soda
   C. soda-acid
   D. water

10. According to the above paragraph, the sodium bicarbonate solution, compared to water, is

    A. *more* effective in putting out fires
    B. *less* effective in putting out fires
    C. *equally* effective in putting out fires
    D. *more* or *less* effective, depending upon the type of fire

Questions 11-13.

DIRECTIONS: Questions 11 through 13 are to be answered SOLELY on the basis of the following paragraph.

The average daily flow of water through public water systems in American cities ranges generally between 40 and 250 gallons per capita, depending upon the underground leakage in the system, the amount of waste in domestic premises, and the qua.ntity used for industrial purposes. The problem of supplying this water has become serious in many cities. Supplies, once adequate, in many cases have become seriously deficient, due to greater demands with increased population and growing industrial use of water. Water works, operating on fixed schedules of water charges, have in many cases not been able to afford the heavy capital expenditures necessary to provide adequate supply, storage, and distribution facilities. Thus, the adequacy of a public water supply for fire protection in any given location cannot properly be taken for granted.

11. The four programs listed below are possible ways by which American communities might try to reduce the seriousness of the water shortage problem.
    The one of the four programs which does NOT directly follow from the paragraph above is the program of

    A. regular replacement of old street water mains by new ones
    B. inspection and repair of leaky plumbing fixtures
    C. fire prevention inspection and education to reduce the amount of water used to extinguish fires
    D. research into industrial processes to reduce the amount of water used in those processes

12. The MAIN conclusion reached by the author of the above paragraph is

    A. there is a waste of precious natural resources in America
    B. communities have failed to control the industrial use of water
    C. a need exists for increasing the revenue of water works to build up adequate supplies of water
    D. fire departments cannot assume that they will always have the necessary supply of water available to fight fires

13. Per capita consumption of water of a community is determined by the formula

    A. $\dfrac{\text{Population}}{\text{Total consumption in gallons}} = \text{per capita consumption in gallons}$

    B. $\dfrac{\text{Total consumption in gallons}}{\text{Population}} = \text{per capita consumption in gallons}$

    C. Total consumption in gallons x population = per capita consumption in gallons
    D. Total consumption in gallons - population = Per capita consumption in gallons

Questions 14-17.

DIRECTIONS: Questions 14 through 17 are to be answered SOLELY on the basis of the following paragraph.

Language performs an essentially social function; it helps us to get along together, to communicate and achieve a great measure of concerted action. Words are signs which have significance by convention, and those people who do not adopt the conventions simply fail to communicate. They do not *get along* and a social force arises which encourages them to achieve the correct associations. *Correct* means as used by other members of the social group. Some of the vital points about language are brought home to an Englishman when visiting America, and vice versa, because our vocabularies are nearly the same—but not quite.

14. *Communicate,* as that word is used in the above paragraph, means to

    A. make ourselves understood
    B. send written messages
    C. move other persons to concerted action
    D. use language in its traditional or conventional sense

15. Usage of a word is *correct*, as that term is defined in the above paragraph, when the word is used as it is

    A. defined in standard dictionaries
    B. used by the majority of persons throughout the world who speak the same language
    C. used by the majority of educated persons who speak the same language
    D. used by other persons with whom we are associating

16. In the above paragraph, the author is concerned PRIMARILY with the 16.____

    A. meaning of words
    B. pronunciation of words
    C. structure of sentences
    D. origin and development of language

17. According to the above paragraph, the MAIN language problem of an Englishman, while 17.____
    visiting America, stems from the fact that an Englishman

    A. uses some words that have different meanings for Americans
    B. has different social values than the Americans
    C. has had more exposure to non-English speaking persons than Americans have had
    D. pronounces words differently than Americans do

Questions 18-21.

DIRECTIONS: Questions 18 through 21 are to be answered SOLELY on the basis of the following paragraph.

   Whenever a social group has become so efficiently organized that it has gained access to an adequate supply of food and has learned to distribute it among its members so well that wealth considerably exceeds immediate demands, it can be depended upon to utilize its surplus energy in an attempt to enlarge the sphere in which it is active. The structure of ant colonies renders them particularly prone to this sort of expansionist policy. With very few exceptions, ants of any given colony are hostile to those of any other community, even of the same species, and this condition is bound to produce preliminary bickering among colonies which are closely associated.

18. According to the above paragraph, a social group is wealthy when it 18.____

    A. is efficiently organized
    B. controls large territories
    C. contains energetic members
    D. produces and distributes food reserves

19. According to the above paragraph, the structure of an ant colony is its 19.____

    A. social organization   B. nest arrangement
    C. territorial extent   D. food-gathering activities

20. It follows from the above paragraph that the LEAST expansionist society would be one 20.____
    that has

    A. great poverty generally
    B. more than sufficient wealth to meet its immediate demands
    C. great wealth generally
    D. wide inequality between its richest and poorest members

21. According to the above paragraph, an ant generally is hostile EXCEPT to other   21._____
    A. insects
    B. ants
    C. ants of the same species
    D. ants of the same colony

Questions 22-25.

DIRECTIONS: Questions 22 through 25 are to be answered SOLELY on the basis of the following paragraph.

Steel used in boiler construction must be of a higher quality than steel used in general construction. The boiler steel must be capable of sustaining loads at elevated temperatures. Temperature has a more serious effect upon the boiler fabrication than has the pressure. The material for bolts and studs is conditioned by tempering. The tempering temperature is at least 100F higher than the service operating temperature. All materials used in boiler construction must be creep resistant to minimize the relaxation in service. Fire box quality plate is used for any part of a boiler exposed to the fire or products of combustion. For parts of the boiler subject to pressure and not exposed to fire or products of combustion, flange quality plate is used. A small percentage of molybdenum is added to steel in the manufacture of superheater tubes, piping, and valves to increase the ability of these parts to withstand high temperature.

22. Material for bolts and studs used on boilers is conditioned for service by   22._____
    A. tempering   B. re-tightening
    C. forging   D. anodizing

23. The part of a boiler that is exposed to products of combustion is made of   23._____
    A. alloy materials   B. firebox quality plate
    C. flange quality plate   D. carbon steel

24. Temperature has a MORE serious effect upon boiler fabrication than has the   24._____
    A. vibration   B. steam   C. relaxation   D. pressure

25. When comparing steel used in boiler construction to steel used in general construction, it   25._____
    can be said that steel used in boiler construction must be of a
    A. high-weld strength   B. low-carbon content
    C. lower quality   D. higher quality

KEY (CORRECT ANSWERS)

1.	C	11.	C
2.	C	12.	D
3.	D	13.	B
4.	D	14.	A
5.	C	15.	D
6.	A	16.	A
7.	D	17.	A
8.	A	18.	D
9.	D	19.	A
10.	C	20.	A

21. D
22. A
23. B
24. D
25. D

TEST 2

Questions 1-3.

DIRECTIONS: Questions 1 through 3 are to be answered SOLELY on the basis of the following paragraph.

    A fire of undetermined origin started in the warehouse shed of a flour mill. Although there was some delay in notifying the fire department, they practically succeeded in bringing the fire under control when a series of dust explosions occurred which caused the fire to spread and the main building was destroyed. The fire department's efforts were considerably handicapped because it was undermanned, and the water pressure in the vicinity was inadequate.

1. From the information contained in the above paragraph, it is MOST accurate to state that the cause of the fire was

    A. suspicious   B. unknown
    C. accidental   D. spontaneous combustion

2. In the fire described above, the MOST important cause of the fire spreading to the main building was the

    A. series of dust explosions
    B. delay in notifying the fire department
    C. inadequate water pressure
    D. wooden construction of the building

3. In the fire described above, the fire department's efforts were handicapped CHIEFLY by

    A. poor leadership
    B. outdated apparatus
    C. uncooperative company employees
    D. insufficient water pressure

Questions 4-6.

DIRECTIONS: Questions 4 through 6 are to be answered SOLELY on the basis of the following paragraph.

    A flameproof fabric is defined as one which, when exposed to small sources of ignition such as sparks or smoldering cigarettes, does not burn beyond the vicinity of the source of the ignition. Cotton fabrics are the materials commonly used that are considered most hazardous. Other materials, such as acetate rayons and linens, are somewhat less hazardous, and woolens and some natural silk fabrics, even when untreated, are about the equal of the average treated cotton fabric insofar as flame spread and ease of ignition are concerned. The method of application is to immerse the fabric in a flameproofing solution. The container used must be large enough so that all the fabric is thoroughly wet and there are no folds which the solution does not penetrate.

4. According to the above paragraph, a flameproof fabric is one which   4._____

   A. is unaffected by heat and smoke
   B. resists the spread of flames when ignited
   C. cannot be ignited by sparks or cigarettes
   D. may smolder but cannot burn

5. According to the above paragraph, woolen fabrics which have not been flameproofed are as likely to catch fire as   5._____

   A. treated silk fabrics
   B. untreated linen fabrics
   C. untreated synthetic fabrics
   D. treated cotton fabrics

6. In the method described above, the flameproofing solution is BEST applied to the fabric by _____ the fabric.   6._____

   A. sponging   B. spraying   C. dipping   D. brushing

Questions 7-10.

DIRECTIONS: Questions 7 through 10 are to be answered SOLELY on the basis of the following paragraph.

There is hardly a city in the country that is not short of fire protection in some areas within its boundaries. These municipalities have spread out and have re-shuffled their residential, business, and industrial districts without readjusting the existing protective fire forces or creating new protection units. Fire stations are still situated according to the needs of earlier times and have not been altered or improved to house modern fire fighting equipment. They are neither efficient for carrying out their tasks nor livable for the men who must occupy them.

7. Of the following, the title which BEST describes the central idea of the above paragraph is   7._____

   A. THE DYNAMIC NATURE OF CONTEMPORARY SOCIETY
   B. THE COST OF FIRE PROTECTION
   C. THE LOCATION AND DESIGN OF FIRE STATIONS
   D. THE DESIGN AND USE OF FIRE FIGHTING EQUIPMENT

8. According to the above paragraph, fire protection is inadequate in the United States in _____ areas _____ cities.   8._____

   A. most; of some   B. some; of most
   C. some; in all   D. most; in most

9. The one of the following criteria for planning of fire stations which is NOT mentioned in the above paragraph is

   A. proper location
   B. design for modern equipment
   C. efficiency of operation
   D. cost of construction

10. Of the following suggestions for improving the fire service, the one which would BEST deal with the problems discussed in the above paragraph would involve

    A. specialized training in the use of modern fire apparatus
    B. replacement of obsolete fire apparatus
    C. longer basic training for probationary firemen
    D. reassignment of fire districts

Questions 11-14.

DIRECTIONS: Questions 11 through 14 are to be answered SOLELY on the basis of the following paragraph.

   Gravity tanks for sprinkler systems shall contain an available quantity of water sufficient to supply 25 percent of the number of sprinkler heads in the average protected fire area for twenty minutes, and in any case at least 5,000 gallons. Where there are more than 200 and not more than 400 sprinklers in such average protected fire area, the available quantity of water in excess of 20,000 gallons need not be greater than an amount sufficient to supply 12 1/2 percent of the sprinklers in excess of 200 in such average protected fire area for a period of twenty minutes. If the number of sprinklers in such average fire area exceeds 400, the available quantity of water in excess of 30,000 gallons need not be greater than an amount sufficient to supply six and one-fourth percent of the sprinklers in excess of four hundred in such average protected fire area for a period of twenty minutes.

11. In establishing the required capacity of the gravity tanks for sprinkler systems, the assumption contained in the above paragraph is that the average discharge per minute from sprinkler heads will be _____ gallons.

    A. 20   B. 22   C. 25   D. 28

12. A sprinkler system containing 500 sprinkler heads requires gravity tanks with a minimum capacity of approximately _____ gallons.

    A. 32,500   B. 35,000   C. 37,500   D. 40,000

13. A sprinkler system contains 600 sprinkler heads in the protected fire area. If the minimum requirements of the above paragraph have been met, the gravity tanks should be able to supply for twenty minutes approximately _____ heads.

    A. 88   B. 94   C. 100   D. 106

14. The one of the following graphs which MOST accurately represents the gravity tanks' capacity requirements for sprinkler systems built in accordance with the requirements of the above paragraph is

14.____

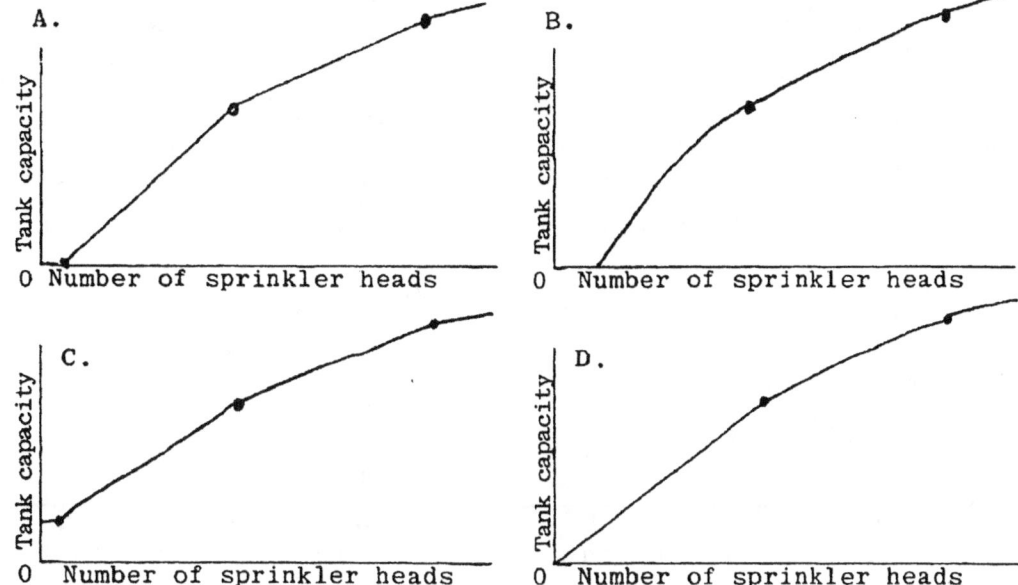

Questions 15-18.

DIRECTIONS: Questions 15 through 18 are to be answered SOLELY on the basis of the following paragraph.

A mixture of a combustible vapor and air will burn only when the proportion of fuel to air lies within a certain range, i.e., between the upper and lower limits of flammability. If a third, non-combustible gas is now added to the mixture, the limits will be narrowed. As increasing amounts of diluent are added, the limits come closer until, at a certain critical concentration, they will converge. This is the peak concentration. It is the minimum amount of diluent that will inhibit the combustion of any fuel-air mixture.

15. If additional diluent is added beyond the peak concentration, the flammable limits of the mixture will

15.____

   A. converge rapidly   B. diverge slowly
   C. diverge rapidly   D. not be affected

16. If the four numbers listed below were peak concentration values obtained in a test of four diluents, then the MOST efficient diluent would have the value of

16.____

   A. 7.5   B. 10   C. 12.5   D. 15

17. The word *inhibit,* as used in the last sentence of the above paragraph, means MOST NEARLY

17.____

   A. slow the rate of
   B. prevent entirely the occurrence of
   C. reduce the intensity of
   D. retard to an appreciable extent the manifestation of

18. The one of the graphs below which BEST represents the process described in the above paragraph is   18._____

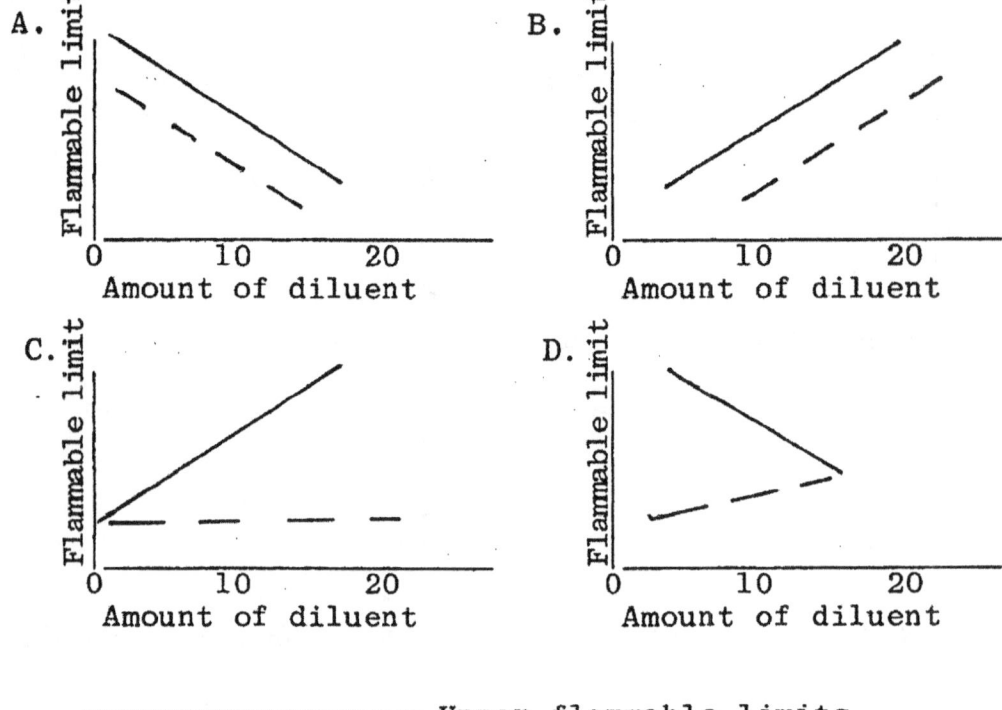

Questions 19-22.

DIRECTIONS: Questions 19 through 22 are to be answered SOLELY on the basis of the following paragraph.

The unadjusted loss per $1000 valuation has only a very limited usefulness in evaluating the efficiency of a fire department, for it depends upon the assumption that other factors will remain constant from time to time and city to city. It might be expected that high fire department operation expenditures would tend to be associated with a low fire loss. A statistical study of the loss and cost data in more than 100 cities failed to reveal any such correlation. The lack of relationship, although to some extent due to failure to make the most efficacious expenditure of fire protection funds, must be attributed in part at least to the obscuring effect of variations in the natural, physical, and moral factors which affect fire risk.

19. One reason for the failure to obtain the expected relationship between fire department expenditures and fire loss data which is stated in the above paragraph is the   19._____

    A. changing dollar valuation of property
    B. unsettling effects of rapid technological innovations
    C. inefficiency of some fire department activities
    D. statistical errors made by the investigators

20. We may conclude that *the unadjusted loss per $1000* figure is useful in comparing the fire departments of two cities

    A. only if the cities are of comparable size
    B. only if adjustments are made for other factors which affect fire loss
    C. under no circumstances
    D. only if properly controlled experimental conditions can be obtained

21. The one of the following factors which affect fire risk that is MOST adequately reflected in the *unadjusted loss per $1000 valuation* index is

    A. fire department operation expenditures
    B. physical characteristics of the city
    C. type of structures most prevalent in the city
    D. total worth of property in the city

22. According to the above paragraph, cities which spend larger sums on their fire departments

    A. tend to have lower fire losses than cities which spend smaller sums on their fire departments
    B. do not tend to have lower fire losses than cities which spend smaller sums on their fire departments
    C. tend to have higher fire losses than cities which spend smaller sums on their fire departments
    D. do not tend to have the same total property valuation as cities which spend smaller sums on their fire departments

Questions 23-25.

DIRECTIONS: Questions 23 through 25 are to be answered SOLELY on the basis of the following paragraph.

Shafts extending into the top story, except those stair shafts where the stairs do not continue to the roof, shall be carried through and at least two feet above the roof. Every shaft extending above the roof, except open shafts and elevator shafts, shall be enclosed at the top with a roof of materials having a fire resistive rating of one hour and a metal skylight covering at least three-quarters of the area of the shaft in the top story, except that skylights over stair shafts shall have an area not less than one-tenth the area of the shaft in the top story, but shall be not less than fifteen square feet in area. Any shaft terminating below the top story of a structure and those stair shafts not required to extend through the roof shall have the top enclosed with materials having the same fire resistive rating as required for the shaft enclosure.

23. The above paragraph states that the elevator shafts which extend into the top story are

    A. not required to have a skylight but are required to extend at least two feet above the roof
    B. neither required to have a skylight nor to extend above the roof
    C. required to have a skylight covering at least three-quarters of the area of the shaft in the top story and to extend at least two feet above the roof
    D. required to have a skylight covering at least three-quarters of the area of the shaft in the top story but are not required to extend above the roof

24. The one of the following skylights which meets the requirements of the above paragraph is a skylight measuring

    A. 4' x 4' over a stair shaft which, on the top story, measures 20' x 9'
    B. 4 1/2' x 3 1/2' over a pipe shaft which, on the top story, measures 5' x 4'
    C. 2 1/2' x 1 1/2' over a dumbwaiter shaft which, on the top story, measures 2 1/2' x 2 1/2'
    D. 4' x 3' over a stair shaft which, on the top story, measures 15' x 6'

25. Suppose that in a Class I building a shaft which does not go to the roof is required to have a three-hour fire resistive rating.
    In regard to the material enclosing the top of this shaft, the above paragraph

    A. states that a one-hour fire resistive rating is required
    B. states that a three-hour fire resistive rating is required
    C. implies that no fire resistive rating is required
    D. neither states nor implies anything about the fire resistive rating

KEY (CORRECT ANSWERS)

1. B		11. A	
2. A		12. A	
3. D		13. A	
4. B		14. C	
5. D		15. D	
6. C		16. A	
7. C		17. B	
8. B		18. D	
9. D		19. C	
10. D		20. B	

21. D
22. B
23. A
24. B
25. B

PREPARING WRITTEN MATERIAL

PARAGRAPH REARRANGEMENT
COMMENTARY

The sentences that follow are in scrambled order. You are to rearrange them in proper order and indicate the letter choice containing the correct answer at the space at the right.

Each group of sentences in this section is actually a paragraph presented in scrambled order. Each sentence in the group has a place in that paragraph; no sentence is to be left out. You are to read each group of sentences and decide upon the best order in which to put the sentences so as to form a well-organized paragraph.

The questions in this section measure the ability to solve a problem when all the facts relevant to its solution are not given.

More specifically, certain positions of responsibility and authority require the employee to discover connection between events sometimes, apparently, unrelated. In order to do this, the employee will find it necessary to correctly infer that unspecified events have probably occurred or are likely to occur. This ability becomes especially important when action must be taken on incomplete information.

Accordingly, these questions require competitors to choose among several suggested alternatives, each of which presents a different sequential arrangement of the events. Competitors must choose the MOST logical of the suggested sequences.

In order to do so, they may be required to draw on general knowledge to infer missing concepts or events that are essential to sequencing the given events. Competitors should be careful to infer only what is essential to the sequence. The plausibility of the wrong alternatives will always require the inclusion of unlikely events or of additional chains of events which are NOT essential to sequencing the given events.

It's very important to remember that you are looking for the best of the four possible choices, and that the best choice of all may not even be one of the answers you're given to choose from.

There is no one right way to solve these problems. Many people have found it helpful to first write out the order of the sentences, as they would have arranged them, on their scrap paper before looking at the possible answers. If their optimum answer is there, this can save them some time. If it isn't, this method can still give insight into solving the problem. Others find it most helpful to just go through each of the possible choices, contrasting each as they go along. You should use whatever method feels comfortable and works for you.

While most of these types of questions are not that difficult, we've added a higher percentage of the difficult type, just to give you more practice. Usually there are only one or two questions on this section that contain such subtle distinctions that you're unable to answer confidently. And you then may find yourself stuck deciding between two possible choices, neither of which you're sure about.

PREPARING WRITTEN MATERIAL PARAGRAPH REARRANGEMENT

EXAMINATION SECTION

TEST 1

DIRECTIONS: The sentences that follow are in scrambled order. You are to rearrange them in proper order and indicate the letter choice containing the CORRECT answer. *PRINT THE LETTER OF THE CORRECT ANSWER IN THE SPACE AT THE RIGHT.*

1. Police Officer Jenner responds to the scene of a burglary at 2106 La Vista Boulevard. He is approached by an elderly man named Richard Jenkins, whose account of the incident includes the following five sentences:
   I. I saw that the lock on my apartment door had been smashed and the door was open.
   II. My apartment was a shambles; my belongings were everywhere and my television set was missing.
   III. As I walked down the hallway toward the bedroom, I heard someone opening a window.
   IV. I left work at 5:30 P.M. and took the bus home.
   V. At that time, I called the police.
   The MOST logical order for the above sentence to appear in the report is
   A. I, V, IV, II, III   B. IV, I, II, III, V   C. I, V, II, III, IV   D. IV, III, II, V, I

   1.____

2. Police Officer LaJolla is writing an Incident Report in which back-up assistance was required. The report will contain the following five sentences:
   I. The radio dispatcher asked what my location was and he then dispatched patrol cars for back-up assistance.
   II. At approximately 9:30 P.M., while I was walking my assigned footpost, a gunman fired three shots at me.
   III. I quickly turned around and saw a white male, approximately 5'10", with black hair, wearing blue jeans, a yellow T-shirt, and white sneaker, running across the avenue carrying a handgun.
   IV. When the back-up officers arrived, we searched the area but could not find the suspect.
   V. I advised the radio dispatcher that a gunman had just fired a gun at me, and then I gave the dispatcher a description of the man
   The MOST logical order for the above sentences to appear in the report is:
   A. III, V, II, IV, I   B. II, III, V, I, IV   C. III, II, IV, I, V   D. II, V, I, III, IV

   2.____

3. Police Officer Durant is completing a report of a robbery and assault. The report will contain the following five sentences:
   I. I went to Mount Snow Hospital to interview a man who was attacked and robbed of his wallet earlier that night.
   II. An ambulance arrived at 82nd Street and 3rd Avenue and took an intoxicated, wounded man to Mount Snow Hospital
   III. Two youths attacked the man and stole his wallet.

   3.____

IV. A well-dressed man left Hanratty's Bar very drunk, with his wallet hanging out of his back pocket.
V. A passerby dialed 911 and requested police and ambulance assistance.
The MOST logical order for the above sentences to appear in the report is
   A. I, II, IV, III, V   B. IV, III, V, II, I   C. IV, V, II, III, I   D. V, IV, III, II, I

4. Police Officer Boswell is preparing a report of an armed robbery and assault which will contain the following five sentences:
   I. Both men approached the bartender and one of them drew a gun.
   II. The bartender immediately went to grab the phone at the bar.
   III. One of the men leaped over the counter and smashed a bottle over the bartender's head.
   IV. Two men in a blue Buick drove up to the bar and went inside.
   V. I found the cash register empty and the bartender unconscious on the floor, with the phone still dangling off the hook.
   The MOST logical order for the above sentences to appear in the report is
      A. IV, I, II, II, V   B. V, IV, III, I, II   C. IV, III, II, V, I   D. II, I, III, IV, V

5. Police Officer Mitzler is preparing a report of a bank robbery, which will contain the following five sentences:
   I. The teller complied with the instructions on the note, but also hit the silent alarm.
   II. The perpetrator then fled south on Broadway.
   III. A suspicious male entered the bank at approximately 10:45 A.M.
   IV. At this time, an undetermined amount of money has been taken.
   V. He approached the teller on the far right side and handed her a note.
   The MOST logical order for the above sentences to appear in the report is:
      A. III, V, I, II, IV   B. I, III, V, II, IV   C. III, V, IV, I, II   D. III, V, II, IV, I

6. A Police Officer is preparing an Accident Report for an accident which occurred at the intersection of East 119th Street and Lexington Avenue. The report will include the following five sentences:
   I. On September 18, while driving ten children to school, a school bus driver passed out.
   II. Upon arriving at the scene, I notified the dispatcher to send an ambulance.
   III. I notified the parents of each child once I got to the station house.
   IV. He said the school bus, while traveling west on East 119th Street, struck a parked Ford which was on the southwest corner of East 119th Street.
   V. A witness by the name of John Ramos came up to me to describe what happened.
   The MOST logical order for the above sentences to appear in the Accident Report is:
      A. I, II, V, III, IV   B. I, II, V, IV, III   C. II, V, I, III, IV   D. II, V, I, IV, III

7. A Police Officer is preparing a report concerning a dispute. The report will contain the following five sentences:
   I. The passenger got out of the back of the taxi and leaned through the front window to complain to the driver about the fare.

II. The driver of the taxi caught up with the passenger and knocked him to the ground; the passenger then kicked the driver and a scuffle ensued.
III. The taxi drew up in front of the high-rise building and stopped.
IV. The driver got out of the taxi and followed the passenger into the lobby of the apartment building.
V. The doorman tried but was unable to break up the fight, at which point he called the precinct.

The MOST logical order for the above sentences to appear in the report is
   A. III, I, IV, II, V   B. III, IV, I, II, V   C. III, IV, II, V, I   D. V, I, III, IV, II

8. Police Officer Morrow is writing an Incident Report. The report will include the following four sentences:
I. The man reached into his pocket and pulled out a gun.
II. While on foot patrol, I identified a suspect, who was wanted for six robberies in the area, from a wanted picture I was carrying.
III. I drew my weapon and fired six rounds at the suspect, killing him instantly.
IV. I called for back-up assistance and told the man to put his hands up.

The MOST logical order for the above sentences to appear in the report is
   A. II, III, IV, I   B. IV, I, III, II   C. IV, I, II, III   D. II, IV, I, III

9. Sergeant Allen responds to a call at 16 Grove Street regarding a missing child. At the scene, the Sergeant is met by Police Officer Samuels, who gives a brief account of the incident consisting of the following five sentences:
I. I transmitted the description and waited for you to arrive before I began searching the area.
II. Mrs. Banks, the mother, reports that she last saw her daughter Julie about 7:30 A.M. when she took her to school.
III. About 6 P.M., my partner and I arrived at this location to investigate a report of a missing 8-year-old girl.
IV. When Mrs. Banks left her, Julie was wearing a red and white striped T-shirt, blue jeans, and white sneakers.
V. Mrs. Banks dropped her off in front of the playground of P.S. 11.

The MOST logical order for the above sentences to appear in the report is
   A. III, V, IV, II, I   B. III, II, V, IV, I   C. III, IV, I, II, V   D. III, II, IV, I, V

10. Police Officer Franco is completing a report of an assault. The report will contain the following five sentences:
I. In the park I observed an elderly man lying on the ground, bleeding from a back wound.
II. I applied first aid to control the bleeding and radioed for an ambulance to respond.
III. The elderly man stated that he was sitting on the park bench when he was attacked from behind by two males.
IV. I received a report of a man's screams coming from inside the park, and I went to investigate.
V. The old man could not give a description of his attackers.

The MOST logical order for the above sentences to appear in the report is
   A. IV, I, II, III, V   B. V, III, I, IV, II   C. IV, III, V, II, I   D. II, I, V, IV, III

11. Police Officer Williams is completing a Crime Report. The report contains the following five sentences:
    I. As Police Officer Hanson and I approached the store, we noticed that the front door was broken.
    II. After determining that the burglars had fled, we notified the precinct of the burglary.
    III. I walked through the front door as Police Officer Hanson walked around to the back.
    IV. At approximately midnight, an alarm was heard at the Apex Jewelry Store.
    V. We searched the store and found no one.
    The MOST logical order for the above sentences to appear in the report is
    A. I, IV, II, III, V   B. I, IV, III, V, II   C. IV, I, III, II, V   D. IV, I, III, V, II

12. Police Officer Clay is giving a report to the news media regarding someone who has jumped from the Empire State Building. His report will include the following five sentences:
    I. I responded to the 86th floor, where I found the person at the edge of the roof.
    II. A security guard at the building had reported that a man was on the roof at the 86th floor.
    III. At 5:30 P.M., the person jumped from the building.
    IV. I received a call from the radio dispatcher at 4:50 P.M. to respond to the Empire State Building.
    V. I tried to talk to the person and convince him not to jump.
    The MOST logical order for the above sentences to appear in the report is
    A. I, II, IV, III, V   B. III, IV, I, II, V   C. II, IV, I, III, V   D. IV, II, I, V, III

13. The following five sentences are part of a report of a burglary written by Police Officer Reed:
    I. When I arrived at 2400 1st Avenue, I noticed that the door was slightly open.
    II. I yelled out, *Police, don't move!*
    III. As I entered the apartment, I saw a man with a TV set passing through a window to another man standing on a fire escape.
    IV. While on foot patrol, I was informed by the radio dispatcher that a burglary was in progress at 2400 1st Avenue.
    V. However, the burglars quickly ran down the fire escape.
    The MOST logical order for the above sentences to appear in the report is
    A. I, III, IV, V, II   B. IV, I, III, V, II   C. IV, I, III, II, V   D. I, IV, III, II, V

14. Police Officer Jenkins is preparing a report for Lost or Stolen Property. The report will include the following five sentences:
    I. On the stairs, Mr. Harris slipped on a wet leaf and fell on the landing.
    II. It wasn't until he got to the token booth that Mr. Harris realized his wallet was no longer in his back pants pocket.
    III. A boy wearing a football jersey helped him up and brushed off the back of Mr. Harris' pants.
    IV. Mr. Harris states he was walking up the stairs to the elevated subway at Queensborough Plaza.
    V. Before Mr. Harris could thank him, the boy was running down the stairs to the street.

5 (#1)

The MOST logical order for the above sentences to appear in the report is
A. IV, III, V, I, II   B. IV, I, III, V, II   C. I, IV, II, III, V   D. I, II, IV, III, V

15. Police Officer Hubbard is completing a report of a missing person. The report will contain the following five sentences:
   I. I visited the store at 7:55 P.M. and asked the employees if they had seen a girl fitting the description I had been given.
   II. She gave me a description and said she had gone into the local grocery store at about 6:15 P.M.
   III. I asked the woman for a description of her daughter.
   IV. The distraught woman called the precinct to report that her daughter, aged 12, had not returned from an errand.
   V. The storekeeper said a girl matching the description had been in the store earlier, but he could not give an exact time.
   The MOST logical order for the above sentences to appear in the report is
   A. I, III, II, V, IV   B. IV, III, II, I, V   C. V, I, II, III, IV   D. III, I, II, IV, V

16. A police officer is completing an entry in his Daily Activity Log regarding traffic summonses which he issued. The following five sentences will be included in the entry:
   I. I was on routine patrol parked 16 yards west of 170th Street and Clay Avenue.
   II. The summonses were issued for unlicensed operator and disobeying a steady red light.
   III. At 8 A.M. hours, I observed an auto traveling westbound on 170th Street not stop for a steady red light at the intersection of Clay Avenue and 170th Street.
   IV. I stopped the driver of the auto and determined that he did not have a valid driver's license.
   V. After a brief conversation, I informed the motorist that he was receiving two summonses.
   The MOST logical order for the above sentences to appear in the report is
   A. I, III, IV, V, II   B. III, IV, II, V, I   C. V, II, I, III, IV   D. IV, V, II, I, III

17. The following sentences appeared on an Incident Report:
   I. Three teenagers who had been ejected from the theater were yelling at patrons who were now entering.
   II. Police Officer Dixon told the teenagers to leave the area.
   III. The teenager said that they were told by the manager to leave the theater because they were talking during the movie.
   IV. The theater manager called the precinct at 10:20 P.M. to report a disturbance outside the theater.
   V. A patrol car responded to the theater at 10:42 P.M. and two police officers went over to the teenagers.
   The MOST logical order for the above sentences to appear in the Incident Report is
   A. I, V, IV, III, II   B. IV, I, V, III, II   C. IV, I, III, V, II   D. IV, III, I, V, II

18. Activity Log entries are completed by police officers. Police Officer Samuels has written an entry concerning vandalism and part of it contains the following five sentences:
    I. The man, in his early twenties, ran down the block and around the corner.
    II. A man passing the store threw a brick through a window of the store.
    III. I arrived on the scene and began to question the witnesses about the incident.
    IV. Malcolm Holmes, the owner of the Fast Service Shoe Repair Store, was working in the back of the store at approximately 3 P.M.
    V. After the man fled, Mr. Holmes called the police.
    The MOST logical order for the above sentences to appear in the Activity Log is
    A. IV, II, I, V, III   B. II, IV, I, III, V   C. II, I, IV, III, V   D. IV, II, V, III, I

18.____

19. Police Officer Buckley is preparing a report concerning a dispute in a restaurant. The report will contain the following five sentences:
    I. The manager, Charles Chin, and a customer, Edward Green, were standing near the register arguing over the bill.
    II. The manager refused to press any charges providing Green pay the check and leave.
    III. While on foot patrol, I was informed by a passerby of a disturbance in the Dragon Flame Restaurant.
    IV. Green paid the $15.00 check and left the restaurant.
    V. According to witnesses, the customer punched the owner in the face when Chin asked him for the amount due.
    The MOST logical order for the above sentences to appear in the report is
    A. III, I, V, II, IV   B. I, II, III, IV, V   C. V, I, III, II, IV   D. III, V, II, IV, I

19.____

20. Police Officer Wilkins is preparing a report for leaving the scene of an accident. The report will include the following five sentences:
    I. The Dodge struck the right rear fender of Mrs. Smith's 2010 Ford and continued on its way.
    II. Mrs. Smith stated she was making a left turn from 40th Street onto Third Avenue.
    III. As the car passed, Mrs. Smith noticed the dangling rear license plate #412AEJ.
    IV. Mrs. Smith complained to police of back pains and was removed by ambulance to Bellevue Hospital.
    V. An old green Dodge traveling up Third Avenue went through the red light at 40th Street and Third Avenue.
    The MOST logical order for the above sentences to appear in the report is
    A. V, III, I, II, IV   B. I, III, II, V, IV   C. IV, V, I, II, III   D. II, V, I, III, IV

20.____

21. Detective Simon is completing a Crime Report. The report contains the following five sentences:
    I. Police Officer Chin, while on foot patrol, heard the yelling and ran in the direction of the man.
    II. The man, carrying a large hunting knife, left the High Sierra Sporting Goods Store at approximately 10:30 A.M.

21.____

III. When the man heard Police Officer Chin, he stopped, dropped the knife, and began to cry.
IV. As Police Officer Chin approached the man, he drew his gun and yelled, *Police, freeze.*
V. After the man left the store, he began yelling, over and over, *I am going to kill myself!*

The MOST logical order for the above sentences to appear in the report is
   A. V, II, I, IV, III   B. II, V, I, IV, III   C. II, V, IV, I, III   D. II, I, V, IV, III

22. Police Officer Miller is preparing a Complaint Report which will include the following five sentences:
    I. From across the lot, he yelled to the boys to get away from his car.
    II. When he came out of the store, he noticed two teenage boys trying to break into his car.
    III. The boys fled as Mr. Johnson ran to his car.
    IV. Mr. Johnson stated that he parked his car in the municipal lot behind Tams Department Store.
    V. Mr. Johnson saw that the door lock had been broken, but nothing was missing from inside the auto.

    The MOST logical order for the above sentences to appear in the report is
       A. IV, I, II, V, III   B. II, III, I, V, IV   C. IV, II, I, III, V   D. I, II, III, V, IV

22.____

23. Police Officer O'Hara completes a Universal Summons for a motorist who has just passed a red traffic light. The Universal Summons includes the following five sentences:
    I. As the car passed the light, I followed in the patrol car.
    II. After the driver stopped the car, he stated that the light was yellow, not red.
    III. A blue Cadillac sedan passed the red light on the corner of 79th Street and 3rd Avenue at 11:25 P.M.
    IV. As a result, the driver was informed that he did pass a red light and that his brake lights were not working.
    V. The driver in the Cadillac stopped his car as soon as he saw the patrol car, and I noticed that the brake lights were not working.

    The MOST logical order for the above sentences to appear in the Universal Summons is
       A. I, III, V, II, IV   B. III, I, V, II, IV   C. III, I, V, IV, II   D. I, III, IV, II, V

23.____

24. Detective Egan is preparing a follow-up report regarding a homicide on 170th Street and College Avenue. An unknown male was found at the scene. The report will contain the following five sentences:
    I. Police Officer Gregory wrote down the names, addresses, and phone numbers of the witnesses.
    II. A 911 operator received a call of a man shot and dispatched Police Officers Worth and Gregory to the scene.
    III. They discovered an unidentified male dead on the street.
    IV. Police Officer Worth notified the Precinct Detective Unit immediately.
    V. At approximately 9:00 A.M., an unidentified male shot another male in the chest during an argument.

24.____

The MOST logical order for the above sentences to appear in the report is
  A. V, II, III, IV, I   B. II, III, V, IV, I   C. IV, I, V, II, III   D. V, III, II, IV, I

25. Police Officer Tracey is preparing a Robbery Report which will include the following five sentences:
   I. I ran around the corner and observe a man pointing a gun at a taxidriver.
   II. I informed the man I was a police officer and that he should not move.
   III. I was on the corner of 125th Street and Park Avenue when I heard a scream coming from around the corner.
   IV. The man turned around and fired one shot at me.
   V. I fired once, shooting him in the arm and causing him to fall to the ground.
   The MOST logical order for the above sentences to appear in the report is
   A. I, III, IV, II, V   B. IV, V, II, I, III   C. III, I, II, IV, V   D. III, I, V, II, IV

KEY (CORRECT ANSWERS)

1.	B	11.	D
2.	B	12.	D
3.	B	13.	C
4.	A	14.	B
5.	A	15.	B
6.	B	16.	A
7.	A	17.	B
8.	D	18.	A
9.	B	19.	A
10.	A	20.	D

21.	B
22.	C
23.	B
24.	A
25.	C

TEST 2

DIRECTIONS: The sentences that follow are in scrambled order. You are to rearrange them in proper order and indicate the letter choice containing the CORRECT answer. *PRINT THE LETTER OF THE CORRECT ANSWER IN THE SPACE AT THE RIGHT*

1. Police Officer Weiker is completing a Complaint Report which will contain the following five sentences:
   I. Mr. Texlor was informed that the owner of the van would receive a parking ticket and that the van would be towed away.
   II. The police tow truck arrived approximately one half hour after Mr. Texlor complained.
   III. While on foot patrol on West End Avenue, I saw the owner of Rand's Restaurant arrive to open his business.
   IV. Mr. Texlor, the owner, called to me and complained that he could not receive deliveries because a van was blocking his driveway.
   V. The van's owner later reported to the precinct that his van had been stolen, and he was then informed that it had been towed.
   The MOST logical order for the above sentences to appear in the report is
   A. III, V, I, II, IV   B. III, IV, I, II, V   C. IV, III, I, II, V   D. IV, III, II, I, V

   1.____

2. Police Officer Ames is completing an entry in his Activity Log. The entry contains the following five sentences:
   I. Mr. Sands gave me a complete description of the robber.
   II. Alvin Sands, owner of the Star Delicatessen, called the precinct to report he had just been robbed.
   III. I then notified all police patrol vehicles to look for a white male in his early twenties wearing brown pants and shirt, a black leather jacket, and black and white sneakers.
   IV. I arrived on the scene after being notified by the precinct that a robbery had just occurred at the Star Delicatessen.
   V. Twenty minutes later, a man fitting the description was arrested by a police officer on patrol six blocks from the delicatessen.
   The MOST logical order for the above sentences to appear in the Activity Log is
   A. II, I, IV, III, V   B. II IV, III, I, V   C. II, IV, I, III, V   D. II, IV, I, V, III

   2.____

3. Police Officer Benson is completing a Complaint Report concerning a stolen taxicab, which will include the following five sentences:
   I. Police Officer Benson noticed that a cab was parked next to a fire hydrant.
   II. Dawson *borrowed* the cab for transportation purposes since he was in a hurry.
   III. Ed Dawson got into his car and tried to start it, but the battery was dead.
   IV. When he reached his destination, he parked the cab by a fire hydrant and placed the keys under the seat.
   V. He looked around and saw an empty cab with the engine running.
   The MOST logical order for the above sentences to appear in the report is
   A. I, III, II, IV, V   B. III, I, II, V, IV   C. III, V, II, IV, I   D. V, II, IV, III, I

   3.____

4. Police Officer Hatfield is reviewing his Activity Log entry prior to completing a report. The entry contains the following five sentences:
   I. When I arrived at Zand's Jewelry Store, I noticed that the door was slightly open.
   II. I told the burglar I was a police officer and that he should stand still or he would be shot.
   III. As I entered the store, I saw a man wearing a ski mask attempting to open the safe in the back of the store.
   IV. On December 16, 2020, at 1:38 A.M., I was informed that a burglary was in progress at Zand's Jewelry Store on East 59th Street.
   V. The burglar quickly pulled a knife from his pocket when he saw me.
   The MOST logical order for the above sentences to appear in the report is
   A. IV, I, III, V, II   B. I, IV, III, V, II   C. IV, III, II, V, I   D. I, III, IV, V, II

5. Police Officer Lorenz is completing a report of a murder. The report will contain the following five statements made by a witness:
   I. I was awakened by the sound of a gunshot coming from the apartment next door and I decided to check.
   II. I entered the apartment and looked into the kitchen and the bathroom.
   III. I found Mr. Hubbard's body slumped in the bathtub.
   IV. The door to the apartment was open, but I didn't see anyone.
   V. He had been shot in the head.
   The MOST logical order for the above sentences to appear in the report is
   A. I, III, II, IV, V   B. I, IV, II, III, V   C. IV, II, I, III, V   D. III, I, II, IV, V

6. Police Officer Baldwin is preparing an accident report which will include the following five sentences:
   I. The old man lay on the ground for a few minutes, but was not physically hurt.
   II. Charlie Watson, a construction worker, was repairing some brick work at the top of a building at 54th Street and Madison Avenue.
   III. Steven Green, his partner, warned him that this could be dangerous, but Watson ignored him.
   IV. A few minutes later, one of the bricks thrown by Watson smashed to the ground in front of an old man, who fainted out of fright.
   V. Mr. Watson began throwing some of the bricks over the side of the building.
   The MOST logical order for the above sentences to appear in the report is
   A. II, V, III, IV, I   B. I, IV, II, V, III   C. III, II, IV, V, I   D. II, III, I, IV, V

7. Police Officer Porter is completing an Incident Report concerning her rescue of a woman being held hostage by a former boyfriend. Her report will contain the following five sentences:
   I. I saw a man holding .25 caliber gun to a woman's head, but he did not see me.
   II. I then broke a window and gained access to the house.
   III. As I approached the house on foot, a gunshot rang out and I heard a woman scream.
   IV. A decoy van brought me as close as possible to the house where the woman was being held hostage.

V. I ordered the man to drop his gun, and he released the woman and was taken into custody.

The MOST logical order for the above sentences to appear in the report is
A. I, III, II, IV, V B. IV, III, II, I, V C. III, II, I, IV, V D. V, I, II, III, IV

8. Police Officer Byrnes is preparing a crime report concerning a robbery. The report will consist of the following five sentences:
   I. Mr. White, following the man's instructions, opened the car's hood, at which time the man got out of the auto, drew a revolver, and ordered White to give him all the money in his pockets.
   II. Investigation has determined there were no witnesses to this incident.
   III. The man asked White to check the oil and fill the tank.
   IV. Mr. White, a gas attendant, states that he was working alone at the gas station when a black male pulled up to the gas pump in a white Mercury.
   V. White was then bound and gagged by the male and locked in the gas station's rest room.

   The MOST logical order for the above sentences to appear in the report is
   A. IV, I, III, II, V B. III, I, II, V, IV C. IV, III, I, V, II D. I, III, IV, II, V

9. Police Officer Gale is preparing a report of a crime committed against Mr. Weston. The report will consist of the following five sentences:
   I. The man, who had a gun, told Mr. Weston not to scream for help and ordered him back into the apartment.
   II. With Mr. Weston disposed of in this fashion, the man proceeded to ransack the apartment.
   III. Opening the door to see who was there, Mr. Weston was confronted by a tall white male wearing a dark blue jacket and white pants.
   IV. Mr. Weston was at home alone in his living room when the doorbell rang.
   V. Once inside, the man bound and gagged Mr. Weston and locked him in the bathroom.

   The MOST logical order for the above sentences to appear in the report is
   A. III, V, II, I, IV B. IV, III, I, V, II C. III, V, IV, II, I D. IV, III, V, I, II

10. A police officer is completing a report of a robbery, which will contain the following five sentences:
    I. Two police officers were about to enter the Red Rose Coffee Shop on 47th Street and 8th Avenue.
    II. They then noticed a male running up the street carrying a brown paper bag.
    III. They heard a woman standing outside the Broadway Boutique yelling that her store had just been robbed by a young man, and she was pointing up the street.
    IV. They caught up with him and made an arrest.
    V. The police officers pursued the male, who ran past them on 8th Avenue.

    The MOST logical order for the above sentences to appear in the report is
    A. I, III, II, V, IV B. III, I, II, V, IV C. IV, V, I, II, III D. I, V, IV, III, II

11. Police Officer Capalbo is preparing a report of a bank robbery. The report will contain the following five statements made by a witness:
    I. Initialing, all I could see were two men, dressed in maintenance uniforms, sitting in the area reserved for bank officers.
    II. I was passing the bank at 8 P.M. and noticed that all the lights were out, except in the rear section.
    III. Then I noticed two other men in the bank, coming from the direction of the vault, carrying a large metal box.
    IV. At this point, I decided to call the police.
    V. I knocked on the window to get the attention of the men in the maintenance uniforms, and they chased the two men carrying the box down a flight of steps.
    The MOST logical order for the above sentences to appear in the report is
    A. IV, I, II, V, III   B. I, III, II, V, IV   C. II, I, III, V, IV   D. II, III, I, V, IV

11._____

12. Police Officer Roberts is preparing a crime report concerning an assault and a stolen car. The report will contain the following five sentences:
    I. Upon leaving the store to return to his car, Winters noticed that a male unknown to him was sitting in his car.
    II. The man then re-entered Winters' car and drove away, fleeing north on 2nd Avenue.
    III. Mr. Winters stated that he parked his car in front of 235 East 25th Street and left the engine running while he went into the butcher shop at that location.
    IV. Mr. Robert Gering, a witness, stated that the male is known in the neighborhood as Bobby Rae and is believed to reside at 323 East 114th Street.
    V. When Winters approached the car and ordered the man to get out, the man got out of the auto and struck Winters with his fists, knocking him to the ground.
    The MOST logical order for the above sentences to appear in the report is
    A. III, II, V, I, IV   B. III, I, V, II, IV   C. I, IV, V, II, III   D. III, II, I, V, IV

12._____

13. Police Officer Robinson is preparing a crime report concerning the robbery of Mr. Edwards' store. The report will consist of the following five sentences:
    I. When the last customer left the store, the two men drew revolvers and ordered Mr. Edwards to give them all the money in the cash register.
    II. The men proceeded to the back of the store as if they were going to do some shopping.
    III. Janet Morley, a neighborhood resident, later reported that she saw the men enter a green Ford station wagon and flee northbound on Albany Avenue.
    IV. Edwards complied after which the gunmen ran from the store.
    V. Mr. Edwards states that he was stocking merchandise behind the store counter when two white males entered the store.
    The MOST logical order for the above sentences to appear in the report is
    A. V, II, III, I, IV   B. V, II, I, IV, III   C. II, I, V, IV, III   D. III, V, II, I, IV

13._____

14. Police Officer Wendell is preparing an accident report for a 6-car accident that occurred at the intersection of Bath Avenue and Bay Parkway. The report will consist of the following five sentences:
    I. A 2016 Volkswagen Beetle, traveling east on Bath Avenue, swerved to the left to avoid the Impala, and struck a 2014 Ford station wagon which was traveling west on Bath Avenue.
    II. The Seville then mounted the curb on the northeast corner of Bath Avenue and Bay Parkway and struck a light pole.
    III. A 2013 Buick Lesabre, traveling northbound on Bay Parkway directly behind the Impala, struck the Impala, pushing it into the intersection of Bath Avenue and Bay Parkway.
    IV. A 2015 Chevy Impala, traveling northbound on Bay Parkway, had stopped for a red light at Bath Avenue.
    V. A 2017 Toyota, traveling westbound on Bath Avenue, swerved to the right to avoid hitting the Ford station wagon, and struck a 2017 Cadillac Seville double-parked near the corner.
    The MOST logical order for the above sentences to appear in the report is
    A. IV, III, V, II, I   B. III, IV, V, II, I   C. IV, III, I, V, II   D. III, IV, V, I, II

14.____

15. The following five sentences are part of an Activity Log entry Police Officer Rogers made regarding an explosion:
    I. I quickly treated the pedestrian for the injury.
    II. The explosion caused a glass window in an office building to shatter.
    III. After the pedestrian was treated, a call was placed to the precinct requesting additional police officers to evacuate the area.
    IV. After all the glass settled to the ground, I saw a pedestrian who was bleeding from the arm.
    V. While on foot patrol near 5th Avenue and 53rd Street, I heard a loud explosion.
    The MOST logical order for the above sentences to appear in the report is
    A. II, V, IV, I, III   B. V, II, IV, III, I   C. V, II, I, IV, III   D. V, II, IV, I, III

15.____

16. Police Officer David is completing a report regarding illegal activity near the entrance to Madison Square Garden during a recent rock concert. The report will obtain the following five sentences:
    I. As I came closer to the man, he placed what appeared to be tickets in his pocket and began to walk away.
    II. After the man stopped, I questioned him about *scalping* tickets.
    III. While on assignment near the Madison Square Garden entrance, I observed a man apparently selling tickets.
    IV. I stopped the man by stating that I was a police officer.
    V. The man was then given a summons, and he left the area.
    The MOST logical order for the above sentences to appear in the report is
    A. I, III, IV, II, V   B. III, I, IV, V, II   C. III, IV, I, II, V   D. III, I, IV, II, V

16.____

17. Police Officer Sampson is preparing a report containing a dispute in a bar. The report will contain the following five sentences:
    I. John Evans, the bartender, ordered the two men out of the bar.
    II. Two men dressed in dungarees entered the C and D Bar at 5:30 P.M.
    III. The two men refused to leave and began to beat up Evans.
    IV. A customer in the bar saw me on patrol and yelled to me to come separate the three men.
    V. The two men became very drunk and loud within a short time.
    The MOST logical order for the above sentences to appear in the report is
    A. II, I, V, III, IV   B. II, III, IV, V, I   C. III, I, II, V, IV   D. II, V, I, III, IV

18. A police officer is completing a report concerning the response to a crime in progress. The report will include the following five sentences:
    I. The officers saw two armed men run out of the liquor store and into a waiting car.
    II. Police Officers Lunty and Duren received the call and responded to the liquor store.
    III. The robbers gave up without a struggle.
    IV. Lunty and Duren blocked the getaway car with their patrol car.
    V. A call came into the precinct concerning a robbery in progress at Jane's Liquor Store.
    The MOST logical order for the above sentence to appear in the report is
    A. V, II, I, IV, III   B. II, V, I, III, IV   C. V, I, IV, II, III   D. I, V, II, III, IV

19. Police Officers Jenkins is preparing a Crime Report which will consist of the following five sentences:
    I. After making inquirie in the vicinity, Smith found out that his next door neighbor, Viola Jones, had seen two local teenagers, Michael Heinz and Vincent Gaynor, smash his car's windshields with a crowbar.
    II. Jones told Smith that the teenagers live at 8700 19th Avenue.
    III. Mr. Smith heard a loud crash at approximately 11:00 P.M., looked out of his apartment window, and saw two white males running away from his car.
    IV. Smith then reported the incident to the precinct, and Heinz and Gaynor were arrested at the address given.
    V. Leaving his apartment to investigate further, Smith discovered that his car's front and rear windshields had been smashed.
    The MOST logical order for the above sentences to appear in the report is
    A. III, IV, V, I, II   B. III, V, I, II, IV   C. III, I, V, II, IV   D. V, III, I, II, IV

20. Sergeant Nancy Winston is reviewing a Gun Control Report which will contain the following five sentences:
    I. The man fell to the floor when hit in the chest with three bullets from 22 caliber gun.
    II. Merriam's 22 caliber gun was seized, and he was given a summons for not having a pistol permit.
    III. Christopher Merriam, the owner of A-Z Grocery, shot a man who attempted to rob him.
    IV. Police Officer Franks responded and asked Merriam for his pistol permit, which he could not produce.

V. Merriam phoned the police to report he had just shot a man who had attempted to rob him.

The MOST logical order for the above sentences to appear in the report is
   A. III, I, V, IV, II   B. I, III, V, IV, II   C. III, I, V, II, IV   D. I, III, II, V, IV

21. Detective John Manville is completing a report for his superior regarding the murder of an unknown male who was shot in Central Park. The report will contain the following five sentences:
   I. Police Officers Langston and Cavers responded to the scene.
   II. I received the assignment to investigate the murder in Central Park from Detective Sergeant Rogers.
   III. Langston notified the Detective Bureau after questioning Jason.
   IV. An unknown male, apparently murdered, was discovered in Central Park by Howard Jason, a park employee, who immediately called the police.
   V. Langston and Cavers questioned Jason.

   The MOST logical order for the above sentences to appear in the report is
   A. I, IV, V, III, II   B. IV, I, V, II, III   C. IV, I, V, III, II   D. IV, V, I, III, II

22. A police officer is completing a report concerning the arrest of a juvenile. The report will contain the following five sentences:
   I. Sanders then telephoned Jay's parents from the precinct to inform them of their son's arrest.
   II. The store owner resisted, and Jay then shot him and ran from the store.
   III. Jay was transported directly to the precinct by Officer Sanders.
   IV. James Jay, a juvenile, walked into a candy store and announced a hold-up.
   V. Police Officer Sanders, while on patrol, arrested Jay a block from the candy store.

   The MOST logical order for the above sentences to appear in the report is
   A. IV, V, II, I, III   B. IV, II, V, III, I   C. II, IV, V, III, I   D. V, IV, II, I, III

23. Police Officer Olsen prepared a crime report for a robbery which contained the following five sentences:
   I. Mr. Gordon was approached by this individual who then produced a gun and demanded the money from the cash register.
   II. The man then fled from the scene on foot, southbound on 5th Avenue.
   III. Mr. Gordon was working at the deli counter when a white male, 5'6", 150-160 lbs., wearing a green jacket and blue pants, entered the store.
   IV. Mr. Gordon complied with the man's demands and handed him the daily receipts.
   V. Further investigation has determined there are no other witnesses to this robbery.

   The MOST logical order for the above sentences to appear in the report is
   A. I, III, IV, V, II   B. I, IV, II, III, V   C. III, IV, I, V, II   D. III, I, IV, II, V

8 (#2)

24. Police Officer Bryant responded to 285 E. 31st Street to take a crime report of a burglary of Mr. Bond's home. The report will contain a brief description of the incident, consisting of the following five sentences:
    I. When Mr. Bond attempted to stop the burglar by grabbing him, he was pushed to the floor.
    II. The burglar had apparently gained access to the home by forcing open the 2nd floor bedroom window facing the fire escape.
    III. Mr. Bond sustained a head injury in the scuffle, and the burglar exited the home through the front door.
    IV. Finding nothing in the dresser, the burglar proceeded downstairs to the first floor, where he was confronted by Mr. Bond who was reading in the dining room.
    V. Once inside, he searched the drawers of the bedroom dresser.
    The MOST logical order for the above sentences to appear in the report is
        A. V, IV, I, II, III   B. II, V, IV, I, III   C. II, IV, V, III, I   D. III, II, I, V, IV

24.____

25. Police Officer Derringer responded to a call of a rape-homicide case in his patrol area and was ordered to prepare an incident report, which will contain the following five sentences:
    I. He pushed Miss Scott to the ground and forcibly raped her.
    II. Mary Scott was approached from behind by a white male, 5'7", 150-160 lbs. wearing dark pants and a white jacket.
    III. As Robinson approached the male, he ordered him to stop.
    IV. Screaming for help, Miss Scott alerted one John Robinson, a local grocer, who chased her assailant as he fled the scene.
    V. The male turned and fired two shots at Robinson, who fell to the ground mortally wounded.
    The MOST logical order for the above sentences to appear in the report is
        A. IV, III, I, II, V   B. II, IV, III, V, I   C. II, IV, I, V, III   D. II, I, IV, III, V

25.____

KEY (CORRECT ANSWERS)

1.	B	11.	C
2.	C	12.	B
3.	C	13.	B
4.	A	14.	C
5.	B	15.	D
6.	A	16.	D
7.	B	17.	D
8.	C	18.	A
9.	B	19.	B
10.	A	20.	A

21. C
22. B
23. D
24. B
25. D

PREPARING WRITTEN MATERIAL

EXAMINATION SECTION

TEST 1

DIRECTIONS: Each question or incomplete statement is followed by several suggested answers or completions. Select the one that BEST answers the question or completes the statement. *PRINT THE LETTER OF THE CORRECT ANSWER IN THE SPACE AT THE RIGHT.*

1. The one of the following sentences which is LEAST acceptable from the viewpoint of correct usage is:
   A. The police thought the fugitive to be him.
   B. The criminals set a trap for whoever would fall into it.
   C. It is ten years ago since the fugitive fled from the city.
   D. The lecturer argued that criminals are usually cowards.
   E. The police removed four bucketfuls of earth from the scene of the crime.

   1.____

2. The one of the following sentences which is LEAST acceptable from the viewpoint of correct usage is:
   A. The patrolman scrutinized the report with great care.
   B. Approaching the victim of the assault, two bruises were noticed by the patrolman.
   C. As soon as I had broken down the door, I stepped into the room.
   D. I observed the accused loitering near the building, which was closed at the time.
   E. The storekeeper complained that his neighbor was guilty of violating a local ordinance.

   2.____

3. The one of the following sentences which is LEAST acceptable from the viewpoint of correct usage is:
   A. I realized immediately that he intended to assault the woman, so I disarmed him.
   B. It was apparent that Mr. Smith's explanation contained many inconsistencies.
   C. Despite the slippery condition of the street, he managed to stop the vehicle before injuring the child.
   D. Not a single one of them wish, despite the damage to property, to make a formal complaint.
   E. The body was found lying on the floor.

   3.____

4. The one of the following sentences which contains NO error in usage is:
   A. After the robbers left, the proprietor stood tied in his chair for about two hours before help arrived.
   B. In the cellar I found the watchman's hat and coat.
   C. The persons living in adjacent apartments stated that they had heard no unusual noises.

   4.____

D. Neither a knife or any firearms were found in the room.
E. Walking down the street, the shouting of the crowd indicated that something was wrong.

5. The one of the following sentences which contains NO error in usage is:
   A. The policeman lay a firm hand on the suspect's shoulder.
   B. It is true that neither strength nor agility are the most important requirement for a good patrolman.
   C. Good citizens constantly strive to do more than merely comply the restraints imposed by society.
   D. No decision was made as to whom the prize should be awarded.
   E. Twenty years is considered a severe sentence for a felony.

6. Which of the following sentences is NOT expressed in standard English usage?
   A. The victim reached a pay-phone booth and manages to call police headquarters.
   B. By the time the call was received, the assailant had left the scene.
   C. The victim has been a respected member of the community for the past eleven years.
   D. Although the lighting was bad and the shadows were deep, the storekeeper caught sight of the attacker.
   E. Additional street lights have since been installed, and the patrols have been strengthened.

7. Which of the following sentences is NOT expressed in standard English usage?
   A. The judge upheld the attorney's right to question the witness about the missing glove.
   B. To be absolutely fair to all parties is the jury's chief responsibility.
   C. Having finished the report, a loud noise in the next room startled the sergeant.
   D. The witness obviously enjoyed having played a part in the proceedings.
   E. The sergeant planned to assign the case to whoever arrived first.

8. In which of the following sentences is a word misused?
   A. As a matter of principle, the captain insisted that the suspect's partner be brought for questioning.
   B. The principle suspect had been detained at the station house for most of the day.
   C. The principal in the crime had no previous criminal record, but his closest associate had been convicted of felonies on two occasions.
   D. The interest payments had been made promptly, but the firm had been drawing upon the principal for these payments.
   E. The accused insisted that his high school principal would furnish him a character reference.

9. Which of the following statements is ambiguous?　　　　　　　　　　　　　　　　9._____
   A. Mr. Sullivan explained why Mr. Johnson had been dismissed from his job.
   B. The storekeeper told the patrolman he had made a mistake.
   C. After waiting three hours, the patients in the doctor's office were sent home.
   D. The janitor's duties were to maintain the building in good shape and to answer tenants' complaints.
   E. The speed limit should, in my opinion, be raised to sixty miles an hour on that stretch of road.

10. In which of the following is the punctuation or capitalization faulty?　　　　　　10._____
    A. The accident occurred at an intersection in the Kew Gardens section of Queens, near the bus stop.
    B. The sedan, not the convertible, was struck in the side.
    C. Before any of the patrolmen had left the police car received an important message from headquarters.
    D. The dog that had been stolen was returned to his master, John Dempsey, who lived in East Village.
    E. The letter had been sent to 12 Hillside Terrace, Rutland, Vermont 05702.

Questions 11-25.

DIRECTIONS:　Questions 11 through 25 are to be answered in accordance with correct English usage; that is, standard English rather than nonstandard or substandard. Nonstandard and substandard English includes words or expressions usually classified as slang, dialect, illiterate, etc., which are not generally accepted as correct in current written communication. Standard English also requires clarity, proper punctuation and capitalization and appropriate use of words. Write the letter of the sentence NOT expressed in standard English usage in the space at the right.

11.　A.　There were three witnesses to the accident.　　　　　　　　　　　　　　　11._____
　　　B.　At least three witnesses were found to testify for the plaintiff.
　　　C.　Three of the witnesses who took the stand was uncertain about the defendant's competence to drive.
　　　D.　Only three witnesses came forward to testify for the plaintiff.
　　　E.　The three witnesses to the accident were pedestrians.

12.　A.　The driver had obviously drunk too many martinis before leaving for home.　12._____
　　　B.　The boy who drowned had swum in these same waters many times before.
　　　C.　The petty thief had stolen a bicycle from a private driveway before he was apprehended.
　　　D.　The detectives had brung in the heroin shipment they intercepted.
　　　E.　The passengers had never ridden in a converted bus before.

13. A. Between you and me, the new platoon plan sounds like a good idea.
    B. Money from an aunt's estate was left to his wife and he.
    C. He and I were assigned to the same patrol for the first time in two months.
    D. Either you or he should check the front door of that store.
    E. The captain himself was not sure of the witness's reliability.

13.____

14. A. The alarm had scarcely begun to ring when the explosion occurred.
    B. Before the firemen arrived at the scene, the second story had been destroyed.
    C. Because of the dense smoke and heat, the firemen could hardly approach the now-blazing structure.
    D. According to the patrolman's report, there wasn't nobody in the store when the explosion occurred.
    E. The sergeant's suggestion was not at all unsound, but no one agreed with him.

14.____

15. A. The driver and the passenger they were both found to be intoxicated.
    B. The driver and the passenger talked slowly and not too clearly.
    C. Neither the driver nor his passengers were able to give a coherent account of the accident.
    D. In a corner of the room sat the passenger, quietly dozing.
    E. the driver finally told a strange and unbelievable story, which the passenger contradicted.

15.____

16. A. Under the circumstances I decided not to continue my examination of the premises.
    B. There are many difficulties now not comparable with those existing in 1960.
    C. Friends of the accused were heard to announce that the witness had better been away on the day of the trial.
    D. The two criminals escaped in the confusion that followed the explosion.
    E. The aged man was struck by the considerateness of the patrolman's offer.

16.____

17. A. An assemblage of miscellaneous weapons lay on the table.
    B. Ample opportunities were given to the defendant to obtain counsel.
    C. The speaker often alluded to his past experience with youthful offenders in the armed forces.
    D. The sudden appearance of the truck aroused my suspicions.
    E. Her studying had a good affect on her grades in high school.

17.____

18. A. He sat down in the theater and began to watch the movie.
    B. The girl had ridden horses since she was four years old.
    C. Application was made on behalf of the prosecutor to cite the witness for contempt.
    D. The bank robber, with his two accomplices, were caught in the act.
    E. His story is simply not credible.

18.____

19. A. The angry boy said that he did not like those kind of friends.
     B. The merchant's financial condition was so precarious that he felt he must avail himself of any offer of assistance.
     C. He is apt to promise more than he can perform.
     D. Looking at the messy kitchen, the housewife felt like crying.
     E. A clerk was left in charge of the stolen property.

19.____

20. A. His wounds were aggravated by prolonged exposure to sub-freezing temperatures.
     B. The prosecutor remarked that the witness was not averse to changing his story each time he was interviewed.
     C. The crime pattern indicated that the burglars were adapt in the handling of explosives.
     D. His rigid adherence to a fixed plan brought him into renewed conflict with his subordinates.
     E. He had anticipated that the sentence would be delivered by noon.

20.____

21. A. The whole arraignment procedure is badly in need of revision.
     B. After his glasses were broken in the fight, he would of gone to the optometrist if he could.
     C. Neither Tom nor Jack brought his lunch to work.
     D. He stood aside until the quarrel was over.
     E. A statement in the psychiatrist's report disclosed that the probationer vowed to have his revenge.

21.____

22. A. His fiery and intemperate speech to the striking employees fatally affected any chance of a future reconciliation.
     B. The wording of the statute has been variously construed.
     C. The defendant's attorney, speaking in the courtroom, called the official a demagogue who contempuously disregarded the judge's orders.
     D. The baseball game is likely to be the most exciting one this year.
     E. The mother divided the cookies among her two children.

22.____

23. A. There was only a bed and a dresser in the dingy room.
     B. John was one of the few students that have protested the new rule.
     C. It cannot be argued that the child's testimony is negligible; it is, on the contrary, of the greatest importance.
     D. The basic criterion for clearance was so general that officials resolved any doubts in favor of dismissal.
     E. Having just returned from a long vacation, the officer found the city unbearably hot.

23.____

24. A. The librarian ought to give more help to small children.
     B. The small boy was criticized by the teacher because he often wrote careless.
     C. It was generally doubted whether the women would permit the use of her apartment for intelligence operations.
     D. The probationer acts differently every time the officer visits him.
     E. Each of the newly appointed officers has 12 years of service.

24.____

25. A. The North is the most industrialized region in the country.
    B. L. Patrick Gray 3d, the bureau's acting director, stated that, while "rehabilitation is fine" for some convicted criminals, "it is a useless gesture for those who resist every such effort."
    C. Careless driving, faulty mechanism, narrow or badly kept roads all play their part in causing accidents.
    D. The childrens' books were left in the bus.
    E. It was a matter of internal security; consequently, he felt no inclination to rescind his previous order.

25.____

KEY (CORRECT ANSWERS)

1.	C		11.	C
2.	B		12.	D
3.	D		13.	B
4.	C		14.	D
5.	E		15.	A
6.	A		16.	C
7.	C		17.	E
8.	B		18.	D
9.	B		19.	A
10.	C		20.	C

21. B
22. E
23. B
24. B
25. D

TEST 2

DIRECTIONS: Each question or incomplete statement is followed by several suggested answers or completions. Select the one that BEST answers the question or completes the statement. *PRINT THE LETTER OF THE CORRECT ANSWER IN THE SPACE AT THE RIGHT.*

Questions 1-6.

DIRECTIONS: Each of Questions 1 through 6 consists of a statement which contains a word (one of those underlined) that is either incorrectly used because it is not in keeping with the meaning the quotation is evidently intended to convey, or is misspelled. There is only one INCORRECT word in each quotation. Of the four underlined words, determine if the first one should be replaced by the word lettered A, the second replaced by the word lettered B, the third replaced by the word lettered C, or the fourth replaced by the word lettered D.

1. Whether one depends on <u>fluorescent</u> or artificial light or both, adequate <u>standards</u> should be <u>maintained</u> by means of <u>systematic</u> tests.
   A. natural   B. safeguards   C. established   D. routine

2. A police officer has to be <u>prepared</u> to assume his <u>knowledge</u> as a social <u>scientist</u> in the <u>community</u>.
   A. forced   B. role   C. philosopher   D. street

3. It is <u>practically</u> impossible to <u>indicate</u> whether a sentence is <u>too</u> long simply by <u>measuring</u> its length.
   A. almost   B. tell   C. very   D. guessing

4. Strong <u>leaders</u> are <u>required</u> to organize a community for delinquency prevention and for <u>dissemination</u> of organized <u>crime</u> and drug addiction.
   A. tactics   B. important   C. control   D. meetings

5. The <u>demonstrators</u> who were taken to the Criminal Courts building in <u>Manhattan</u> (because it was large enough to <u>accommodate</u> them), contended that the arrests were <u>unwarranted</u>.
   A. demonstraters   B. Manhatten
   C. accomodate   D. unwarranted

6. They were <u>guaranteed</u> a calm <u>atmosphere</u>, free from <u>harassment</u>, which would be conducive to quiet consideration of the <u>indictments</u>.
   A. guarenteed   B. atmspher
   C. harassment   D. inditements

Questions 7-11.

DIRECTIONS: Each of Questions 7 through 11 consists of a statement containing four words in capital letters. One of these words in capital letters is not in keeping with the meaning which the statement is evidently intended to carry. The four words in capital letters in each statement are reprinted after the statement. Print the capital letter preceding the one of the four words which does MOST to spoil the true meaning of the statement in the space at the right.

7. Retirement and pension systems are essential not only to provide employees with with a means of support in the future, but also to prevent longevity and CHARITABLE considerations from UPSETTING the PROMOTIONAL opportunities RETIRED members of the career service.
   A. charitable   B. upsetting   C. promotional   D. retired

7.____

8. Within each major DIVISION in a properly set up public or private organization, provision is made so that each NECESSARY activity is CARED for and lines of authority and responsibility are clear-cut and INFINITE.
   A. division   B. necessary   C. cared   D. infinite

8.____

9. In public service, the scale of salaries paid must be INCIDENTAL to the services rendered, with due CONSIDERATION for the attraction of the desired MANPOWER and for the maintenance of a standard of living COMMENSURATE with the work to be performed.
   A. incidental   B. consideration
   C. manpower   D. commensurate

9.____

10. An understanding of the AIMS of an organization by the staff will AID greatly in increasing the DEMAND of the correspondence work of the office, and will to a large extent DETERMINE the nature of the correspondence.
    A. aims   B. aid   C. demand   D. determine

10.____

11. BECAUSE the Civil Service Commission strongly feels that the MERIT system is a key factor in the MAINTENANCE of democratic government, it has adopted as one of its major DEFENSES the progressive democratization of its own procedures in dealing with candidates for positions in the public service.
    A. Because   B. merit   C. maintenance   D. defenses

11.____

Questions 12-14.

DIRECTIONS: Questions 12 through 14 consist of one sentence each. Each sentence contains an incorrectly used word. First, decide which is the incorrectly used word. Then, from among the options given, decide which word, when substituted for the incorrectly used word, makes the meaning of the sentence clear.
EXAMPLE:
The U.S. national income exhibits a pattern of long term deflection.
   A. reflection   B. subjection   C. rejoicing   D. growth

The word *deflection* in the sentence does not convey the meaning the sentence evidently intended to convey. The word *growth* (Answer D), when substituted for the word *deflection*, makes the meaning of the sentence clear. Accordingly, the answer to the question is D.

12. The study commissioned by the joint committee fell compassionately short of the mark and would have to be redone.
    A. successfully
    B. insignificantly
    C. experimentally
    D. woefully

13. He will not idly exploit any violation of the provisions of the order.
    A. tolerate   B. refuse   C. construe   D. guard

14. The defendant refused to be virile and bitterly protested service.
    A. irked   B. feasible   C. docile   D. credible

Questions 15-25.

DIRECTIONS: Questions 15 through 25 consist of short paragraphs. Each paragraph contains one word which is INCORRECTLY used because it is NOT in keeping with the meaning of the paragraph. Find the word in each paragraph which is INCORRECTLY used and then select as the answer the suggested word which should be substituted for the incorrectly used word.

SAMPLE QUESTION:
In determining who is to do the work in your unit, you will have to decide just who does what from day to day. One of your lowest responsibilities is to assign work so that everybody gets a fair share and that everyone can do his part well.
    A. new   B. old   C. important   D. performance

EXPLANATION:
The word which is NOT in keeping with the meaning of the paragraph is *lowest*. This is the INCORRECTLY used word. The suggested word *important* would be in keeping with the meaning of the paragraph and should be substituted for *lowest*. Therefore, the CORRECT answer is choice C.

15. If really good practice in the elimination of preventable injuries is to be achieved and held in any establishment, top management must refuse full and definite responsibility and must apply a good share of its attention to the task.
    A. accept   B. avoidable   C. duties   D. problem

16. Recording the human face for identification is by no means the only service performed by the camera in the field of investigation. When the trial of any issue takes place, a word picture is sought to be distorted to the court of incidents, occurrences, or events which are in dispute.
    A. appeals   B. description   C. portrayed   D. deranged

17. In the collection of physical evidence, it cannot be emphasized too strongly that a haphazard systematic search at the scene of the crime is vital. Nothing must be overlooked. Often the only leads in a case will come from the results of this search.
    A. important
    B. investigation
    C. proof
    D. thorough

17.____

18. If an investigator has reason to suspect that the witness is mentally stable, or a habitual drunkard, he should leave no stone unturned in his investigation to determine if the witness was under the influence of liquor or drugs, or was mentally unbalanced either at the time of the occurrence to which he testified or at the time of the trial.
    A. accused   B. clue   C. deranged   D. question

18.____

19. The use of records is a valuable step in crime investigation and is the main reason every department should maintain accurate reports. Crimes are not committed through the use of departmental records alone but from the use of all records, of almost every type, wherever they may be found and whenever they give any incidental information regarding the criminal.
    A. accidental   B. necessary   C. reported   D. solved

19.____

20. In the years since passage of the Harrison Narcotic Act of 1914, making the possession of opium amphetamines illegal in most circumstances, drug use has become a subject of considerable scientific interest and investigation. There is at present a voluminous literature on drug use of various kinds.
    A. ingestion   B. derivatives   C. addiction   D. opiates

20.____

21. Of course, the fact that criminal laws are extremely patterned in definition does not mean that the majority of persons who violate them are dealt with as criminals. Quite the contrary, for a great many forbidden acts are voluntarily engaged in within situations of privacy and go unobserved and unreported.
    A. symbolic   B. casual   C. scientific   D. broad-gauged

21.____

22. The most punitive way to study punishment is to focus attention on the pattern of punitive action: to study how a penalty is applied, too study what is done to or taken from an offender.
    A. characteristic   B. degrading   C. objective   D. distinguished

22.____

23. The most common forms of punishment in times past have been death, physical torture, mutilation, branding, public humiliation, fines, forfeits of property, banishment, transportation, and imprisonment. Although this list is by no means differentiated, practically every form of punishment has had several variations and applications.
    A. specific   B. simple   C. exhaustive   D. characteristic

23.____

5 (#2)

24. There is another important line of inference between ordinary and professional criminals, and that is the source from which they are recruited. The professional criminal seems to be drawn from legitimate employment and, in many instances, from parallel vocations or pursuits.
   A. demarcation   B. justification   C. superiority   D. reference

24.____

25. He took the position that the success of the program was insidious on getting additional revenue.
   A. reputed   B. contingent   C. failure   D. indeterminate

25.____

KEY (CORRECT ANSWERS)

1.	A		11.	D
2.	B		12.	D
3.	B		13.	A
4.	C		14.	C
5.	D		15.	A
6.	C		16.	C
7.	D		17.	D
8.	D		18.	C
9.	A		19.	D
10.	C		20.	B

21. D
22. C
23. C
24. A
25. B

TEST 3

DIRECTIONS: Each question or incomplete statement is followed by several suggested answers or completions. Select the one that BEST answers the question or completes the statement. *PRINT THE LETTER OF THE CORRECT ANSWER IN THE SPACE AT THE RIGHT.*

Questions 1-5.

DIRECTIONS: Questions 1 through 5 are to be answered on the basis of the following.

You are a supervising officer in an investigative unit. Earlier in the day, you directed Detectives Tom Dixon and Sal Mayo to investigate a reported assault and robbery in a liquor store within your area of jurisdiction.

Detective Dixon has submitted to you a preliminary investigative report containing the following information:

- At 1630 hours on 2/20, arrived at Joe's Liquor Store at 350 SW Avenue with Detective Mayo to investigate A & R.
- At store interviewed Rob Ladd, store manager, who stated that he and Joe Brown (store owner) had been stuck up about ten minutes prior to our arrival.
- Ladd described the robbers as male whites in their late teens or early twenties. Further stated that one of the robbers displayed what appeared to be an automatic pistol as he entered the store, and said, *Give us the money or we'll kill you*. Ladd stated that Brown then reached under the counter where he kept a loaded .38 caliber pistol. Several shots followed, and Ladd threw himself to the floor.
- The robbers fled, and Ladd didn't know if any money had been taken.
- At this point, Ladd realized that Brown was unconscious on the floor and bleeding from a head wound.
- Ambulance called by Ladd, and Brown was removed by same to General Hospital.
- Personally interviewed John White, 382 Dartmouth Place, who stated he was inside store at the time of occurrence. White states that he hid behind a wine display upon hearing someone say, *Give us the money*. He then heard shots and saw two young men run from the store to a yellow car parked at the curb. White was unable to further describe auto. States the taller of the two men drove the car away while the other sat on passenger side in front.
- Recovered three spent .38 caliber bullets from premises and delivered them to Crime Lab.
- To General Hospital at 1800 hours but unable to interview Brown, who was under sedation and suffering from shock and a laceration of the head.
- Alarm #12487 transmitted for car and occupants.
- Case Active.

Based solely on the contents of the preliminary investigation submitted by Detective Dixon, select one sentence from the following groups of sentences which is MOST accurate and is grammatically correct.

1. A. Both robbers were armed.
   B. Each of the robbers were described as a male white.
   C. Neither robber was armed.
   D. Mr. Ladd stated that one of the robbers was armed.

2. A. Mr. Brown fired three shots from his revolver.
   B. Mr. Brown was shot in the head by one of the robbers.
   C. Mr. Brown suffered a gunshot wound of the head during the course of the robbery.
   D. Mr. Brown was taken to General Hospital by ambulance.

3. A. Shots were fired after one of the robbers said, *Give us the money or we'll kill you.*
   B. After one of the robbers demanded the money from Mr. Brown, he fired a shot.
   C. The preliminary investigation indicated that although Mr. Brown did not have a license for the gun, he was justified in using deadly physical force.
   D. Mr. Brown was interviewed at General Hospital.

4. A. Each of the witnesses were customers in the store at the time of occurrence.
   B. Neither of the witnesses interviewed was the owner of the liquor store.
   C. Neither of the witnesses interviewed were the owner of the store.
   D. Neither of the witnesses was employed by Mr. Brown.

5. A. Mr. Brown arrived at General Hospital at about 5:00 P.M.
   B. Neither of the robbers was injured during the robbery.
   C. The robbery occurred at 3:30 P.M. on February 10.
   D. One of the witnesses called the ambulance.

Questions 6-10.

DIRECTIONS: Each of Questions 6 through 10 consists of information given in outline form and four sentences labeled A, B, C, and D. For each question, choose the one sentence which CORRECTLY expresses the information given in outline form and which also displays PROPER English usage.

6. Client's Name: Joanna Jones
   Number of Children: 3
   Client's Income: None
   Client's Marital Status: Single

   A. Joanna Jones is an unmarried client with three children who have no income.
   B. Joanna Jones, who is single and has no income, a client she has three children.
   C. Joanna Jones, whose three children are clients, is single and has no income.
   D. Joanna Jones, who has three children, is an unmarried client with no income.

7. Client's Name: Bertha Smith
   Number of Children: 2
   Client's Rent: $1050 per month
   Number of Rooms: 4

   A. Bertha Smith, a client, pays $1050 per month for her four rooms with two children.
   B. Client Bertha Smith has two children and pays $1050 per month for four rooms.
   C. Client Bertha Smith is paying $1050 per month for two children with four rooms.
   D. For four rooms and two children client Bertha Smith pays $1050 per month.

7.____

8. Name of Employee: Cynthia Dawes
   Number of Cases Assigned: 9
   Date Cases were Assigned: 12/16
   Number of Assigned Cases Completed: 8

   A. On December 16, employee Cynthia Dawes was assigned nine cases; she has completed eight of these cases.
   B. Cynthia Dawes, employee on December 16, assigned nine cases, completed eight.
   C. Being employed on December 16, Cynthia Dawes completed eight of nine assigned cases.
   D. Employee Cynthia Dawes, she was assigned nine cases and completed eight, on December 16.

8.____

9. Place of Audit: Broadway Center
   Names of Auditors: Paul Cahn, Raymond Perez
   Date of Audit: 11/20
   Number of Cases Audited: 41

   A. On November 20, at the Broadway Center 41 cases was audited by auditors Paul Cahn and Raymond Perez.
   B. Auditors Raymond Perez and Paul Cahn has audited 41 cases at the Broadway Center on November 20.
   C. At the Broadway Center, on November 20, auditors Paul Cahn and Raymond Perez audited 41 cases.
   D. Auditors Paul Cahn and Raymond Perez at the Broadway Center, on November 20, is auditing 41 cases.

9.____

10. Name of Client: Barbra Levine
    Client's Monthly Income: $2100
    Client's Monthly Expenses: $4520

    A. Barbra Levine is a client, her monthly income is $2100 and her monthly expenses is $4520.
    B. Barbra Levine's monthly income is $2100 and she is a client, with whose monthly expenses are $4520.

10.____

C. Barbra Levine is a client whose monthly income is $2100 and whose monthly expenses are $4520.
D. Barbra Levine, a client, is with a monthly income which is $2100 and monthly expenses which are $4520.

Questions 11-13.

DIRECTIONS: Questions 11 through 13 involve several statements of fact presented in a very simple way. These statements of fact are followed by 4 choices which attempt to incorporate all of the facts into one logical statement which is properly constructed and grammatically correct.

11. I. Mr. Brown was sweeping the sidewalk in front of his house.
    II. He was sweeping it because it was dirty.
    III. He swept the refuse into the street.
    IV. Police Officer gave him a ticket.

    Which one of the following BEST presents the information given above?
    A. Because his sidewalk was dirty, Mr. Brown received a ticket from Officer Green when he swept the refuse into the street.
    B. Police Officer Green gave Mr. Brown a ticket because his sidewalk was dirty and he swept the refuse into the street.
    C. Police Officer Green gave Mr. Brown a ticket for sweeping refuse into the street because his sidewalk was dirty.
    D. Mr. Brown, who was sweeping refuse from his dirty sidewalk into the street, was given a ticket by Police Officer Green.

11.____

12. I. Sergeant Smith radioed for help.
    II. The sergeant did so because the crowd was getting larger.
    III. It was 10:00 A.M. when he made his call.
    IV. Sergeant Smith was not in uniform at the time of occurrence.

    Which one of the following BEST presents the information given above?
    A. Sergeant Smith, although not on duty at the time, radioed for help at 10 o'clock because the crowd was getting uglier.
    B. Although not in uniform, Sergeant Smith called for help at 10:00 A.M. because the crowd was getting uglier.
    C. Sergeant Smith radioed for help at 10:00 A.M. because the crowd was getting larger.
    D. Although he was not in uniform, Sergeant Smith radioed for help at 10:00 A.M. because the crowd was getting larger.

12.____

13. I. The payroll office is open on Fridays.
    II. Paychecks are distributed from 9:00 A.M. to 12 Noon.
    III. The office is open on Fridays because that's the only day the payroll staff is available.
    IV. It is open for the specified hours in order to permit employees to cash checks at the bank during lunch hour.

13.____

The choice below which MOST clearly and accurately presents the above idea is:
A. Because the payroll office is open on Fridays from 9:00 A.M. to 12 Noon, employees can cash their checks when the payroll staff is available.
B. Because the payroll staff is only available on Fridays until noon, employees can cash their checks during their lunch hour.
C. Because the payroll staff is available only on Fridays, the office is open from 9:00 A.M. to 12 Noon to allow employees to cash their checks.
D. Because of payroll staff availability, the payroll office is open on Fridays. It is open from 9:00 A.M. to 12 Noon so that distributed paychecks can be cashed at the bank while employees are on their lunch hour.

Questions 14-16.

DIRECTIONS: In each of Questions 14 through 6, the four sentences are from a paragraph in a report. They are not in the right order. Which of the following arrangements is the BEST one?

14. I. An executive may answer a letter by writing his reply on the face of the letter itself instead of having a return letter typed.
    II. This procedure is efficient because it saves the executive's time, the typist's time, and saves office file space.
    III. Copying machines are used in small offices as well as large offices to save time and money in making brief replies to business letters.
    IV. A copy is made on a copy machine to go into the company files, while the original is mailed back to the sender.

    The CORRECT answer is:
    A. I, II, IV, III   B. I, IV, II, III   C. III, I, IV, II   D. III, IV, II, I

14.____

15. I. Most organizations favor one of the types but always include the others to a lesser degree.
    II. However, we can detect a definite trend toward greater use of symbolic control.
    III. We suggest that our local police agencies are today primarily utilizing material control.
    IV. Control can be classified into three types: physical, material, and symbolic.

    The CORRECT answer is:
    A. IV, II, III, I   B. II, I, IV, III   C. III, IV, II, I   D. IV, I, III, II

15.____

16. I. They can and do take advantage of ancient political and geographical boundaries, which often give them sanctuary from effective policy activity.
    II. This country is essentially a country of small police forces, each operating independently within the limits of its jurisdiction.
    III. The boundaries that define and limit police operations do not hinder the movement of criminals, of course.
    IV. The machinery of law enforcement in America is fragmented, complicated, and frequently overlapping.

16.____

The CORRECT answer is:
A. III, I, IV   B. II, IV, I, III   C. IV, II, III, I   D. IV, III, II, I

17. Examine the following sentence, and then choose from below the words which should be inserted in the blank spaces to produce the best sentence.
The unit has exceeded _____ goals and the employees are satisfied with _____ accomplishments.
A. their, it's   B. it's; it's   C. its, there   D. its, their

17._____

18. Examine the following sentence, and then choose from below the words which should be inserted in the blank spaces to produce the best sentence.
Research indicates that employees who _____ no opportunity for close social relationships often find their work unsatisfying, and this _____ of satisfaction often reflects itself in low production.
A. have; lack   B. have; excess   C. has; lack   D. has; excess

18._____

19. Words in a sentence must be arranged properly to make sure that the intended meaning of the sentence is clear.
The sentence below that does NOT make sense because a clause has been separated from the word on which its meaning depends is:
A. To be a good writer, clarity is necessary.
B. To be a good writer, you must write clearly.
C. You must write clearly to be a good writer.
D. Clarity is necessary to good writing.

19._____

Questions 20-21.

DIRECTIONS: Each of Questions 20 and 21 consists of a statement which contains a word (one of those underlined) that is either incorrectly used because it is not in keeping with the meaning the quotation is evidently intended to convey, or is misspelled. There is only one INCORRECT word in each quotation. Of the four underlined words, determine if the first one should be replaced by the word lettered A, the second one replaced by the word lettered B, the third one replaced by the word lettered C, or the fourth one replaced by the word lettered D.

20. The alleged killer was occasionally permitted to excercise in the corridor.
A. alledged   B. ocasionally   C. permited   D. exercise

20._____

21. Defense counsel stated, in affect, that their conduct was permissible under the First Amendment.
A. council   B. effect   C. there   D. permissable

21._____

Question 22.

DIRECTIONS: Question 22 consists of one sentence. This sentence contains an incorrectly used word. First, decide which is the incorrectly used word. Then, from among the options given, decide which word, when substituted for the incorrectly used word, makes the meaning of the sentence clear.

22. As today's violence has no single cause, so its causes have no single scheme. 22._____
    A. deference   B. cure   C. flaw   D. relevance

23. In the sentence, *A man in a light-grey suit waited thirty-five minutes in the ante-room for the all-important document*, the word IMPROPERLY hyphenated is 23._____
    A. light-grey
    B. thirty-five
    C. ante-room
    D. all-important

24. In the sentence, *The candidate wants to file his application for preference before it is too late*, the word *before* is used as a(n) 24._____
    A. preposition
    B. subordinating conjunction
    C. pronoun
    D. adverb

25. In the sentence, *The perpetrators ran from the scene*, the word *from* is a 25._____
    A. preposition   B. pronoun   C. verb   D. conjunction

KEY (CORRECT ANSWERS)

1. D
2. D
3. A
4. B
5. D

6. D
7. B
8. A
9. C
10. C

11. D
12. D
13. D
14. C
15. D

16. C
17. D
18. A
19. A
20. D

21. B
22. B
23. C
24. B
25. A

SPECIAL CHARACTERISTICS OF TREES

CONTENTS

		PAGE
I.	Trees With Excellent Fall Color	1
II.	Trees With Attractive Winter Silhouette	1
III.	Summer-flowering Trees	2
IV.	Small Garden and Patio Trees	2
V.	Trees With Interesting Bark	2
VI.	Trees With Attractive Fruits or Berries	3
VII.	Trees For Fragrance	3
VIII.	Trees For Screens and Buffers	3
IX.	Trees That Attract Birds	3
X.	Trees That Tolerate Seashore Conditions	4
XI.	Trees With Color for Many Seasons	4
XII.	Wall Trees	4
XIII.	Trees that Stand City Conditions	5
XIV.	Trees Essentially Pest-free	5
XV.	Trees That Will Stand Abuse	6
XVI.	Skyline Trees	6

I. Trees With Excellent Fall Color
   In many parts of the North, trees and fall colors are inseparable.

Acer spp.	Maple
Amelanchier spp.	Serviceberry
Betula spp.	Birch
Carpinus caroliniana	Hornbeam
Carya ovata	Shagbark hickory
Cercidiphyllum japonicum	Katsura tree
Cornus florida	Flowering dogwood
Cotinus Coggygria	Smoke tree
Diospyros virginiana	Common persimmon
Fraxinus spp.	Ash
Ginkgo biloba	Maidenhair tree
Larix Kaempferi	Japanese larch
Liquidamba Styraciflua	Sweet gum
Liriodendron tulipifera	Tulip tree
Nyssa sylvatica	Sour gum
Oxydendrum arboretum	Sourwood
Populus spp.	Poplar
Pyrus Calleryana	Callery pear
Quercus spp.	Oak
Rhus Typhina	Sumac
Sassafras albidum	Sassafras

II. Trees With Attractive Winter Silhouette
   Leafless, these trees provide a handsome outline against the open sky or a background of evergreens. They are winter's visual delights

Acer spp.	Maple
Aesculus Hippocastanum	Horse chestnut
Betula spp.	Birth
Carya ovata	Shagbark hickory
Cercidiphyllum japonicum	Katsura tree
Cladrastis lutea	Yellowwood
Cornus florida	Flowering dogwood
Fagus grandifolia	American beech
Ginkgo biloba	Maidenhair tree
Gleditsia triacanthos inermis	Thornless honey locust
Gymnocladus dioica	Kentucky coffee tree
Ilex opaca	American holly
Liqauidambar Styraciflua	Sweet gum
Liriodendron tulipifera	Tulip tree
Magnolia spp.	Magnolia
Malus spp.	Crab apple
Nyssa sylvatica	Sour gum
Phellodendron amurense	Amur cork tree
Platanus spp.	Sycamore
Populus spp.	Poplar
Quercus spp.	Oak
Salix spp.	Willow

III. Summer-flowering Trees
Many trees are colorful long after the first spring blossoms are over. Here are some summer-flowering trees.

Albizia Julibrissin	Silk tree
Catalpa spp.	Catalpa
Chionanthus virginicus	Fringe tree
Cladrastis lutea	Yellowwood
Cornus Kousa	Kousa dogwood
Cotinus Coggygria	Smoke tree
Crataegus Phaenopyrum	Washington thorn
Franklinia Alatamaha	Franklin tree
Koelreuteria paniculata	Golden-rain tree
Laburnum Watereri "Vossiii"	Golden-chain tree
Liriodendron Tulipifera	Tulip tree
Oxydendrum arboretum	Sourwood
Sophora japonica	Japanese pagoda tree
Syringa reticulate	Japanese lilac tree

IV. Small Garden and Patio Trees
Small, well-behaved trees that provide shade and seasonal show while allowing for patio and garden activities.

Acer spp.*	Maple**
Amelanchier spp.	Serviceberry
Betula populifolia	Gray birch
Cercidiphyllum japonicum	Katsura tree
Cercis canadensis	Redbud
Chionanthus virginicus	Fringe tree
Cornus spp.	Dogwood
Cotinus Coggygria	Smoke tree
Crataegus spp.	Hawthorn
Halesia carolina	Snowdrop tree
Koelreuteria paniculata	Golden-rain tree
Magnolia spp.	Magnolia
Malus spp.	Crab apple
Ostrya virginiana	Hop hornbeam
Oxydendrum	Sourwood
Prunus spp.	Flowering fruit trees
Pyrus Calleryana	Gallery pear
Styrax japonicas	Japanese snowbell
Syringa reticulata	Japanese lilac tree
Viburnum Sieboldii	Siebold viburnum

V. Trees With Interesting Bark
Texture, color, and patterns of bark are important considerations when selecting landscape trees.

Acer griseum	Paperbark maple
Betula spp.	Birch
Carpinus caroliniana	American hornbeam
Carya ovata	Shagbark hickory
Cladrastis lutea	Yellowwood
Diospyros virgianina	Common persimmon
Fagus grandifolia	American beech
Ostrya virginiana	Hop hornbeam
Pinus Bungeana	Lacebark pine
Platanus spp.	Sycamore
Populus spp.	Cottonwood
Prunus serrulata	Oriental cherry
Salix alba tristis	Golden weeping willow

VI. Trees With Attractive Fruits or Berries

Bright colors are not limited to foliage and flowers. Fruits and berries, edible and inedible, can be just as attractive and sometime last longer.

Amelanchier spp.	Serviceberry
Chionanthus virginicus	Fringe tree
Cornus spp.	Dogwood
Crataegus spp.	Hawthorn
Elaeagnus angustifolia	Russian olive
Ilex spp.	Holly
Malus spp.	Crab apple
Oxydendrum arboretum	Sourwood
Prunus spp.	Flowering fruit trees
Sorbus Aucuparia	European mountain ash

VII. Trees For Fragrance

Although some of these trees have flowers that are inconspicuous, their presence in the garden is a pleasure.

Acer Ginnala	Amur maple
Chionanthus	Fringe tree
Cladrastis lutea	Yellowwood
Elaeagnus angustifolia	Russian olive
Magnolia spp.	Magnolia
Oxydendrum arboretum	Sourwood
Prunus spp.	Flowering fruit trees
Robinia Pseudoacacia	Japanese pagoda tree
Syringa reticulate	Japanese lilac tree
Tilia spp.	Linden

VIII. Trees For Screens and Buffers

These trees are selected for their ability to hide unattractive, but necessary, areas.

Abies spp.	Fir
Carpinus Betulus 'Fastigiata'	Columnar European hornbeam
Cedrus Deodara	Deodar cedar
x Cupressocyparis Leylandii	Leyland cypress
Juniperus spp.	Juniper (columnar forms)
Ilex spp.	Holly
Picea spp.	Spruce
Pinus spp.	Pine
Populus spp.	Poplar
Rhamnus Frangula	Alder buckthorn
Taxus spp.	Yew
Thuja occidentalis	American arborvitae
Tsuga canadensis	Canada hemlock

IX. Trees That Attract Birds

All trees attract birds, but these trees provide abundant fruit as well as cover.

Amelanchier spp.	Serviceberry
Cornus spp.	Dogwood
Crataegus spp.	Hawthorn
Elaeagnus angusifolia	Russian olive
Elaeagnus umbellate	Wild olive
Ilex spp.	Holly
Juniperus virginiana	Red cedar
Malus spp.	Crab apple
Morus spp.	Mulberry
Prunus spp.	Flowering fruit trees
Viburnum Sieboldii	Siebold viburnum

X. **Trees That Tolerate Seashore Conditions**
Use these trees as your first line of defense along the coast.

Acer platanoides	Norway maple
Acer pseudoplatanus	Sycamore maple
Acer rubrum	Red maple
Ailanthus altissima	Tree-of-heaven
Betula populifolia	Gray birch
Carpinus Betulus	European hornbeam
Cryptomeria japonica	Japanese cedar
Juniperus virginiana	Red cedar
Nyssa sylvatica	Sour gum
Picea glauca	White spruce
Pinus nigra	Austrian pine
Pinus thunbergiana	Japanese black pine
Platanus x acerifolia	London plane tree
Populus deltoids	Cottonwood
Salix alba	White willow
Sciadopitys verticillata	Umbrella pine

XI. **Trees With Color For Many Seasons**
These trees provide interest with their flowers, fruits, autumn color, or bark.

Amelanchier spp.	Serviceberry
Betula spp.	Birch
Cercis canadensis	Redbud
Chionanthus virginicus	Fringe tree
Cornus spp.	Dogwood
Crataegus spp.	Hawthorn
Halesia carolina	Snowdrop tree
Malus spp.	Crab apple
Oxydendrum arboretum	Sourwood
Prunus spp.	Flowering fruit trees
Styrax japonicas	Japanese snowbell

XII. **Wall Trees**
Trees on this list have well-behaved root system and habits that allow for close planting to walls.

Acer spp.	Maple (columnar forms)
Betula spp.	Birch
Carpinus Betulus 'Fastigiata'	Columnar European hornbeam
Chamaecyparis Lawsoniana	Lawson cypress
Crataegus Phaenopyrum	Washington thorn
Ginkgo biloba 'Fastigiata'	Columnar ginkgo
Ilex opaca	American holly
Malus spp.	Crab apple
Picea glauca	White spruce
Pyrus Calleryana	Gallery pear
Quercus robur 'Fastigiata'	Columnar English oak

XIII. **Trees That Stand City Conditions**
All are resistant to air pollution, reflected heat, limited open soil surface for water.

Acer spp.	Maple
Aesculus x carnea	Horse chestnut
Carpinus Betulus	European hornbeam
Catalpa speciose	Western catalpa
Celtis occidentalis	Hackberry
Cotinus Coggygria	Smoke tree
Crataegus Phaenopyrum	Washington thorn
Fraxinus spp.	Ash
Ginkgo biloba	Maidenhair tree
Gleditsia triacanthos inermis	Thornless honey locust
Ilex opaca	American holly
Koelreuteria paniculata	Golden-rain tree
Malus spp.	Crab apple
Ostrya virginiana	Hop hornbeam
Phellodendron amurense	Amur cork tree
Pinus nigra	Austrian pine
Pinus sylvestris	Scotch pine
Platanus x acerifolia	London plane tree
Pyrus Calleryana	Gallery pear
Quercus spp.	Oak
Sophora japonica 'Regent'	Japanese pagoda tree
Tilia cordata	Small-leaved European linden
Ulmus parvifolia	Chinese elm
Zelkova serrata	Saw-leaf zelkova

XIV. **Trees Essentially Pest-free**
Choose a tree for more reasons than just freedom from pests. "Pest-free" is a relative term depending on locality.

Carpinus Betulus	European hornbeam
Cedrus spp.	Cedar
Cercidiphyllum japonicum	Katsura tree
Chionanthus virginicus	Fringe tree
Ginkgo biloba	Maidenhair tree
Gymnocladus dioica	Kentucky coffee tree
Koelreuteria paniculata	Golden-rain tree
Metasequoia glyptostroboides	Dawn redwood
Ostrya virginiana	Hop hornbeam
Phellodendron amurense	Amur cork tree
Pseudolarix Kaempferi	Golden larch
Taxodium distichum	Bald cypress

XV. Trees That Will Stand Alone
Whether you call some of these trees "undesirables" or not won't stop them from growing where all else fails.

Ailanthus altissima	Tree-of-heaven
Elaeagnus angustifolia	Russian olive
Fraxinus spp.	Ash
Ginkgo biloba	Maidenhair tree
Gleditsia triacanthos inermis	Thornless honey locust
Juniperus virginiana	Red cedar
Maclura pomifera	Osage orange
Malus spp.	Crab apple
Melia azedarach	Chinaberry
Morus alba	White mulberry
Platanus spp.	Sycamore
Populus spp.	Poplar
Robinia Pseudoacacia	Black locust
Salix spp.	Willow
Ulmus spp.	elm

XVI. Skyline Trees
These are giants that need lots of space to grow in and be appreciated.

Acer spp.	Maple
Carya ovata	Shagbark hickory
Fagus grandifolia	American beech
Gleditsia triacanthos inermis	Thornless honey locust
Liqidambar Styraciflua	Sweet gum
Liriodendron Tulipifera	Tulip tree
Picea spp.	Spruce
Pinus spp.	Pine
Quercus spp.	Oak
Taxodium distichum	Bald cypress
Tsuga canadensis	Canada hemlock

How to
Recognize Hazardous Tree Defects

Contents	Page
Introduction	1
Inspecting Trees	2
What to Look For	3
Dead Wood	3
Cracks	4
Weak Branch Unions	5
Decay	7
Cankers	8
Root Problems	9
Poor Tree Architecture	11
Multiple Defects	12
Corrective Actions	12
Move the Target	13
Prune the Tree	13
Remove the Tree	14
Cabling and Bracing	14
Topping and Tipping--Poor Pruning Practices	15
Suggested Reading	16

Introduction

Trees add to our enjoyment of outdoor experiences whether in forests, parks, or urban landscapes. Too often, we are unaware of the risks associated with defective trees, which can cause personal injury and property damage. Interest in hazard tree management has increased in recent years due to safety and liability concerns resulting from preventable accidents. Recognizing hazardous trees and taking proper corrective actions can protect property and save lives.

A "hazard tree" is a tree with structural defects likely to cause failure of all or part of the tree, which could strike a "target." A target can be a vehicle, building, or a place where people gather such as a park bench, picnic table, street, or backyard.

This brochure was created to help home owners and land managers in recognizing hazardous defects in trees and to suggest possible corrective actions. We recommend that corrective actions be undertaken by professional arborists.

Because of the natural variability of trees, the severity of their defects, and the different sites upon which they grow, evaluating trees for hazardous defects can be a complex process. This publication presents guidelines, not absolute rules for recognizing and correcting hazardous defects. When in doubt, consult an arborist.

Inspecting Trees

Inspect trees under your responsibility every year. Tree inspections can be done at any time of year, leaf-on or leaf-off. To be thorough, inspect trees after leaf drop in fall, after leaf-out in spring, and routinely after severe storms.

Inspect trees carefully and systematically. Examine all parts of the tree, including the roots, root or trunk flare, main stem, branches, and branch unions. Be sure to examine all sides of the tree. Use a pair of binoculars to see branches high off the ground.

Consider the following factors when inspecting trees:

Tree Condition: Trees in poor condition may have many dead twigs, dead branches, or small, off-color leaves. Trees in good condition will have full crowns, vigorous branches, and healthy, full-sized leaves; however, green foliage in the crown does not ensure that a tree is safe. Tree trunks and branches can be quite defective and still support a lush green crown.

Tree Species: Certain tree species are prone to specific types of defects. For example, some species of maple and ash in the Northeast often form weak branch unions (page 5), and aspen is prone to breakage at a young age (50-70 years) due to a variety of factors, including decay (page 7) and cankers (page 8).

Tree Age and Size: Trees are living organisms subject to constant stress. Pay particular attention to older trees, which may have accumulated multiple defects and extensive decay.

What to Look For

Hazardous defects are visible signs that the tree is failing. We recognize seven main types of tree defects: dead wood, cracks, weak branch unions, decay, cankers, root problems, and poor tree architecture. A tree with defects is not hazardous, however, unless some portion of it is within striking distance of a target.

Dead wood

Dead wood is "not negotiable"-- dead trees and large dead branches must be removed immediately! Dead trees and branches are unpredictable and can break and fall at any time (Fig. 1). Dead wood is often dry and brittle and cannot bend in the wind like a living tree or branch. Dead branches and tree tops that are already broken off ("hangers" or "widow makers") are especially dangerous!

Take immediate action if...

- A broken branch or top is lodged in a tree.
- A tree is dead.
- A branch is dead and of sufficient size to cause injury (this will vary with height and size of branch).

Figure 1. Dead branches can break and fall at any time.

Cracks

A crack is a deep split through the bark, extending into the wood of the tree. Cracks are extremely dangerous because they indicate that the tree is already failing (Fig. 2).

Take action if...

- A crack extends deeply into, or completely through the stem.
- Two or more cracks occur in the same general area of the stem.
- A crack is in contact with another defect.
- A branch of sufficient size to cause injury is cracked.

Figure 2. A serious crack like this one indicates that the tree is already failing!

Weak Branch Unions

Weak branch unions are places where branches are not strongly attached to the tree. A weak union occurs when two or more similarly-sized, usually upright branches grow so closely together that bark grows between the branches, inside the union. This ingrown bark does not have the structural strength of wood, and the union is much weaker than one that does not have included bark (Fig. 3). The included bark may also

Figure 3. This weak branch union has failed, creating a highly hazardous situation.

act as a wedge and force the branch union to split apart. Trees with a tendency to form upright branches, such as elm and maple, often produce weak branch unions.

Weak branch unions also form after a tree or branch is tipped or topped (page 15), i.e., when the main stem or a large branch is cut at a right angle to the direction of growth leaving a large branch stub. The stub inevitably decays, providing very poor support for new branches ("epicormic" branches) that usually develop along the cut branch.

Take action if...

- A weak branch union occurs on the main stem.
- A weak branch union is cracked.
- A weak branch union is associated with a crack, cavity, or other defect.

Decay

Decaying trees can be prone to failure, but the presence of decay, by itself, does not indicate that the tree is hazardous. Advanced decay, i.e., wood that is soft, punky, or crumbly, or a cavity where the wood is missing can create a serious hazard (cover photo). Evidence of fungal activity including mushrooms, conks, and brackets growing on root flares, stems, or branches are indicators of advanced decay.

A tree usually decays from the inside out, eventually forming a cavity, but sound wood is also added to the outside of the tree as it grows. Trees with sound outer wood shells may be relatively safe, but this depends upon the ratio of sound to decayed wood, and other defects that might be present. Evaluating the safety of a decaying tree is usually best left to trained arborists (Fig. 4).

Take action if...

- Advanced decay is associated with cracks, weak branch unions, or other defects.
- A branch of sufficient size to cause injury is decayed.

Figure 4. This seriously decayed tree should have been evaluated and removed before it failed.

- The thickness of sound wood is less than 1" for every 6" of diameter at any point on the stem.

Cankers

A canker is a localized area on the stem or branch of a tree, where the bark is sunken or missing. Cankers are caused by wounding or disease. The presence of a canker increases the chance of the stem breaking near the canker (Fig. 5). A tree with a canker that encompasses more than half of the tree's circumference may be hazardous even if exposed wood appears sound.

Take action if...

- A canker or multiple cankers affect more than half of the tree's circumference.

Figure 5. The large canker on this tree has seriously weakened the stem.

- A canker is physically connected to a crack, weak branch union, a cavity, or other defect.

Root Problems

Trees with root problems may blow over in wind storms. They may even fall without warning in summer when burdened with the weight of the tree's leaves. There are many kinds of root problems to consider, e.g., severing or paving-over roots (Fig. 6); raising or lowering the soil grade near the tree; parking or driving vehicles over the roots; or extensive root decay.

Soil mounding (Fig. 7), twig dieback, dead wood in the crown, and off-color or smaller

Figure 6. Severing roots decreases support and increases the chance of failure or death of the tree.

than normal leaves are symptoms often associated with root problems. Because most defective roots are underground and out of sight, aboveground symptoms may serve as the best warning.

Take action if...

- A tree is leaning with recent root exposure, soil movement, or soil mounding near the base of the tree.

- More than half of the roots under the tree's crown have been cut or crushed. These trees are dangerous because they do not have adequate structural support from the root system.

Figure 7. The mound (arrow) at the base of this tree indicates that the tree has recently begun to lean, and may soon fail.

- Advanced decay is present in the root flares or "buttress" roots.

Poor Tree Architecture

Poor architecture is a growth pattern that indicates weakness or structural imbalance. Trees with strange shapes are interesting to look at, but may be structurally defective. Poor architecture often arises after many years of damage from storms, unusual growing conditions, improper pruning, topping, and other damage (Fig. 8).

A leaning tree may be a hazard. Because not all leaning trees are dangerous, any leaning tree of concern should be examined by a professional arborist.

Take action if...

- A tree leans excessively.
- A large branch is out of proportion with the rest of the crown.

Figure 8. This tree is decayed and badly out of balance because of poor maintenance. It is dangerous, and extremely unattractive!

Multiple Defects

The recognition of multiple defects in a tree is critical when evaluating the tree's potential to fail. Multiple defects that are touching or are close to one another should be carefully examined. If more than one defect occurs on the tree's main stem, you should assume that the tree is extremely hazardous.

Corrective Actions

Corrective actions begin with a thorough evaluation. If a hazardous situation exists, there are three recommended options for correcting the problem: move the target, prune the tree, or remove the tree.

Move the Target

Removing the target is often an inexpensive and effective treatment for correcting a hazard tree. Easily moved items like play sets and swings, RV's, and picnic tables can be placed out of the reach of the hazardous tree with little effort and expense.

If the target cannot be moved and a serious hazard exists, consider blocking access to the target area until the hazard can be properly eliminated.

Prune the Tree

A hazardous situation may be caused by a defective branch or branches, even though the rest of the tree is sound. In this case, pruning the branch solves the problem.

Prune when...

- A branch is dead.
- A branch of sufficient size to cause injury is cracked or decayed.
- A weak branch union exists and one of the branches can be removed.
- Branches form a sharp angle, twist, or bend.
- A branch is lopsided or unbalanced with respect to the rest of the tree.
- A broken branch is lodged in the crown. Remove the branch and prune the stub.

Pruning a tree properly early in its life is a good way to effectively avoid many potential problems when the tree is older and larger. When done correctly, routine pruning of trees does not promote future defects. If done improperly, immediate problems may be removed, but cracks, decay, cankers, or poor architecture will be the ultimate result, creating future hazards.

We recommend that the "natural target" pruning method be used. This pruning method is fully described in How to Prune Trees (Bedker, O'Brien & Mielke, 1995).

Remove the Tree

Before cutting a tree down, carefully consider the alternatives. The effects of removing a tree are often pronounced in landscape situations and may result in reduced property values. Tree removal should be considered as the final option and used only when the other two corrective actions will not work. Tree removal is inherently dangerous and is even more serious when homes and other targets are involved. Removal of hazardous trees is usually a job for a professional arborist.

Cabling and Bracing

Cabling and bracing does not repair a hazard tree, but when done correctly by a trained arborist, it can extend the time a tree or its parts are safe. Done incorrectly, it creates a more serious hazard. We do **not** recommend cabling or bracing as treatment for a hazard tree unless the tree has significant historic or landscape value.

Topping and Tipping--Poor Pruning Practices

Topping is the practice of pruning large upright branches at right angles to the direction of growth, sometimes used to reduce the height of the crown. Tipping is the cutting of lateral branches at right angles to the direction of growth to reduce crown width. Both of these practices are harmful and should **never** be used. The inevitable result of such pruning wounds is decay in the remaining stub, which then serves as a very poor support to any branches that subsequently form. Trees that are pruned in this manner are also misshapen and esthetically unappealing (see Fig. 8).

Conclusions

Evaluating and treating hazard trees is complicated, requiring a certain knowledge and expertise. This publication outlines some of the basic problems that may alert you to a hazardous situation. Never hesitate if you think a tree might be hazardous. If you are not sure, have it evaluated by a professional. Consult your phone book under "Arborists" or "Tree Service."

Remember that trees do not live forever. Design and follow a landscape plan that includes a cycle of maintenance and replacement. This is the best way to preserve the health of our trees and ensure a safe and enjoyable outdoor experience.

UNDERSTANDING FOREST ECOSYSTEMS

Contents

- 1 **The Forest Ecosystem**
- 2 Living Components
- 2 The Environment
- 4 Component Requirements
- 8 Component Interrelationships
- 10 Environmental Relationships with Plants and Animals
- 12 Forest Dynamics
- 13 **The Forest as a Renewable Resource**
- 15 **Forest Description and Inventory**
- 15 Plot Location
- 15 History
- 16 Conducting the Inventory
- 20 Forest Evaluation Inventory Sheet
- 22 Review of Forest Inventory
- 26 **Forest Management**
- 28 Control of Undesirable Vegetation
- 28 Growth Enhancers
- 29 Pest and Disease Control
- 29 Fire
- 29 Harvest Systems
- 31 Regeneration Methods
- 33 Exercise in Forest Management
- 34 **Conclusion**
- 35 **Glossary**
- 36 **Appendix 1.** How to Construct and Use a Biltmore Stick
- 38 **Appendix 2.** How to Construct and Use a Clinometer
- 39 **Appendix 3.** Volume Tables

Understanding Forest Ecosystems

A forest, according to dictionaries, is an area populated by trees and underbrush. A real forest is much more than that. It is a community of many plants and animals interacting, often in complex ways. A forest exists in a physical environment that directly influences the composition and growth of the forest community.

Humans attach value to forests. This value is determined by how people use the forest and by which resources they extract from it. Traditionally, the forest's worth has been based mainly on the dollar value of the volume and species of trees present. Forest inventories have been developed to tabulate these factors for a particular wooded area. As defined by the Society of American Foresters (SAF), a *forest inventory** is "an inventory of forest land to determine area, condition, timber volume, and species for specific purposes such as timber purchase, forest management or as a basis for forest policies and programs." Taking tree measurements to estimate the volume of valuable wood is termed *timber cruising*.

People's attitudes are changing. Although wood fiber is still a major resource extracted from a forest, the importance of other forest-derived resources such as wildlife habitat, water quality, aesthetics, recreation, Christmas trees, maple sirup, and other special products is being recognized. A simple timber cruise will not give an accurate inventory of resources other than commercial trees. The method of forest evaluation presented here is designed with a broader scope than the traditional inventory. It involves a description of all major components of the forest, the physical environment of the forest, and major interactions among them. The purpose is to help youth look at the forest as an ecosystem, view the forest as the producer of many renewable resources, and recognize the intangible as well as the tangible values of the forest. It also proposes to develop a basic understanding of how forest management can be employed to maintain the renewability of the forest and to guide the forest to produce the desired resources.

The Forest Ecosystem

The key to a good forest evaluation is a background knowledge of the forest ecosystem. The *forest ecosystem* is a community in which all organisms and their environment interact. It consists of both living parts (components) and nonliving parts (the environment) that interact in an exchange of material (fig. 1).

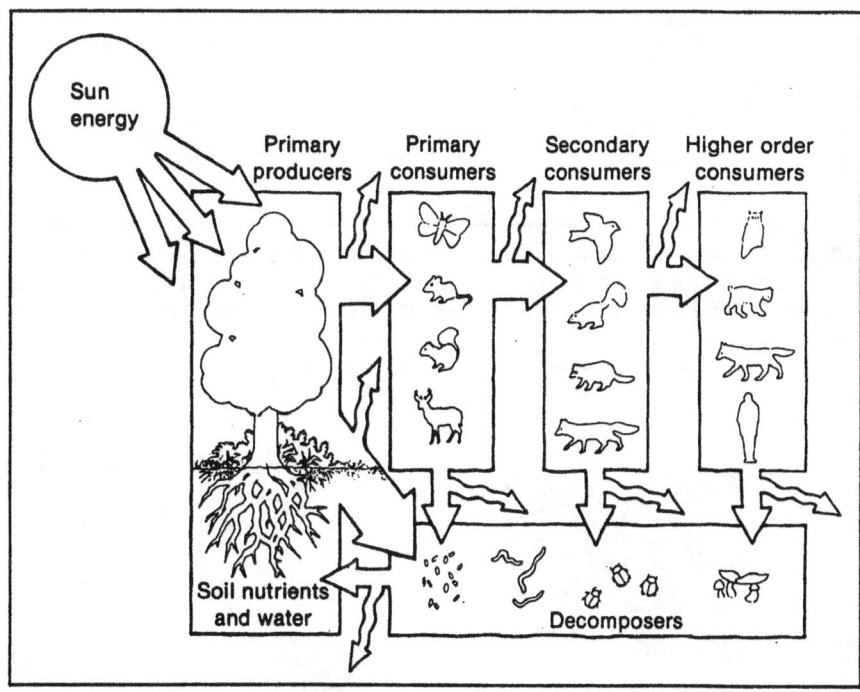

Figure 1. A forest ecosystem consisting of living components and nonliving parts (the environment).

Living Components

The living components of a forest ecosystem can be divided into two broad categories, flora and fauna. Flora includes all the plant life from trees to tiny mosses, lichens, and fungi.

Trees are woody perennials with an erect stem and a height of at least 7.62 meters (25 feet). Crowns of the taller trees in a stand form the main *canopy;* trees in the *understory* are those growing below the main canopy. Trees are classified as being either coniferous or broadleaf. Conifers have needlelike leaves, bear their seeds in cones, and are usually evergreen. They are also called evergreens or *softwoods.* Broadleaf trees, often called *hardwoods* (fig. 2) or deciduous trees, have seeds that develop in an enclosed ovary. Although many hardwoods are deciduous, that is, they lose all their leaves at one time, there are also many evergreen hardwoods.

Shrubs are woody perennials that have one or more spreading stems and grow not more than 7.62 meters (25 feet) in height. In addition to trees and shrubs, the forest floor includes many leafy, herbaceous plants that are nonwoody and generally die back every winter. These plants, called forbs, include wildflowers and grasses. Other vegetation, such as mosses, fungi, lichens, and even bacteria, as well as roots in the soil, is also a part of the flora.

Fauna includes the animal life, which may be found in the soil, on the forest floor, in the undergrowth, or overhead in the forest canopy. It includes both vertebrates (mammals, birds, fishes, reptiles, amphibians) and invertebrates (insects, mollusks, worms, and protozoans, for example).

The Environment

The environment of the forest will determine which components can exist in that particular forest community. It will also influence the growth and vigor of those organisms. Sunlight, atmospheric conditions (climate), water, and soil are all prominent environmental factors.

The sun is the primary source of energy for the forest. The amount of energy available to a forest depends on the intensity of light reaching it and the duration of exposure to this light. The quality of light is influenced by the geographic position of a forest. *Slope* and *aspect* are the terms used to describe geographic position. Slope is the steepness or flatness of the land in the forest. Aspect is the direction that the land is sloping. For example, if you were standing facing downhill on a slope with a south aspect, your face would be towards the south. The slope and aspect (fig. 3) of a piece of forested land determine at which angle the sun's rays will strike the forest. The closer this angle is to perpendicular, the more energy is available to the forest. To illustrate this principle, think of a clear winter day and a clear summer day and of the difference in the temperature: the more direct angle of the summer sun warms your skin much faster.

The atmosphere is composed of particles and gases such as oxygen, nitrogen, carbon dioxide, and various pollutants that come into contact with the forest. The air is mixed and passed through the forest by wind flows. Air temperature is not constant. It fluctuates both daily and seasonally. The geographic position of a forest influences wind strength, direction of flow, and air temperature. The top of a high ridge may be much windier than a protected valley. Rolling topography can help to break up a fierce wind

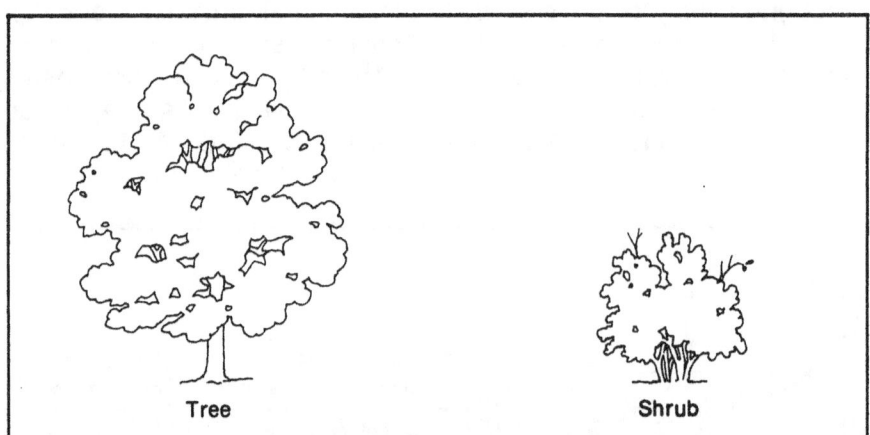

Figure 2. Above: A tree is a woody perennial that grows at least 7.62 meters tall; a shrub is a woody perennial that spreads and grows not more than 7.62 meters tall. Below: Conifers, or softwoods, have needlelike leaves; hardwoods are broadleafed.

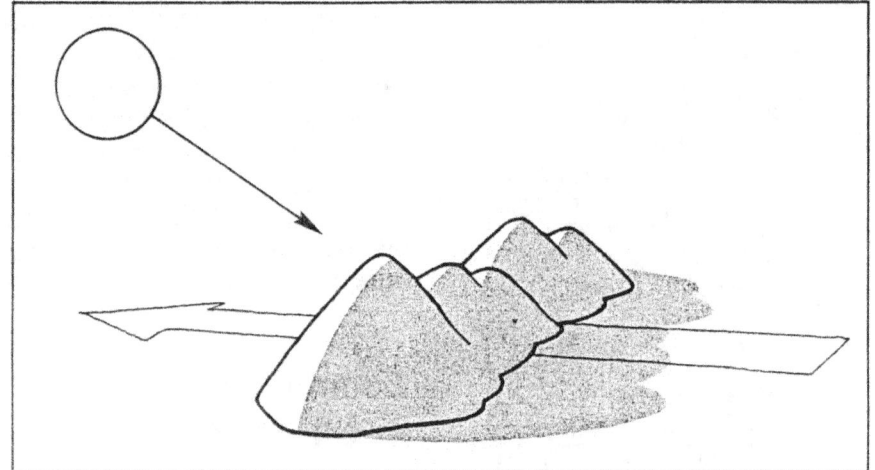

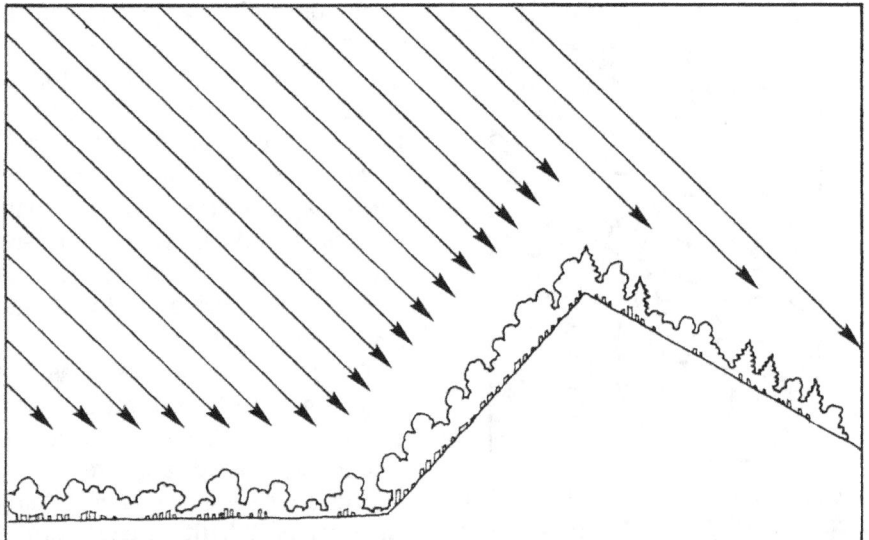

Figure 3. The slope and aspect (above) of a piece of land determine the angle at which the sun's rays will strike a forest (below).

driving across an open plain. Valley bottoms and depressions in the land are settling spots for cold air because it is denser (heavier) than warm air.

Water comes to the forest in the form of rain, snow, dew, overground flow (streams, rivers), or underground flows (seeps). The amount of water varies with seasons, dry spells, and wet spells. Water may come in large quantities in a short period of time, or it may come to the forest in small quantities but over a longer period of time. The temperature of water in open bodies affects how much oxygen is dissolved in it. Aquatic life, such as fish, is sensitive to water temperature and available oxygen. Depth of water and sun intensity are factors in water temperature. Deep water tends to be cooler than shallow water; water that is shaded by trees is cooler than unshaded water.

Just as the sun is the primary source of energy, soil is the primary source of nutrients for land organisms. Soil is a product of climate, the rock from which the soil has formed, and the plants and animals that live and die on it. Plants and animals contribute organic matter to the soil. Climate affects the rate at which organic matter decays and at which the rock is broken down into its mineral components. The *relief* of the land and passage of time also play a part in the formation of soil. There are two broad classifications of soil — transported soils and soils derived directly from underlying rock.

Transported soils are developed from weathered rock fragments that have been brought to their present location by water, ice, wind, or gravity. Since they are transported, the rock fragments are well mixed. A transported soil, then, contains mixed fragments of many kinds of rocks and minerals and of many sizes.

A soil that has been derived directly from underlying rock can be identified by distinct horizontal layers of different colors and textures. The layers, also called *horizons*, can be viewed in a bank cut along a road or in a pit dug into the soil (fig. 4). (An old transported soil can also be layered. The layers, however, are usually less distinct.) There are three major horizons — the *A*, *B*, and *C* horizons. Overlying them is usually a layer of forest debris, or *duff*. The debris consists of identifiable leaves, twigs, feathers, fur, feces, and whatever else may fall on the forest floor. As this organic matter begins to decompose, earthworms and other small animals help to mix it into the *A* horizon of the soil. In this uppermost layer, or topsoil, as it is called, partly decomposed organic matter is mixed with mineral particles. As water percolates through the *A* horizon, it carries with it organic and inorganic compounds, which mix with fine clay and silt particles in the subsoil or *B* horizon. Most of a tree's roots are found in the *A* and *B* horizons. Immediately below the *B* horizon is the *C* horizon — the parent material of the soil. It consists of slightly weathered rock and grades into unweathered bedrock at its depths.

The nutrients and water required for the life of the forest are available mainly in the *A* and *B* horizons of the soil. The parent material and organic matter found at a particular site determine the soil's mineral and nutrient con-

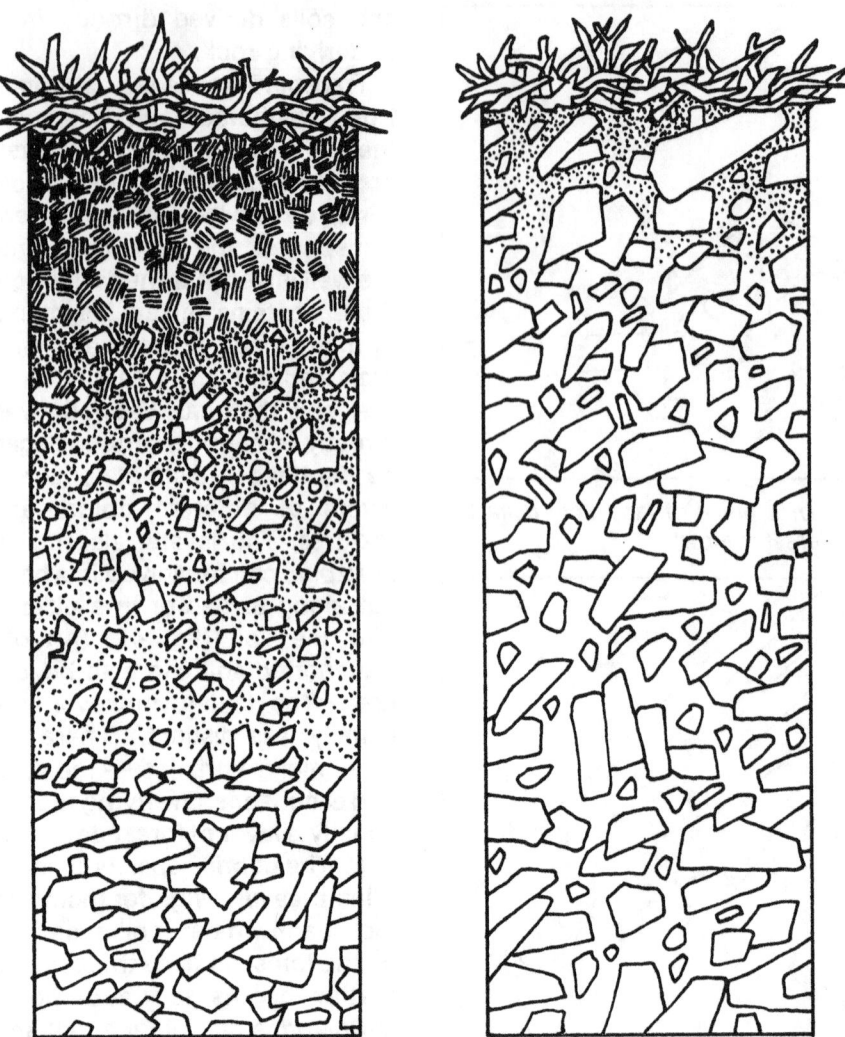

Figure 4. Left: *a soil derived directly from underlying rock, showing distinct horizons, or layers.* Right: *a transported soil, showing well-mixed rock fragments.*

tent. The amount and availability of these nutrients and of water are influenced by such characteristics of the soil as depth, texture, and pH.

A deep soil has a larger quantity of nutrients and water than a shallow soil of similar structure and content. The depth of the soil is affected by the slope of the land. On a ridge or steep slope, the soil tends to be shallower than in a valley bottom or over a flat plain.

Texture refers to the different-sized particles in a soil and is classified as ranging from sand to loam to clay. The texture affects the amount of water available, the aeration (the amount of gases in the soil — roots require oxygen to grow and absorb), and the drainage of the soil. A sandy soil holds less water than clay. Clay particles, being smaller than sand particles, have a stronger adhesion (attraction) to water and "hold" it more tightly than do sand particles. Thus a clay soil tends to hold water and be poorly drained. A clay-type soil also has fewer air spaces than a sandier soil. If such a soil is saturated with water, little oxygen will be available to roots. Without oxygen the roots are not able to absorb water or nutrients properly.

The pH, a measure of how acidic a soil is, varies between different locations in the soil and can vary seasonally. The acidity of a soil affects the availability of certain nutrients to vegetation. For example, in a strongly acidic soil, iron and manganese are more available to vegetation than in a slightly alkaline soil, and nitrogen and phosphorus are less available.

Component Requirements

All plants and animals have basic requirements that must be satisfied for them to live. These requirements vary depending upon the individual. All the organisms found in a forest exist there because their requirements for life are met in that forest environment. If you examine the forest space that an organism occupies and observe its behavior, you can learn something about the requirements of that particular organism.

To become established as part of a forest, a plant must be transported there in some form — usually as a seed, a spore, or as a vegetative segment (fig. 5). Cherry or berry-type fruits are likely to be eaten by animals and carried to a new location where the seed is deposited in the animal's scat. Sticky or burlike seeds often ride in an animal's fur or on a person's socks to a new location where they fall or are picked off. Wind transports a great many light, winged seeds and spores of mosses, fungi, and ferns. Water and gravity are other transporting agents.

A vegetative segment of a parent plant can also be responsible for more individuals of that species. For example, a cutting from a willow branch can sprout roots and develop into a tree if it is stuck into a sandy wet soil.

Plants found in a forest can also be there as a result of a "parent plant" that was already established in the forest. Roots and

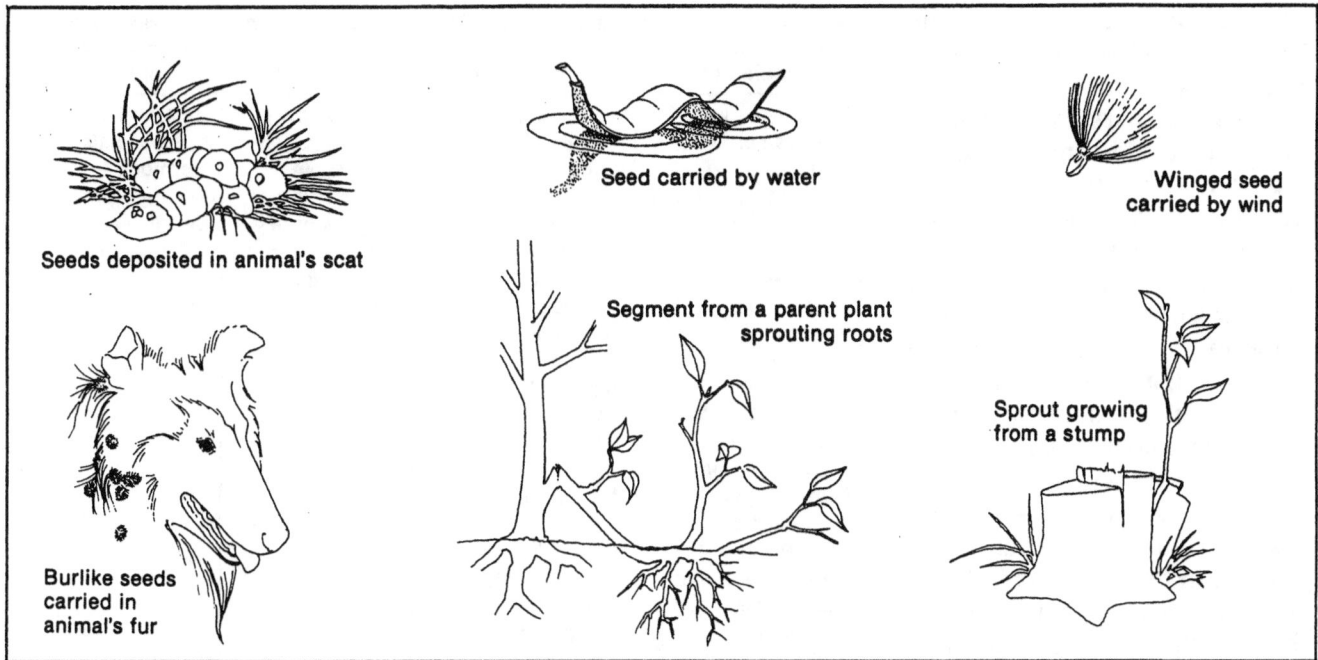

Figure 5. Plants disperse and reproduce themselves in a variety of ways.

stumps of many plants sprout. Because of the advantage of an established, mature root system, such sprouts have the potential to grow faster than a seed-started individual.

For a plant to get started and grow in a new environment, all of its basic life requirements must be met. These requirements include energy, nutrients, gases, and water (fig. 6).

Energy is required by all life. Green plants contain chlorophyll and are able to capture all their required energy from the sun. This light energy is converted to chemical energy through the process of *photosynthesis*. Photosynthesis, in Greek, means "put together with light." During photosynthesis, water and carbon dioxide are combined to form glucose, a simple sugar. Chemical energy is stored in the bonds that hold the molecules of glucose together. The glucose is then available to be transported to all parts of the plant (fig. 7).

Energy requirements of plants vary depending upon the needs and size of the plant. A tree, for example, requires much more total energy to build and main-

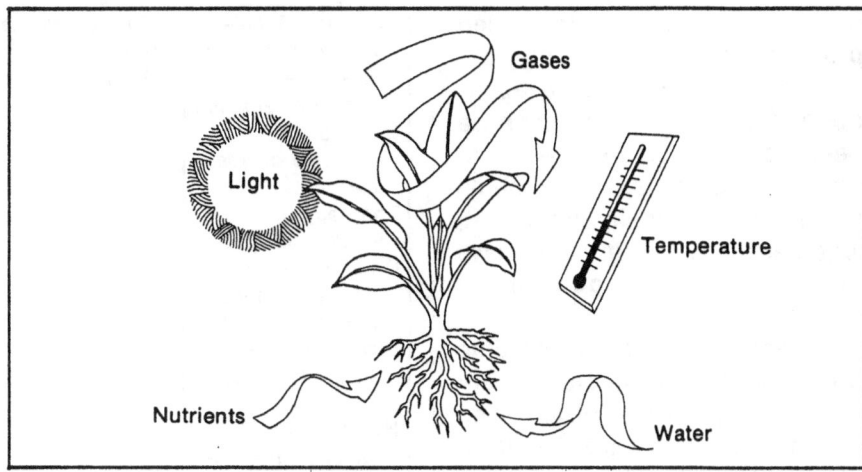

Figure 6. A plant's requirements for growth are energy, nutrients, gases, and water.

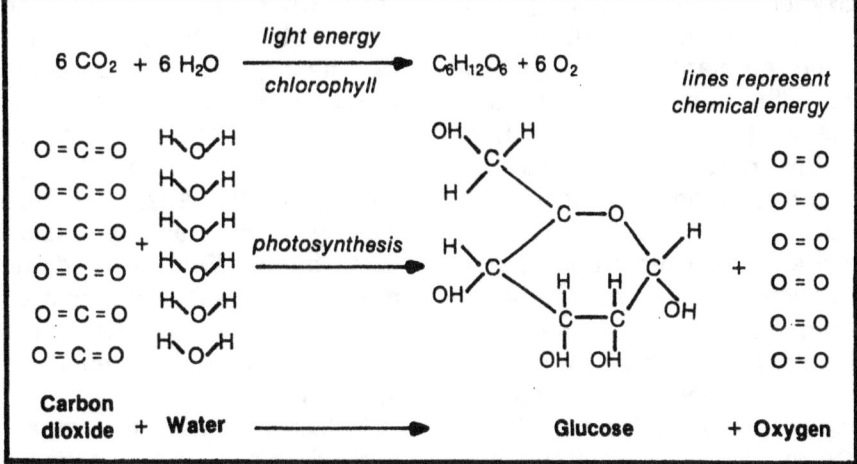

Figure 7. In photosynthesis, water and carbon dioxide are combined to form glucose.

tain itself than does a grass plant. Therefore, the tree has more green area than the grass.

Leaves of different plant species vary in how efficient they are at capturing the sun's energy. A term to indicate this relative efficiency is *tolerance*. Some plant species are able to use the energy found in subdued sunlight. They are able to survive in the shade and, in fact, may not grow well or at all in direct sunlight. These plants are called *tolerant*, that is, they are tolerant to shade. Tolerant trees, such as beech and basswood, are most often found growing in the forest understory. *Intolerant* plant species are not able to use indirect light and instead require full sunlight. Intolerant tree species, such as oaks and aspen, are often called pioneer species because they are the first trees to grow in abandoned fields or in areas that have been recently cleared. Why do you suppose pines, with needle leaves, are typically intolerant, whereas many tolerant trees have horizontally arranged broad leaves?

Nutrients — that is, organic compounds and minerals — are the building blocks of all living organisms. All throughout a plant's life, nutrients are required for growth and maintenance. Some of the most important elements required by plants besides oxygen, carbon, and nitrogen are potassium, phosphorus, and calcium. All plants, however, do not have the same mineral requirements. For example, beech requires more calcium, potassium, and phosphorus than most pines do.

Plants also require the proper atmospheric gases. Carbon dioxide is essential for photosynthesis, and oxygen is consumed by plants because all their live cells respire just like animal cells. Some gases, such as sulfur dioxide, may cause damage to plants.

Table 1. Relative Tolerance of Some Common Northeastern Hardwood Trees

Intolerant	Intermediate	Tolerant	Very Tolerant
Pines — *Pinus* sp.	White Spruce — *Picea glauca*	Red Spruce — *Picea rubens*	Balsum Fir — *Abies balsamea*
Red Cedar — *Juniperus virginiana*	White Oak — *Quercus alba*	Red Maple — *Acer rubrum*	Hemlock — *Tsuga canadensis*
Black Willow — *Salix nigra*	Red Oak — *Q. rubra*	Sugar Maple — *A. saccharum*	Beech — *Fagus grandifolia*
Larch — *Larix laricina*	Black Oak — *Q. velutina*	Blue Beech — *Carpinus* sp.	
Aspens — *Populus* sp.	Scarlet Oak — *Q. coccinea*	Hop Hornbeam — *Ostrya* sp.	
Cottonwood — *Populus deltoides*	Slippery Elm — *Ulmus rubra*		
Black Walnut — *Juglans nigra*	White Ash — *Fraxinus americana*		
Butternut — *Juglans cinerea*	Black Ash — *F. nigra*		
Gray Birch — *Betula populifolia*	Paper Birch — *Betula lenta*		
Black Birch — *B. lenta*	Yellow Birch — *B. alleghaniensis*		
Tulip Tree — *Liriodendron tulipifera*	Hickories — *Carya* sp.		
Cucumber Tree — *Magnolia acuminata*	Basswood — *Tilia americana*		
Sassafras — *Sassafras albidum*	Arborvitae — *Thuja occidentalis*		
Sycamore — *Platanus occidentalis*			
Thornapple — *Crataegus* sp.			
Cherries — *Prunus serotina* *P. pennsylvanica*			
Black Locust — *Robinia pseudoacacia*			
Honey Locust — *Gleditsia triacanthos*			

Water is another essential for life. Water requirements vary among plant species. Trees such as willows, alders, and cottonwoods grow mainly where much water is available. They are most typically found along seeps, creeks, or river beds. These trees usually have spreading, shallow root systems. Other trees do not require as much water and are able to survive in drier areas. They tend to have deeper root systems.

All living cells require temperatures within a certain range to survive. Extremely hot or cold temperatures can actually cause damage to cells. Temperature affects the rate of the life processes of *metabolism*, photosynthesis, *respiration*, growth, and reproduction. At colder temperatures all life processes slow down; photosynthesis and respiration occur at slower rates. The temperature of the soil is as important as is the air temperature to plants. Roots are not able to absorb water and nutrients so quickly when the soil is cold as when the soil is warmer.

Growth and reproduction are sensitive to air temperature. The sudden surge of spring greenery and flowers attests to this. If a plant were to grow during the bitter cold of winter, the succulent new growth would freeze and die and thus waste the plant's energy. Seeds are especially sensitive to temperature. The seeds of some species must be *stratified;* that is, they must be exposed to a cold temperature for a period of time and then to a warmer temperature before they will germinate. The temperatures activate sensitive growth *hormones.*

Animals also require energy, nutrients, gases, water, and a certain temperature range; but unlike plants, most animals are highly mobile. The forest in which you find them does not need to satisfy all their requirements; however, those requirements that are satisfied in the forest may be essential for the survival of that particular animal. Wildlife biologists classify the requirements of the animals they study into the categories of food, water, cover, and habitat (fig. 8).

The number and variety of animals that a forest can support are determined by the size and diversity of the forest. A diverse forest is composed of many different types of vegetation, which is usually distributed in different patterns throughout the forest. Vegetation may be spaced evenly (which usually indicates human planting), in clumps, or interspersed with openings. A forest that has different kinds of vegetation interspersed with openings represents the most diverse type of forest. The more diverse a forest is, the more different types of fauna will be found in it.

Food provides the necessary energy and nutrients for an animal to live, grow, and reproduce. The forest provides food in the form of either vegetation or other animals found in the forest. Some animals have very limited diets, like the white pine weevil, an insect that bores only into the new shoot at the tip of the main stem of a white pine. Other animals have a more varied diet, such as the sharp-shinned hawk, which eats vireos and other small birds and mammals.

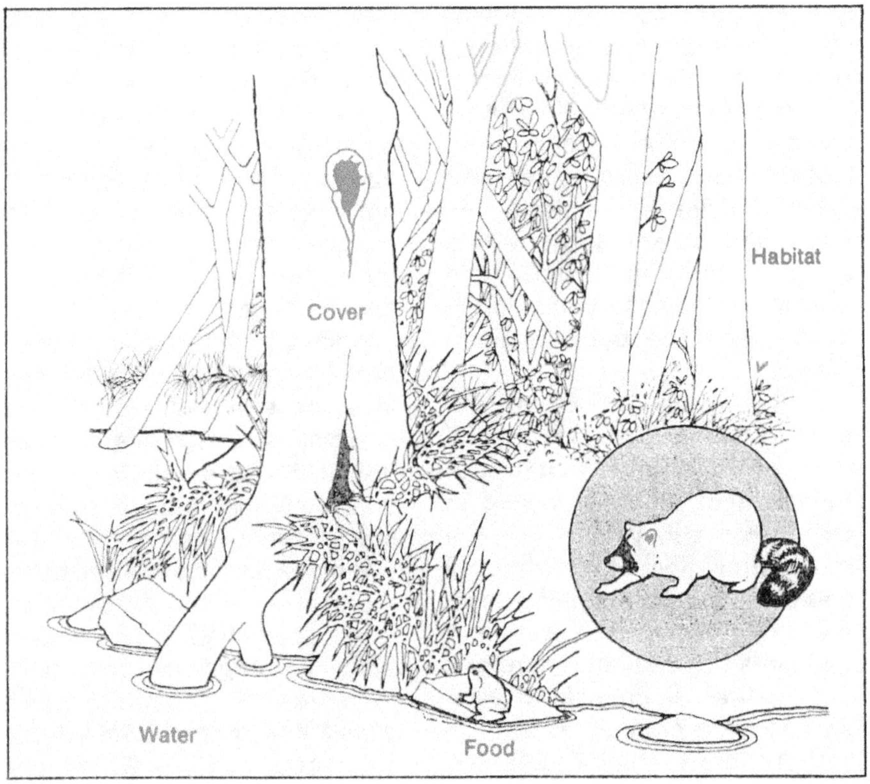

Vital water may be consumed either directly or indirectly. Direct sources of water that might be found in a forest include streams, ponds, other open bodies of water, and raindrops or dew that clings to vegetation. Succulent vegetation or the water found in bodies of prey provides all the water required by some animals.

Shrubs, a dense herbaceous layer, and tree canopies provide protective cover for animals from the weather and from predators. Small animals such as chipmunks and mice prefer to carry out their activities under the cover of shrubs. Because deer are much larger, they cannot always feed and water under cover. Therefore, they usually stick close to cover and rely on their quick legs to jump to safety. A doe with newborn fawns uses the cover of grass and ferns to hide them from danger. Just as vegetation provides protective cover from predators, it also provides a place for bobcats and foxes to hide and wait to ambush their prey. Burrows, blowdowns, and hollow trees found in the forest also become important hiding places for many animals.

The forest is a living space and breeding place for many animals. Hollowed logs provide homes for animals such as skunks and porcupines. Animals such as ground squirrels and chipmunks hibernate over winter in a nest of grass under the forest floor. Many animals reproduce in the forest. Birds nest among branches, on the forest floor, or, as in the case of woodpeckers and wood ducks, in holes in dead trees called *snags.* Weasels bear their young in burrows in the forest. Animals require a certain amount of space in which to forage for food and to carry out their other activities. Because forest resources are limited, many animals make territorial claims to a habitat, which they defend from other animals requiring the same resources as they do.

Figure 8. Wildlife requirements for life are food, water, cover, and habitat.

Component Interrelationships

The mere listing of the components of the forest does not suggest the essence of the forest community. It is like listing the ingredients to make a loaf of raisin bread without discussing how to put them together. Anyone can put raisins, flour, yeast, salt, oil, sugar, and spices into a bowl, but to make a loaf of delicious raisin bread is an art. Likewise, a forest is not a collection of plants and animals tossed together in a location. The components of a forest are related to each other with highly complex and often elusive links. How they are related is determined mainly by their individual requirements, but may, in turn, be modified by the environment.

The idea of interrelatedness implies an exchange of materials or energy, as seen in the food chain (fig. 9). Plants are the producers. The energy, nutrients, and organic matter of which they are made are passed on to the animals that eat them. Every part of a plant is a food source for some animal. Seeds, buds, and bark are eaten by mice, squirrels, and insects. Leaves may be eaten by caterpillars, deer, or rabbits. These animals then provide energy and nutrients for their predators, which, in turn, fall prey to other predators. Though plants are the primary link in the chain, some carnivorous plants attract and trap insects in cuplike structures containing a pool of digestive juices.

Even as plants and animals die, they are linked to other organisms in the forest. Scavengers obtain their energy from the wastes and remains of plants and animals. Flies and other insects lay eggs in dead animals. Opossums supplement their diets with dead animals. *Saprophytic* plants such as pine drops and invertebrates such as slugs feed on dead plants.

As these scavengers break down plant and animal remains into smaller pieces, a host of decomposers continue the chemical and mechanical breakdown. Mushrooms, other fungi, and bacteria all decompose such matter into its basic chemical elements—carbon, hydrogen, nitrogen, iron, and calcium — and other reusable forms. Worms and insects mix these minerals and nutrients into the soil and thus make them available to be absorbed by plant roots. Thus the cycle is completed.

In this whole process of exchange along the food chain, most of the organic matter, nutrients, and minerals remain in the forest ecosystem. On the other hand, most of the chemical energy and water are being used; and along each link, a portion of energy is lost as heat. Therefore, the number of animals at each successive level decreases.

In the forest, relations between plants and animals and among animals themselves are not limited solely to consumption. As mentioned before, forest vegetation provides cover and habitat for animals. Moose, deer, and elk also use the trunks of trees to scrape the velvet from their antlers. Trees are claw-sharpening posts for mountain lions, territorial markers for bears, and construction material for beavers. When a woodpecker excavates a nesting hole in a snag, it is creating a future nesting site for other birds such as nuthatches and chickadees.

Animals provide benefit for vegetation by controlling the population sizes of insects and animals that feed on the vegetation. Chickadees seen hanging upside down on branches are busy eating insects off leaves and branches of the tree. The fact that animals destroy vegetation is a benefit to the remaining plants of the forest. When a porcupine kills a whole tree by girdling it, he is making available additional sunlight, nutrients, water, and growing space, which the surviving plants can use for growth and reproduction. Animals also benefit vegetation by dispersing seeds to new locations. The red cedar berries eaten by a bird will pass through its digestive system and be deposited in a location away from the parent plant. Although squirrels dig up most of the acorns they bury, those overlooked have a fair chance of germinating.

Animal - plant relationships become harmful when population levels cause a strain on a resource or when a foreign element does not fit into the existing ecosystem. If the population of an animal species increases to the point where the animals are consuming more of a certain resource at a rate faster than it is being replaced, a negative drain on the forest results. The effects can be devastating. For example, in more than one location where predators have been reduced, deer

Figure 9. The transfer of energy through a food web.

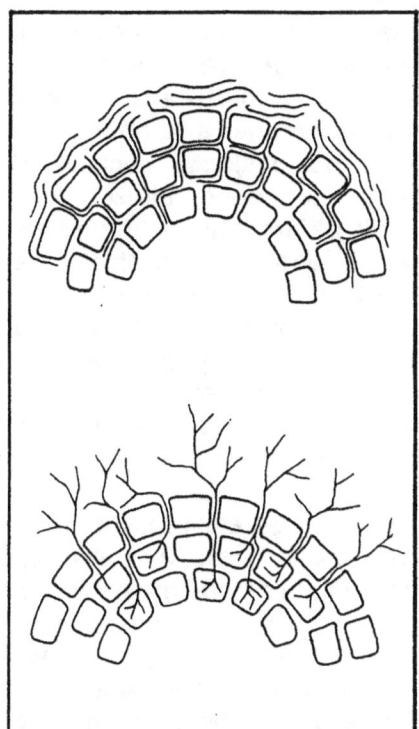

Figure 10. Diagram of mycorrhizal fungi, which absorb sugars from the host plant but also allow the tree to absorb more minerals and water because of greater root surface area.

herds have increased to the point where the deer have destroyed their favored foods and have been forced to eat and destroy less palatable vegetation. As a result, massive die-offs have occurred through starvation and disease. Insects normally do not kill the trees they feed on except an occasional scattered tree. Abnormally high numbers of insects, however, can kill whole stands.

Relations among plants in the forest can be either harmful or beneficial to one or more of the individuals involved. A mutually beneficial relationship exists between *mycorrhizal fungi* and root systems. Roots inoculated (fig. 10) with mycorrhizae are able to absorb more minerals and water because of increased root surface area and actions of the fungus itself. The mycorrhizae benefit by absorbing sugars that the tree makes. Other types of fungi may be harmful to live trees by causing heartrot and other rots. These rotted, hollow trees are then susceptible to wind breakage.

Some tree species form root grafts among different individuals. Though such grafts may aid in absorption of water and nutrients and allow the exchange of genetic material, they may also be pathways for fungal infections. Grapes and other vine plants seeking sunlight grow into the crowns of taller trees. The vines may become heavy enough to kill the supporting tree.

Plants indirectly influence the growth and survival of their neighbors by modifying the immediate environment. As trees grow taller, they create a shelter from temperature extremes, wind, heavy rain, and direct sunlight for the plants growing under them. Their leaf litter may provide nutrients not available in the soil but required by other species. Some trees such as alder even have bacterial nodules on their roots that add usable nitrogen to the soil. As a result, plants that otherwise could not grow in the understory can grow there. This relationship is not always beneficial, however. Roots of certain plants secrete chemical substances called *allelopaths* into the soil; these are toxic to other plants trying to become established nearby. The establishment of seedlings is affected in another manner. *Damping-off fungi*, which exist under certain conditions in leaf litter, attack and kill the newly germinated seedlings of some species.

Within a certain area, only a fixed amount of water, light, and nutrients is available for a plant to draw upon to satisfy its requirements. As plants grow closer together, a *competition* arises in which two or more plants must draw on the same supply. One organism is detrimental to its competitor by making similar demands on the same environmental resources (fig. 11). The larger and rapidly growing plants are often better able to satisfy their demands and thus cause slower growth and even death to their neighbors. Growing space becomes limited. As trees begin to crowd their neighbors, the growth rate of all trees drops dramatically and dense "dog-hair" thickets of thin, closely spaced trees develop. Trees in such thickets may appear to be young because of their small size, but actually they may be quite old.

Plants modify the environment in other ways. Trees along streams and rivers shade the water. When trees are removed, the water may become warmer, and fish species

Figure 11. Left: competition arises when two or more plants must draw on the same supply of water, light, and nutrients. Right: plants that do not have to compete grow taller and larger than those that must compete.

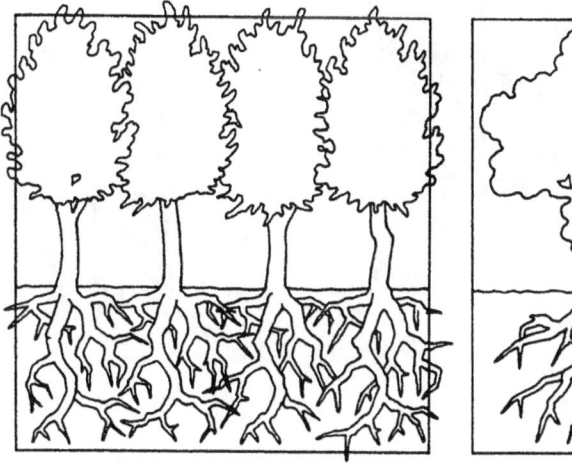

may change from cold-water species to those more tolerant of of warm water. Trees are also important in helping to control soil erosion. A vegetative cover reduces the impact of rain drops, which actually displace soil where they hit bare ground. Vegetation also prevents the wind from blowing away dry top soil. The roots of plants help hold the soil in place and prevent erosion.

Plants affect the formation of soil. Leaf litter and plant wastes add organic matter and return minerals to the soil. Roots add minerals to the developing soil by chemically and mechanically breaking down rocks. Roots also extract nutrients from the soil and thus change the soil fertility. In fact, most of the nutrients in jungle forests are thought to be tied up in the lush vegetation. Jungle soils are actually low in those minerals required by plants.

Environmental Relationships with Plants and Animals

The environment has a direct relationship with the forest community. It controls the establishment, growth, and survival of plants and animals in the forest by satisfying the requirements of some organisms and not of others. Because of the varied environments across the continent, there are different types of regional forests — boreal, western, northeastern mixed, central deciduous, and southeastern mixed forests (see map). On a smaller scale, the light, temperature, water, soil type, and depth of soil vary from ridge top to slope to valley bottom to slope to the next ridge top. Ridges tend to be drier and the soil tends to be shallower than in the valley bottom, where water often flows and soil is deposited. Slopes range somewhere in between, but south-facing slopes tend to be drier and hotter than north-facing slopes because of the direct angle of the sun. As a result, different types of trees are likely to be found on each of these locations. For example, in a northeastern mixed forest, oaks and hickories are likely to be found on dry, warm ridges and slopes; hemlocks and birches will grow in the colder, moister valley bottoms (fig. 12).

Differences are present on an even smaller scale. The environment within a stand of trees is, in a sense, a microenvironment. Trees in the upper canopy influence how much water and light fall on the vegetation below them. The climate within the stand is different from that outside it. The forest floor is not uniform. It may have a pit-mound relief created

Map 1. Types of forests growing in different regions.

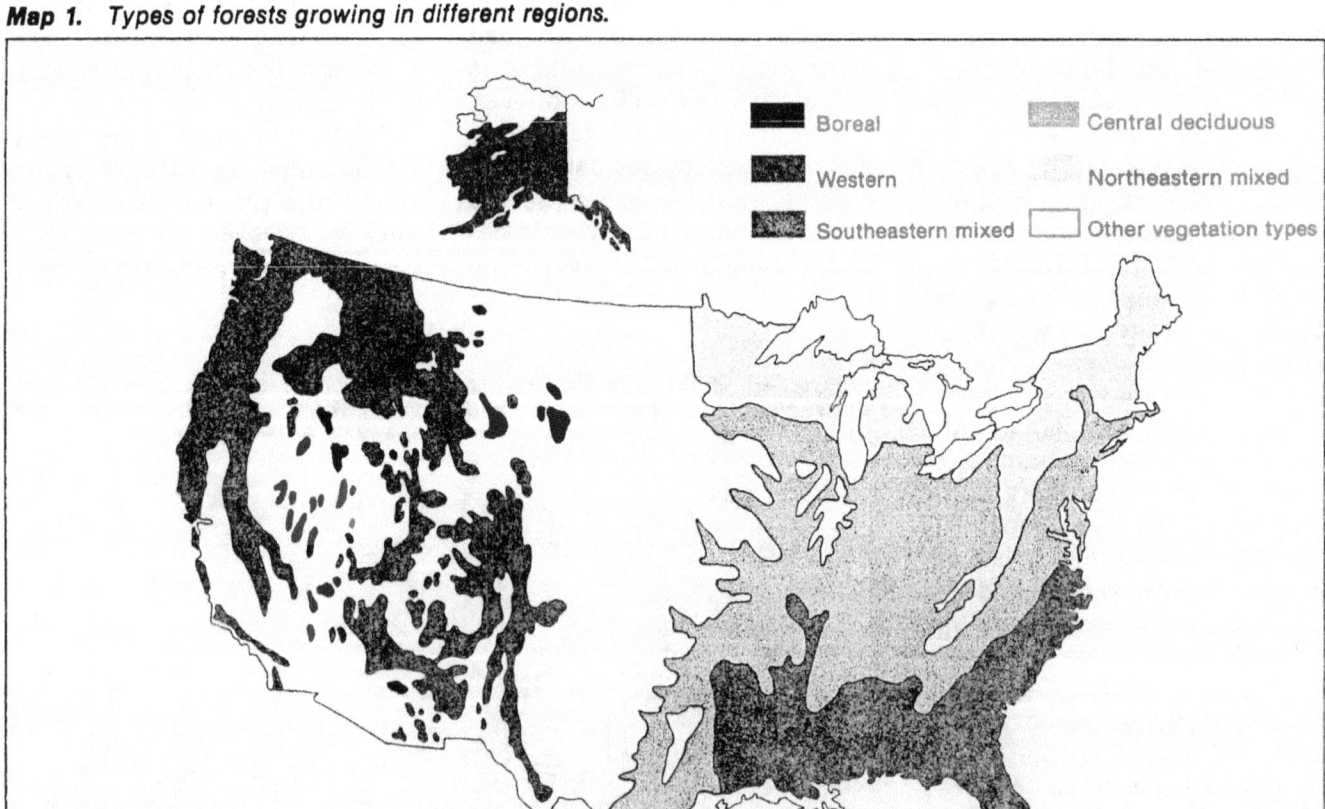

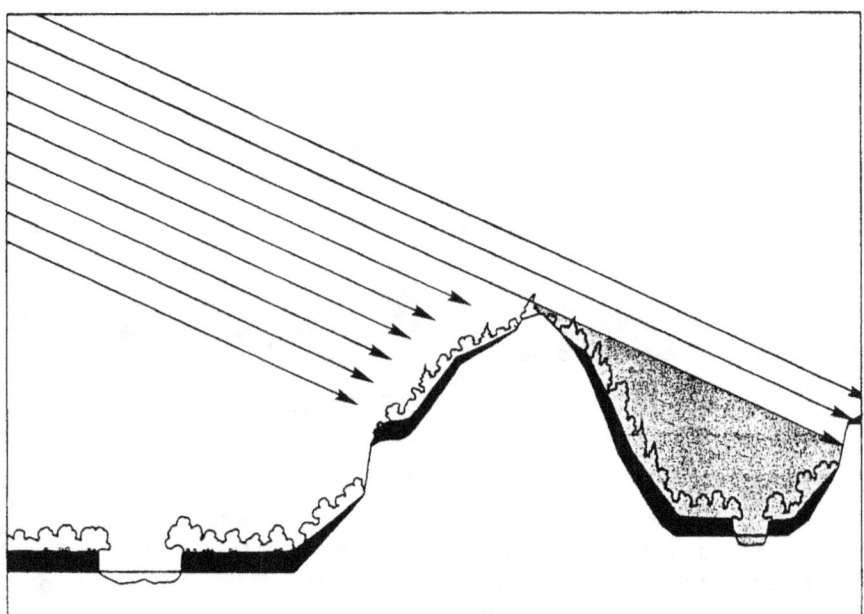

Figure 12. Schematic of local factors that influence soil depth and sunlight available to plants.

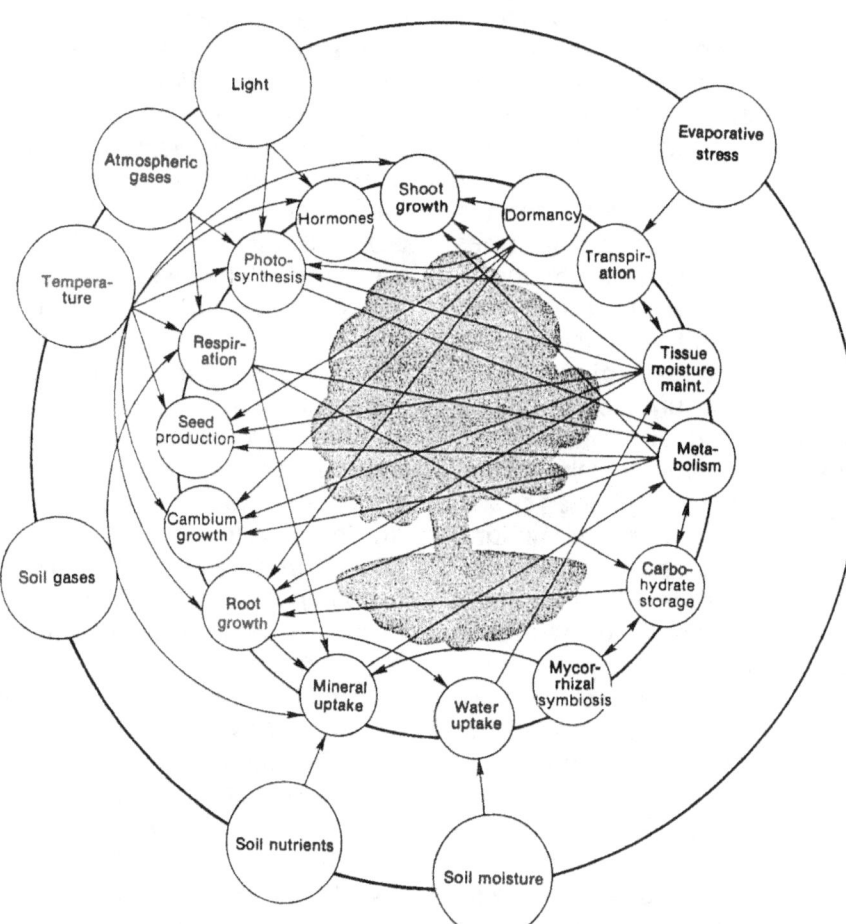

Figure 13. Interacting environmental factors that influence the life processes of forest plants.

by fallen trees. When a tree falls, the roots pull up the soil surrounding them; a mound of soil is made with a pit behind. A 3-meter transect of the soil will most likely show differences in structure, texture, acidity, and water and mineral content. Thus each individual potential growing space is unique and not suitable for every type of plant.

All life processes of forest plants are regulated to some extent by the environment. The uptake of water, minerals, and nutrients; metabolism; photosynthesis; respiration; growth; and reproductive systems are all affected by atmospheric gases, light, air temperature, humidity, and by nutrients, gases, and moisture in the soil (fig. 13). The ranges or amounts of those essentials and their combination in the environment affect the rate at which the above systems proceed. For example, growth and photosynthesis slow down when the temperature gets cold. On the other hand, certain life processes are triggered by temperature extremes. The sap that makes delicious maple sirup requires subfreezing temperatures at night and above 4.4°C (40°F) temperatures during the day to flow.

Photoperiod, the length of exposure to light per day, plays an important role in the growth, dormancy, and reproduction of a plant. As the days get shorter, hormones in plants respond to the briefer exposure to light and cause the plant to cease growing and become dormant. During this time, deciduous trees lose all their leaves, and the sap flows to the roots for overwinter storage. As longer days signal the beginning of spring, buds swell and open to flowers and leaves.

It is important for their survival that plants do respond to the environment. As each new season approaches, a plant must be prepared to adjust to changes. It must become dormant to survive the winter, and it must take advantage of the favorable spring and summer climates to reproduce and grow as it competes with its neighbors for survival.

Questions for thought:

How are animals attuned to the environment? Do you think that their relationship with the environment is as direct as the relationship between plants and the environment?

Forest Dynamics

A forest is dynamic, constantly changing. What you see when you walk into a forest is a balance of the components and their requirements, the environment, and interrelations. It exists only at that instant of time. The changes may not be noticeable. The process of decay and growth proceeds so slowly that you usually cannot tell the differences from day to day. New leaves are growing as others fall or are eaten. Minerals and water are continually recycling through the forest. New seedlings are sprouting; old veterans are dying.

Some changes can be quite noticeable and even catastrophic. An ice storm might hit and cause many broken branches or topped trees. A landslide, a fire, or logging can change a lush forest into a cleared open area overnight. When such an opening occurs, a process called succession begins its cycle. Many resources are available in a clearing: sunlight, air, water, and soil nutrients — if the soil was not eroded badly — are not being used. The seeds of many plants fall into the area. If bare mineral soil is exposed, those seedlings susceptible to damping-off fungi can survive. Tree, shrub, and herbaceous seedlings that start growing must be able to grow in intense sunlight; otherwise, they will die. These plants, known as pioneers, include such species as goldenrod, viburnums, aspen, oaks, cherries, and certain pines. As the trees grow taller, they begin to change the environment below them. The shrubs and herbaceous plants begin to die from lack of sun, water, and nutrients. "Open spots" appear. Many different seeds continue falling into the area. A layer of organic matter accumulates on the forest floor and damping-off fungi are present. In the Northeast, only certain species such as maple, birches, and spruces are able to thrive in less-intense light and moister conditions. The forest continues growing. Less sunlight reaches the forest floor and only the seeds of tolerant trees are able to survive. An understory forms, made up of hemlock, basswood, and sugar maple. The older, taller trees begin to die off. Trees in the understory whose small size might be masking their true age are able to take advantage of the newly released space, nutrients, and increased sunlight. These spruces, beeches, and maples now become the dominant trees of the stand. If the area is again disturbed — if a fire burns through, a windstorm blows down a stand of tall, shallow-rooted trees, or the weather changes — the succession cycle will occur again. If, however, the final vegetation is able to replace itself and the forest composition stays relatively constant, a *climax forest* is said to have been achieved (fig. 14).

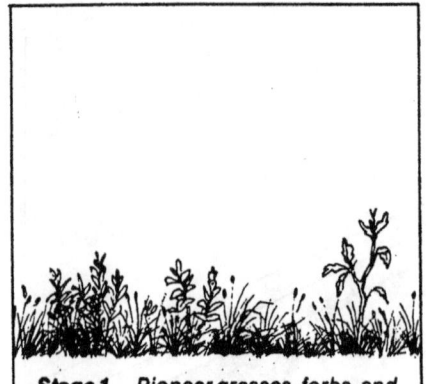

Stage 1. Pioneer grasses, forbs, and shrubs.

Stage 2. Shrub stage with invasion of intolerant seedlings.

Things to do:

1. Take a trip into a forested area. Observe the forest environment. Sit in one place for awhile and observe closely around you. Walk around the area and list components of the forest. Try to observe the things that you have read about. After at least ½–1 hour, discuss with your group what you have found.

2. Go to an open field. Observe it closely as you walk around and then sit down for awhile. How is the open area different from the forest observed in #1?

3. Pick a tree species and read about it. Jot down its requirements for life. Go to a forested area with your group and look at the forest. If you were that tree, would you be able to survive in this forest? Explain why or why not. Select a forest animal and do the same thing.

4. With your group, have each member choose a living component or environmental factor of the forest. Allow each person to take a turn to explain how his or her component or factor is related to all the others represented by club members.

5. Look at the forest environment section of *Environmental Awareness*. Do any of the activities that interest you and your group.

6. Go to an open or abandoned field that is not being plowed, mowed, or grazed. Do you see signs of succession taking place? What are they? If succession is not taking place, why?

Stage 3. Mixed species stand of young intolerant trees.

Stage 4. Mature stand of intolerant trees with understory of tolerant seedlings.

Stage 5. Mature stand of tolerant species with understory of their own seedlings.

Figure 14. Typical succession in a northeastern forest.

The Forest as a Renewable Resource

The forest ecosystem satisfies the requirements of many animals. It also provides many useful materials for the human animal. We call these materials *forest resources*.

Since the beginning of human history, forest-dwelling people have found a rich source of food, clothing, tools, shelter, and fuel in the forest. In North America, native Americans and pioneers depended upon the wild animals and the nuts, berries, fruits, buds, and roots from the forest to supplement their food supply. Maple sirup, which the pioneers learned to make from the Indians, provided a valuable sugar source. Roots, bark, and herbs were also important for their medicinal properties. Today many people still gather berries, mushrooms, and other special products from the forests. The wildlife and fish populations of forested lands are now managed by our government to assure sport and meat from fishing and hunting.

Fur and hides from forest animals in the past were an important source of clothing for Indians and settlers alike. Today trappers supply the fur industry with the hides of forest animals. Also, rayon, a product of wood pulp, is used to make fabrics for the clothing industry.

Tools of the past were made mainly from wood. Pails, baskets, handles, and brooms were all shaped from wood. Although metals have replaced some of the uses of wood, many tools today have wooden handles or are made of wood-derived synthetics.

The need for shelter has been served for centuries by wood. Pole frames thatched with bark, branches, grass, or hides were the homes of primitive people. The settlers built log cabins furnished with wooden furniture. Even today, many houses are made of wood, or they at least contain some wood or wood product. Insulation, wood finishes, stains, and other building accessories are made from wood products.

Fire used for heating and cooking has greatly expanded the adaptability of humans by allowing them to live in many climates and to eat various foods. Wood was the main source of fuel for fire until the 1900s when other sources of heat and power were developed. Because of increasing costs of coal, gas, heating oil, and electricity, some people in the U.S. are beginning to convert their homes to wood heat. Wood fuel is again renewing its importance among the many uses of wood.

Today, forest resources provide direct income for many people. The growing, cutting, preparing, transporting, and selling of such wood products as timber, pulpwood, firewood, charcoal, and Christmas trees employs a large number of people. Many individuals supplement their income with the sale of special products including floral greenery, maple sirup, seed cones, and tree burls. The money derived from forest resources can in fact indirectly support an entire community. For example, a local sawmill may provide employment for members of most families in a small town. Because these families need services such as stores, hospitals, and gas stations, their money earned from timber goes towards supporting the commercial establishments in town. This is known as the multiplier effect of money. Recreation is another important forest use. A growing number of people enjoy hiking, skiing, camping, hunting, and fishing in our forests. Recreation also provides income for those who operate private campsites and recreation facilities.

Forests supply a clean source of water for many communities. A forest cover absorbs and slowly releases water from rain and snow. The forest floor helps to filter the water. Forests also prevent erosion and the resultant sedimentation of streams, rivers, and lakes.

Many people value the *aesthetics* or beauty of the forest. An intangible forest resource, aesthetics is a combination of visual quality and the emotional feelings one has about a place. Its worth truly is in the eye of the beholder. Some people prefer forest vistas, others prefer an old growth forest of a single or mixed species. The solitude, the filtered sunlight, the wildness, and spiritual feelings are all reasons why people enjoy being in a forest.

The forest provides something that is often taken for granted — environmental improvement. Trees serve as windbreaks and noise and vision buffers. Besides providing us with oxygen, they act as air filters. Branches and leaves collect particles from the air, and leaves actually absorb some pollutants. Homesites benefit from the shade and beauty provided by trees.

Forest resources are special (fig. 15). Most are *renewable*, that is, resources that are properly removed can be naturally replaced. The appropriate environment and appropriate seed (plant) or population (animal) sources assure the regeneration of that which was removed. We need only wait for time to pass as the forest grows and renews itself. The forest environment, however, can be altered significantly by a sloppy job of resource removal or by overuse. It may take several human generations to replace itself. In such cases, the forest can be considered to be nonrenewable. Abuse and overuse, the story of our past, should be avoided. If unwise practices do cause a forest resource to become nonrenewable, the decision of use then becomes ethical.

Questions to consider:

1. How do you feel about using a nonrenewable resource?
2. What do you think about conserving resource supplies for future generations?
3. What nonrenewable resources do you currently use? How do you feel about it? Is there anything you can do to avoid using them? What if it means an inconvenience to you?
4. What renewable resources do you use? How do you feel about it? Because they are renewable, does that mean you can use them frivolously?

Things to do:

1. Tour a wood-using mill or factory. Find out what kinds of trees they use as raw materials.
2. Have a forester take you out in the woods to show you what types of trees are appropriate for sawlogs, pulpwood, firewood, and other wood products.
3. Have a hunter, trapper, or naturalist take you through the woods to show you how to look for animal signs.

Figure 15. *Forest resources.*

Forest Description and Inventory

With the understanding of forest ecosystems and forest resources you have developed, you now have the background to proceed with the forest inventory. For the inventory you will be sampling a piece of a forest ecosystem. Objectives of the inventory are as follows:

1. To see what exists in the forest — to examine the components and environment of the ecosystem, and to study the possible forest resources in your forest;
2. To measure the timber resources;
3. To look at the dynamics of the forest ecosystem;
4. To see how forest dynamics affect the growth, quality, and renewability of forest resources.

Equipment you need to conduct the inventory:

- pencils
- hammer
- wooden or pipe stake
- Bright flagging — plastic, cloth, toilet paper (be sure to remove flagging when finished)
- a 22.86-m (75-ft) tape measure or a rope knotted 16.06 m (52.7 ft) from the end
- compass (optional but handy)
- slope-measuring device (see Appendix 2 for construction details)
- *Biltmore* stick for measuring tree diameter and height (see Appendix 1 for construction details)
- chalk or a sock filled with powdered chalk to mark trees that have been measured
- shovel
- ruler
- clipboard to write on

Be sure to keep track of all equipment out in the field. It is hard to see them lying on the forest floor. If they are flagged with a bright color, they are much easier to find.

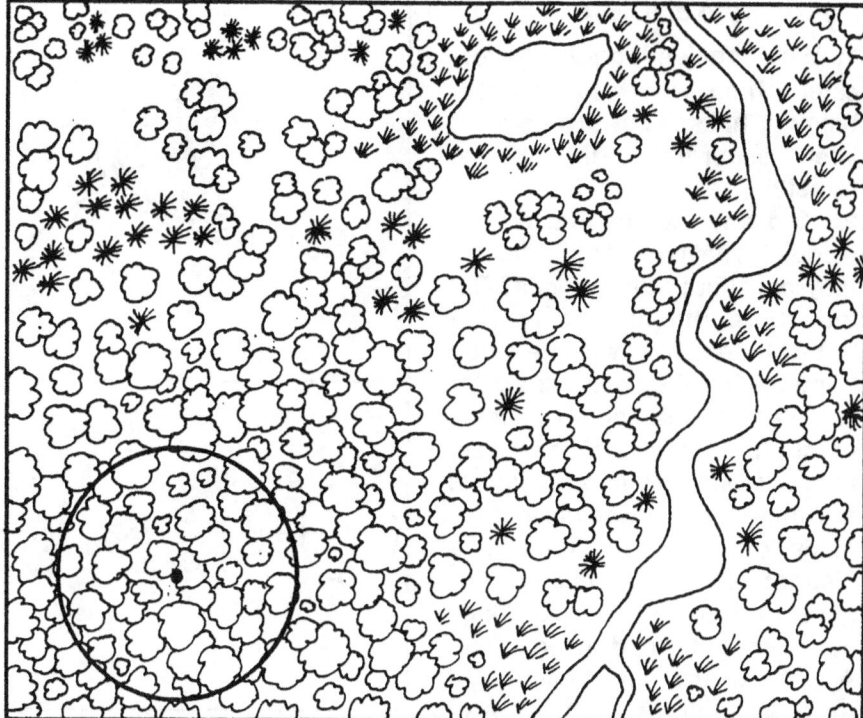

Figure 16. Sample plots should be typical of the area being studied.

Plot Location

Locate a wooded area in your own or a neighbor's backyard or on state land; or ask a private woodlot owner for permission to carry out this exercise on his or her land. Walk through the area to get an idea of what the forest looks like. To choose the location for your plot, try to find an area that represents the rest of the forest. (Do not pick the only hemlock stand in the middle of a hardwood-cover type unless you are measuring other "typical" hardwood plots.) Do not locate the plot on the edge of a stream unless that is typical of the forest you are sampling (fig. 16).

For a more accurate sample of your woods, it is best to measure more than one plot. Measure as many plots as you wish or have the time for; the more plots, the more complete your information will be. These plots should all be located to represent typical stands of your woods.

You may wish to sample a variety of different forest types. To do this, locate one plot in a hardwood stand, one in a conifer stand, and one in a mixed hardwood - conifer stand. Compare the differences among these plots. If you are interested in the effect of environment on the forest, locate one plot on a ridge top, one in a valley bottom, and one on each a north- and south-facing slope. Compare any differences. *Hypothesize* why they might occur.

History

To help give you some possible insights about the forest you are sampling, learn something about the land-use history of the area. Libraries or land ownership records will provide you with some information. You may have to deduce past land-use practices by using clues and evidence you actually find in the woods.

Questions to consider:

1. Was the land originally forested? If so, what was the forest type? (What species of trees most likely occurred in the original forest?)
2. Did any Indians live in your woods? What type of activities did they carry out in the woods? Did they burn the area to provide habitat for the wildlife they hunted? Did they plant crops?
3. Was the area cleared for fields or cut for timber? If the forest floor is relatively smooth, chances are that the area was cleared for fields or pasture. If there is a distinct pit-mound relief, it was never plowed and was most likely cut over or burned at one time. Are there any cut stumps? Are there any signs of fire? Any charred stumps?
4. What resources did this forest supply in the past to white people?
5. When was the forest last cut, or when was it abandoned if it was cleared? Ages of trees will give a good approximation of this. Ages can be estimated by counting the growth rings on recently cut stumps or by counting the whorls of branches on conifers. The whorl is the level at which several branches are attached around the trunk of the tree. Each whorl represents 1 year.
6. Is there evidence of soil erosion? Gullies or streams running down old roads indicate erosion.
7. Was the area planted or did it naturally seed in with trees? Rows of trees indicate planting.
8. What does the history indicate about the renewability of the forest?

Conducting the Inventory

The inventory can be done by one person, although it is much easier and less frustrating to do with two people.

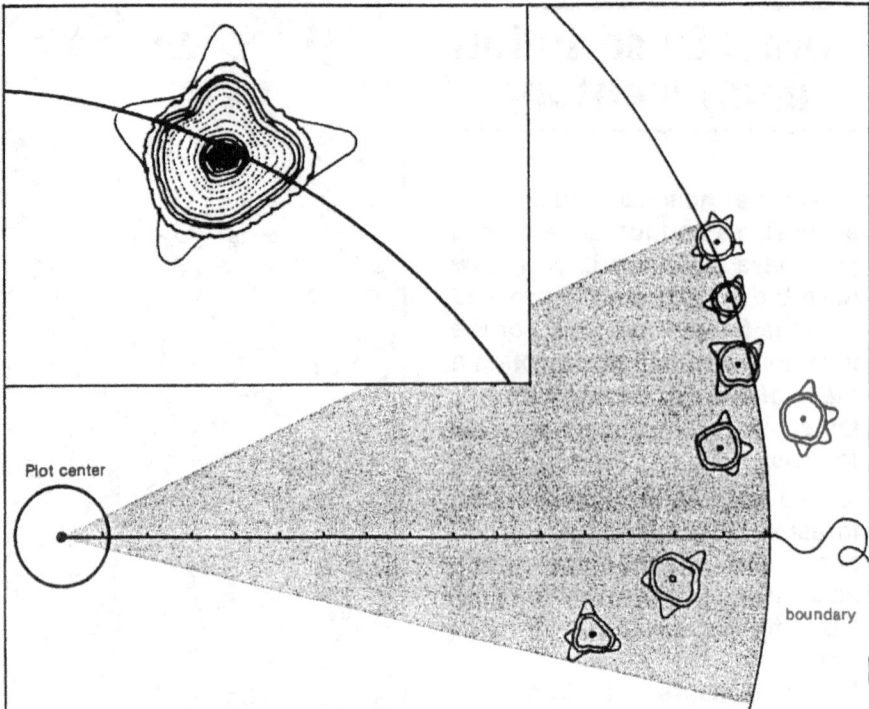

Figure 17. *Plot boundaries should be marked carefully.*

Set up the plot.

After you have found an appropriate location, drive a stake into the ground to mark the center of a 2/25-hectare (1/5-acre) circular plot. A flagged tree can also serve as a plot center. To establish the plot boundary, use a tape measure or a knotted rope to measure out from the plot center 16.06 m (52.7 ft). Flag all trees close to the boundary that are in the plot. Carefully measure borderline trees. Should the distance from the stake to the center of the tree be greater than 16.06 m (52.7 ft), the tree is outside the plot (fig. 17).

Inventory form.

Once the plot has been established, fill in the inventory (see p. 20), using the following guidelines:

A. Technical data.
Record the plot number, the date, and the field crew. If you are working with more than one person, only one form should be filled out for each plot measured. Property owner and town and county should be recorded.

B. Environmental factors.
• Indicate if the general *topography* (the configuration of the land's surface) of the area is flat or hilly. If it is hilly, is it steep are the hills rolling hills or is it a gradually rising slope?
• Topographic site refers to the specific site of the plot. Indicate where the plot is located.
• Slope indicates how steeply the land rises. Slope, measured here in percentage, is the number of meters rise (upward) for each 100 meters level distance. A 45° angle is a 100% slope. Take a measure of the average slope of the plot using the clinometer you made.
• Record the aspect of the slope that the plot is on. Face downhill as you stand at the plot center. Use a compass or the position of the sun to determine which direction you are facing, and record this direction.

C. Vegetation.
• Record the general forest type of your plot: hardwood, conifer, or mixed hardwood-conifer.
• Origin of stand — Look first at the overstory to determine how most of these trees became estab-

lished. Indicate if they originated from seeds or root sprouts (these will look like individual, independent trees), from stump sprouts (stump sprouts are all of the same species and will share either a common base or will be closely clustered together at their bases), or if they were planted (planted trees are usually arranged in rows).

Indicate which category most of the overstory trees fall into and mark it with an *O*. Determine the origin of the understory trees, if any exist, and mark the appropriate category with a *U*.

• Vegetation other than trees — Give a brief description of the shrub layer and the ground cover of forbs, grasses, mosses, mushrooms, lichens, and so forth. Give an idea of species present and of how dense the shrub layer and ground cover are.

D. Forest floor and soil.

• Indicate the absence or presence of organic litter (leaves, branches, humus, etc.). Measure its depth in centimeters from top to mineral soil, and describe its composition. Identify the leaves if you can.

• Dig a deep pit into the ground. Ideally, the soil pit should be dug to the bedrock to expose all soil layers. In some cases, only a backhoe would work; give it a good effort by hand, but you don't need to break your back or the shovel. Bury the pit when you are done; otherwise, it could become a trap for small animals. Determine if the soil has been developed from the underlying rock (indicated by distinct layers) or if it was transported to the site (no distinct layers, mixed rock fragments).

• For the first instance, measure in centimeters the depth of each layer and describe its color (fig. 18).

• Test the texture of the soil at each layer (see table 2). Squeeze a bit of moistened soil in your hand. Which category does it fit into?

• For transported soil, give a description of rock color, type, and sizes. Are they all the same size or does the size vary greatly? If you have any idea of how the soil was transported, write it down.

• Note where you find most of the roots. How well drained is the soil? Is it mucky, does the pit fill in with water, or is it fairly well drained?

• Is there a distinct pit-mound topography (fig. 19)? When a tree falls over, it creates a hole or pit where the roots were and a mound from the soil that is wrenched out of the ground by the roots. In most cases, the tree will have decomposed and no longer be evident. This pit-mound topography is very common in northeastern forests. (Make sure that you have not dug your soil pit in a pit or mound.)

• Water — Indicate the presence of open bodies of water nearby or on the plot. Describe the color, depth, and width of the water. Note any fish or other aquatic animal life dependent on this water.

E. Note signs of wildlife and signs of human activity.

F. Damage.

Look around at the vegetation. Pay particular attention to the trees. Look up into the tops, at the base ends, and along the trunks of trees. Describe the presence of damage, its cause, its extent, and relative abun-

Figure 18. Soil pit showing soil horizons.

Figure 19. Pit and mound topography resulting from decay of windthrown trees.

Table 2. Soil textures

Texture	Characteristics
Sand	Loose; squeezed in the hand when dry, it will fall apart when pressure is released; squeezed when moist, it will form a cast* which will crumble when touched.
Loam	Somewhat gritty, yet fairly smooth and able to hold a form when moist; squeezed when dry, the cast will not break if handled carefully; when moist, a cast can be handled freely without breaking.
Clay	Forms hard lumps when dry; when wet, is sticky and able to hold a form; moist clay can be pinched out between thumb and finger to form a long, flexible ribbon.

Source: K. A. Armson. 1977. *Forest Soils: Properties and Processes.* University of Toronto Press.
*Cast: a form, a mold

dance in the stand. Keep an eye out for cankers, rot, wounds, insects, animal damage, storm damage, and so forth. Mushrooms and other growths on living trees indicate fungal diseases. An abundance of broken tree tops may be the result of ice storm damage. The presence of many uprooted trees indicate wind storm damage.

Tree Measurements

Two types of tree surveys are conducted for this inventory. First, a survey of small trees is taken to give an idea of regeneration. Second, all trees of commercial value are measured to determine the volume of valuable wood in the forest.

Regeneration Survey.

The purpose of this survey (p. 21) is to focus on the abundance and species of trees regenerating in the forest. This information is important because it helps to determine when to cut and which harvest and regeneration systems to use. A simple tally is taken of the regeneration on a 1/2500-hectare (1/1000-acre) plot.

Procedure: The regeneration plot is a subplot of the main 2/25-hectare (1/5-acre) plot. Using the same plot center, set up a circular plot with a 1.13-m (3.71-ft) radius. Within this plot, tally all seedlings and trees according to their species and size class. All seedlings less than 1 m (3 ft) tall are categorized by their height. Taller trees are categorized by diameter class. Be sure to measure diameter at 1.37 m (4.5 ft) from the ground whenever possible (this is the *DBH* — Diameter Breast Height). (See instructions for making and using a Biltmore stick in Appendix 1.)

Merchantable Tree Inventory.

The purpose of this inventory (p. 21) is to assess the quality and wood volume of trees of commercial value. Diameter and height

Figure 20. *The size and shape of trees determine what wood products can be obtained from them.*

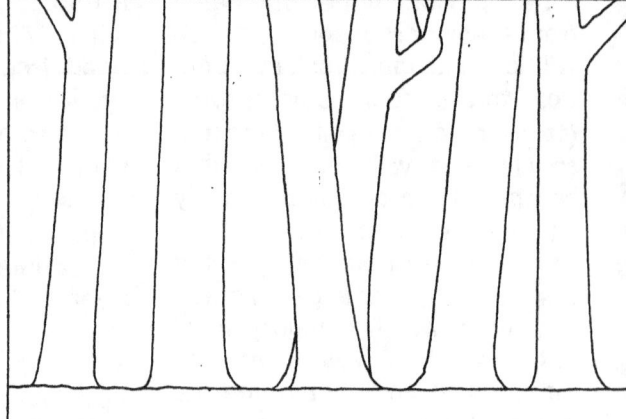

Sawlogs are taken from large, clean-boled trees.

Pulpwood makes use of trees that are crooked, forked, or otherwise defective for sawlogs.

Fuelwood can come from small trees taken in thinning operations or from trees too poor in form for sawlogs or pulpwood.

measurements are taken, and a qualitative description of each tree is made. With this information, the forest manager can assess the quality and amount of wood products the forest is producing. This helps him/her to decide when to harvest trees and which harvest system to use.

For this inventory, all trees of merchantable size — that is, large enough to be sold as a specific wood product — in the 1/25-hectare (1/5-acre) plot boundary are measured with a Biltmore stick. The merchantable size limit varies depending upon the wood product. Therefore, before measuring any trees, you must decide which wood product(s) you prefer from the forest.

Sawlogs: trees that are to be sold for lumber. Sawlogs should have fair to good form — that is, long, straight trunks that are mostly free of branches. Measure only

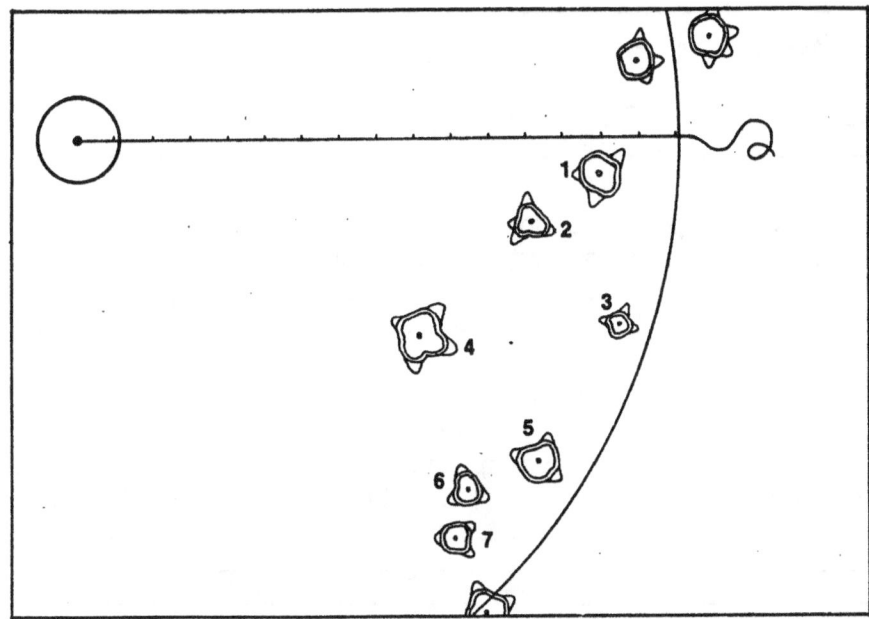

Figure 21. Measure trees in sequence, starting along a radius and measuring all merchantable trees in a clockwise progression. Only trees with their center inside the plot should be measured.

those trees that are 30 cm (11.8 in) DBH or greater. Record the diameter and the height. The recorded height is equal to the number of logs (5-m or 16.3-ft segments) in the tree up to a 15-cm (6-in) top. Trees with excessively poor form are best measured as pulpwood.

Pulpwood: trees that are to be sold as pulp for paper and fiber products. Form is not as important for pulpwood as for sawlogs. Trees that are 15 cm (5.91 in) DBH or greater qualify for pulpwood. Height is measured to the closest meter up to a 9-cm (3.54-in) top.

Firewood: form is not important here. Any size tree will qualify for firewood, but for your purposes, measure only those trees that are 10 cm (3.94 in) at DBH or greater. Measure height to the nearest meter up to an 8-cm (3.14-in) top.

When deciding which wood products to measure, consider the relative value of the products (fig. 20). Large trees of good form and valuable species bring in more money if sold as sawlogs than as pulpwood or firewood. You may wish to combine all three products. In such a case, measure all trees on the plot that are 10 cm or greater. Trees that are at least 10 cm and less than 15 cm should be measured as firewood. Those that are from 15 cm to 29 cm should be measured as pulpwood. Any larger trees should be considered as sawlogs. You may also decide to measure your trees solely for pulpwood or firewood. Whichever product or combination of products you wish to measure is perfectly valid.

Procedure: Stand at the plot center and face in one direction (such as north). Measure all trees of merchantable size, proceeding in a clockwise direction from the plot center. Ignore trees that are less than merchantable size. Mark each measured tree with chalk to avoid remeasurement (fig. 21). For each tree, record the following information on the Merchantable Tree Inventory (p. 21):

- Species — record species. Use *Know Your Trees* if you have difficulties.
- Diameter — be sure to measure at DBH — 1.37 m (4.5 ft) from the ground.
- Height — record height up to a merchantable height in logs or meters, as specified previously. Be sure to include the units.
- Form — Record the form as good, fair, or poor (fig. 22).

Good — a hardwood that is branched only at the top and has a straight trunk; a conifer that is not excessively branched with a straight trunk.

Fair — a tree that has minor defects of form. Note defects.

Poor — a tree that is excessively forked, twisted, branchy. State why.

- Damage — record any rot, wounds, or damage to the tree. Note cause (if detectable) and extent of damage.
- Animal signs — Note any signs of animal use of the tree, such as nests, claw marks, actual sightings.
- Miscellaneous — Record anything unusual about the tree that has not been covered by the previous categories.

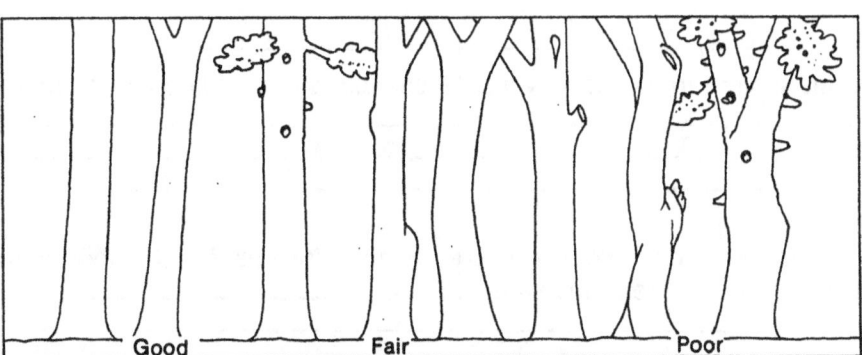

Figure 22. Tree form depends upon size, straightness, length of clean bole, and freedom from disease, damage, or holes.

Forest Evaluation Inventory Sheet

A. Technical Data
Plot #_____ Date measured_____ Field crew _____
Property owner_____ Location _____

B. Environmental Factors
General topography: Flat_____ Hilly_____ (Steep_____ Rolling_____ Gradual_____)
Topographic site: Ridge top_____ Mid-slope_____ Valley bottom_____ Riverbank_____
              Other_____
Slope_____ Aspect _____

C. Vegetation
Forest Type: Hardwood_____   Origin of Stand: Seeds or root sprouts_____
              Conifer _____   Planted_____
              Mixed _____   Stump sprouts_____

Vegetation other than trees: Brief description of shrubs, forbs, leafy, and other vegetation present. Give some idea of abundance. _____
_____
_____

D. Forest Floor and Soil
Litter: Absent (mineral soil)_____
      If present, Depth_____ Composition _____
Soil: Developed from underlying rock_____ Transported _____
     Description: _____
_____

	Depth	Color	Texture
A Horizon	_____	_____	_____
B Horizon	_____	_____	_____
C Horizon	_____	_____	_____

Description of soil drainage and where most of the roots are located.
_____
_____
_____

Evidence of pit-mound topography:_____
Water: Description of open bodies of water — color, depth, width. Note animal life associated with it.
_____
_____
_____

E. Animal Activity
Wildlife: Note scats, evidence of feeding (browsing of limbs, pile of seed shells, etc.), actual sightings, nests, songs, snags with woodpecker holes, bones, etc._____
_____
_____

Regeneration Survey

1/2500-hectare (1/1000-acre) plot. Tally all trees including sprouts by species and size class within this plot.

Species   **Size Class**

	Less than .3 tall	.3 – 1 m tall	>1 m and ≤2.5 cm in diameter	2.5 – 8.0 cm in diameter	9 – 15 cm DBH

		16 – 30 cm DBH	31 – 45 cm DBH	46 – 60 cm DBH	61 + cm DBH

Merchantable Tree Inventory

2/25-hectare (1/5-acre) plot. Measure all trees 15 cm (5.9 in) or greater in DBH.

Species	Diameter	Height	Form	Damage	Animal Signs	Miscellaneous

Review of Forest Inventory

1. Forest Summary. Using points A-D as a guide, summarize the information you have gathered.

A. Summarize the forest stand that you inventoried. Give a brief description of its composition of plants and animals and its environment. Briefly describe the condition of the forest.

B. Regeneration Survey. Using the data you obtained, calculate the number of trees per hectare for each species and age class.

Multiply the total number of trees for each category by 2,500. For example:

Species

	Less than .3 m tall
Sugar maple	
Beech	

Sugar maple 9 × 2,500 = 22,000 TPH (trees per hectare).

Fill in the following table:

Trees per hectare

Species	Less than .3 m tall	.3 - 1 m tall	>1 m & ≤2.5 cm DBH	2.5 - 8.0 cm in diameter	9 - 15 cm DBH

Species	16 - 30 cm DBH	31 - 45 cm DBH	46 - 60 cm DBH	61+ cm DBH

From the table, make a graph like this one:

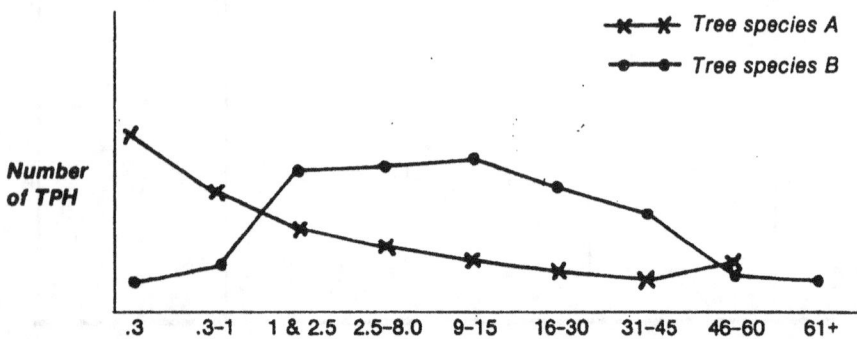

Answer the following questions:
- Is there any pattern in size distribution of specific tree species?
- Which tree species are regenerating?
- Which species of trees are of merchantable size?

C. Volume of Merchantable Trees. To determine the volume of wood on the plot, first organize your data according to wood products. Using the Volumes of Wood Products form (p. 23), make a list of the diameter and height dimensions of each tree under each category. Using these dimensions, look up the volume for each tree on the appropriate volume tables in Appendix 3. Add these figures to calculate the total volume of wood for each wood product. Multiply this number by 2.0235 to get the volume of wood per hectare. Use the form to show your volume calculations, and record the total volume of each wood product per hectare.

Firewood volume is measured in cords. A cord is a stack of wood 4 ft (1.46 m) by 4 ft by 8 ft (2.92 m). Traditionally, pulpwood volume has been measured in either cords or cubic feet and the volume of sawlogs measured in board feet. The board foot is equivalent to a plane 1 inch thick and 1 foot square. In the metric system, both of these volumes are measured in cubic meters. Be sure to use the correct metric units of measure in determining volume.

Remember that the final volumes you come up with are estimates. They would be correct only if the whole forest was exactly like the plot you measured. Each tree would also have to be measured with complete accuracy.

Questions to consider:
- Why are volume estimates important?
- Is it important to be accurate with volume estimates? When? Why?
- What causes volume estimates to be inaccurate?

D. Basal Area. Basal area, like volume estimates, is a numerical way of describing what the forest is like. Basal area is the total cross-sectional area of trees in the stand (fig. 23). In other words, if every tree on 1 hectare of land was cut off at DBH and you were to look down on it from the sky and measure the area of the hectare occupied by the flat tops of the stumps, you would get the basal area of trees per hectare. Basal area is therefore a general measure of stocking or density. The portion of basal area occupied by each species is a measure of relative dominance for each species.

Volumes of Wood Products

Wood product _____			Wood product _____			Wood product _____		
DBH cm	Height	Volume	DBH cm	Height	Volume	DBH cm	Height	Volume
	Total			Total			Total	
	× 2.0235			× 2.0235			× 2.0235	
Total vol./hectare			Total vol./hectare			Total vol./hectare		

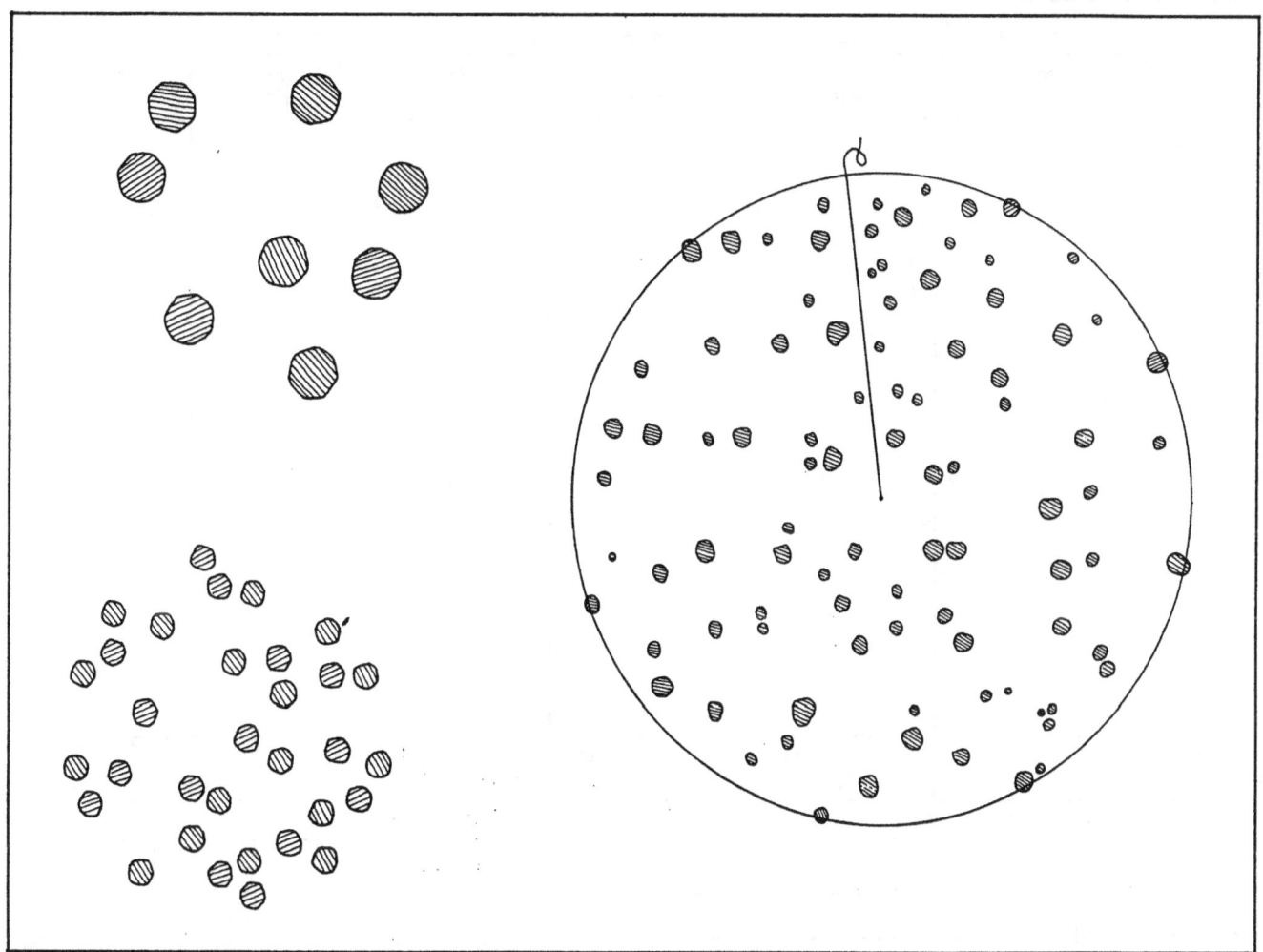

Figure 23. Basal area includes the total area of the plot covered by trees if they were measured as stumps. As seen on the left, where shaded areas are equal, basal area measures can be misleading.

Using the Basal Area Calculation form below, calculate the basal area of each species and the total basal area of your forest per hectare as follows:

- First organize a list of the trees you measured on the large plot by species. Record the diameters for each tree. Then use the Basal Area Table in Appendix 3 to calculate the basal area for each tree. Record.
- Add to find the total BA/species. Multiply each of these numbers by 2.0235 to obtain BA/species/hectare. Record these and sum them to find the BA of all trees/hectare.

Basal area calculations are important when planning forest management. It gives the forester an idea of how densely the trees are arranged in the forest. From this information, she or he can determine how much basal area to harvest from a stand to create a favorable environment for desired tree species.

But basal area can be confusing. If the basal area is the only information provided, it does not say anything about the size of trees in the stand. For example, a forest with a basal area of 3.76 m²/hectare (100 ft²/acre) may be composed of 62 trees/hectare (152 trees/acre) that are 27.9 cm (11 in) in diameter, or of 116 trees/hectare (287 trees/acre) that are 20.3 cm (8 in) in diameter. More information is provided, therefore, if basal area is accompanied by the average diameter of trees in the stand, called average stand diameter (ASD).

To calculate the ASD for your forest, sum all the diameters of trees measured in the large plot and divide by the total number of trees. Compare this with the basal area of all trees/hectare.

Questions to consider:

- Think back to your stand. Does the ASD really represent your forest? What other information might be useful to include to more accurately describe your forest?
- Explain the value of using an estimate for basal area. Explain some pitfalls of the use of such an estimate.

2. If you measured more than one plot, complete the analysis for each and compare the plots as follows.

Basal Area Calculations

	*Species*_____		*Species*_____		*Species*_____	
	Diameter (cm)	BA (m²)	Diameter (cm)	BA (m²)	Diameter (cm)	BA (cm²)
Total	cm	m² × 2.0235	cm	m² × 2.0235	cm	m² × 2.0235
BA/hectare		m²/ha		m²/ha		m²/ha

Total BA of all trees/hectare _____

Total diameters (cm) _____

Total number of trees   ÷   _____

Average stand diameter   _____

A. For plots that represent different forest types, such as conifer and hardwood, or that represent different environments, such as ridge, hillside, and valley bottom, compare the estimates of regeneration, volume, and basal area.
- Is there more regeneration in a certain forest type or environment?
- How do volumes differ between plots?
- Do different plots offer different resources? If so, what are they? Why?
- Summarize any other differences or similarities among plots.

B. For plots that represent the same type of forest, calculate average estimates as shown below.

Regeneration Survey: Set up a table showing average trees per hectare, and fill in the average number of trees for each species in each size class. For example:

Plot 1

	Trees per hectare
Size class	Less than .3 m tall
Species Maple	22,000

Plot 2

	Trees per hectare
Size class	Less than .3 m tall
Species Maple	25,000

$$\text{Average} = \frac{a + b + c \ldots}{\text{number of plots}}$$

$$= \frac{22,000 + 25,000}{2}$$

$$= 23,500 \text{ trees per hectare}$$

Average number of trees per hectare

Size class	Less than .3 m tall
Species Maple	23,500

Make a graph of regeneration by species as you did before, but use the data from the table showing average trees per hectare.

Volume Estimates: Take the final estimates of total volume per hectare calculated for each wood product and average them. For example:

Plot 1

Sawlogs
0

Pulpwood
108.5 m³/hectare

Firewood
8.4 cords/hectare

Plot 2

Sawlogs
20.3 m³/hectare

Pulpwood
79.6 m³/hectare

Firewood
17.2 cords/hectare

Average

Sawlogs
$$\frac{20.3 + 0}{2} = 10.2 \text{ m}^3/\text{hectare}$$

Pulpwood
$$\frac{108.5 + 79.6}{2} = 94.2 \text{ m}^3/\text{hectare}$$

Firewood
$$\frac{8.4 + 17.2}{2} = 12.8 \text{ cords/hectare}$$

Basal Area: Determine the average basal area per hectare from all plots by adding up BA estimates and dividing by the number of plots. Total the average stand diameter from all plots, and divide by the number of plots. This will give you an estimate of the average diameter of trees in the forest where your plots are located.

By sampling more than one plot and calculating average estimates as above, your final estimate is more representative of the whole forest. Sampling just one plot can give you an inaccurate picture of the total forest because the plot you measure may have certain peculiarities that are not common throughout the forest, or it may be lacking a character that is present in the rest of the forest. By calculating an average estimate from several similar plots, these peculiarities will have less influence on the final estimate, and any character that one plot is lacking most likely will show up on another plot.

3. Consider the dynamics of the forest ecosystem you have just evaluated.

A. How do you think past human history has influenced the forest as it exists now?

B. If you measured a mixed stand of trees, what can be said about each group of species? How are the species mixed? Do they occur in clumps together? Where do different species occur — on ridgetops, valley bottoms, slopes, wet spots, dry spots, other? Which species are intolerants, intermediate tolerants, and tolerants? Where do they occur? In which layer of the forest — understory, upper canopy?

C. Choose the three major species of your forest. Describe how each of these species reproduces, by seeds or by sprouts. How are the seeds dispersed? What are the requirements of each of these species to become established and grow?

D. How have plants, animals, and environmental factors influenced the development of your forest into what it is now?

E. What evidence is there that the forest is not static? How is it changing? Why do certain species and individual trees survive while others die off throughout the growth of the forest?

F. What will the forest be like in the future if allowed to grow without any modifications such as harvesting or fire?

G. What unusual or unexpected things did you see in your forest?

4. What renewable resources exist in this forest?

A. Wildlife resources:
What animals live in the forest now?
What are their requirements for life?
Which requirements are satisfied by this particular forest?

B. Recreation:
What types of recreation exist now in the forest?
Does there exist potential for other recreational activities?
What requirements must be met for these kinds of activities?

C. Water:
How does this forest affect the water cycle?
Does it supply water for direct usage?
How does the forest affect nearby open bodies of water?
Does it affect water temperature and aquatic life?

D. Aesthetics:
Is this forest unique?
Does it offer a view?
Does it have potential for a nature trail?
Should the forest be thinned and/or cleaned to make it more pleasing to the eye?

E. Special Products:
What special products does this forest provide?
Is there any potential to supply other special products?
Could this forest provide Christmas trees?

F. Environmental Improvement:
Is this forest located close to cities, towns, villages?
How does it directly or indirectly affect environmental quality?

G. Wood Products
Timber —
What valuable timber species exist in this forest for sawlogs and for pulpwood?
Are they of good form?
What is the volume of sawlogs? of pulpwood?
What is the basal area of sawlogs? of pulpwood?

Firewood —
Which species in this forest will make the best firewood?
In which size class are they?
How much basal area do they represent?
Would they be more valuable as sawlogs or pulpwood?
How much volume of firewood exists per hectare on your forest?
Do you wish to produce firewood for sale or just for your own needs?

Forest Management

To survive, humans have always modified their environment in some way to produce what they need. Unfortunately, too many times these changes have been unorganized and have led to deterioration of the world around us. Land management is a more organized way of modifying the environment. Land management is based on a plan that uses scientific knowledge about the ecosystem. It analyzes a situation, agrees on objectives, adopts a plan, and measures the results of the plan (fig. 24).

Forest management is defined by the Society of American Foresters (SAF) as "the application of business methods and technical forestry principles to the operation of a forest property." Forest management works to keep forest land productive and to maintain the *renewability* of the forest resources. Since forest lands can produce a variety of resources, they are usually managed to provide us with more than just one resource. *Multiple use* conflicts arise, however, when certain forest resources are *mutually exclusive* — that is, they cannot be produced at the same time on the same piece of land. The forest manager must weigh the conflicts to determine the best use of the land. This decision demands skill, technical knowledge, responsibility, and open-mindedness. It's not easy, especially when we realize that managers do not know all the answers. The amount of information is vast,

Figure 24. Flow chart of forest management process.

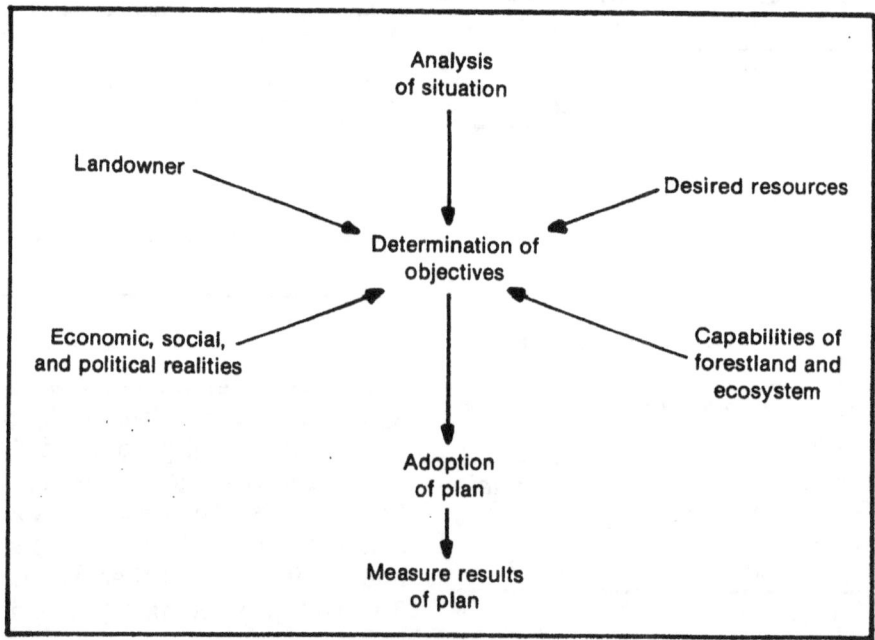

and we still have much to learn about ecosystems. The forest ecosystem is much more complex than we realize; we can only know the tip of the vast iceberg of knowledge to be had.

Forest management includes everything from intense management to neglect. If a forest stand is unmanaged or neglected, chance occurrences in nature will shape it. Such a stand might be presumed to be "natural". However, it is probably being influenced indirectly by the actions of people. If it is not a virgin forest, past uses of the land have shaped what the forest is today. Previous harvest or land clearing could affect forest composition and the fertility of the land. Our policy of stopping all fires and controlling flooding also indirectly affects forests today. Fires, floods, and other natural "disasters" have always played a part in the cycles of ecosystems. Also, heavily polluted air from our cities drifts to outlying areas and enters forest ecosystems. The effects may not be noticeable, but in many cases, damage has been documented. For example, some trees in the San Bernadino Mountains close to the Los Angeles basin are unhealthy and are dying because of air pollution. The acid precipitation in the Northeast is affecting forests and even the acidity of lakes in the Adirondack Mountains. This effect, in turn, is causing fish in these lakes to die off. Neglect is sometimes the worst form of management because in doing so we are not aware of how we are indirectly changing the system. Irreversible damages can result if we are not aware of the effects of our actions.

After nonmanagement comes every type of management from low level (such as the removal of diseased trees) to intensive management (as displayed in tree plantations). The intensity of management depends on the management objectives and, in most cases, on how much money is available for management.

Questions to consider:

1. Is the forest you inventoried managed? If so, how is it managed? Ask the landowner.
2. If the forest is unmanaged, are there any indirect forces influencing its development? What are they? How are they affecting the forest?

The key to good forest management is to start with a clear idea of the reason for management. Objectives must be set. The objectives vary depending upon (1) what resources are desired from the forest, (2) what the forest land and ecosystem are capable of producing, (3) who owns the land, and (4) what is realistic economically, socially, and politically.

Take, for example, the owner of a woodlot who wishes to establish a red pine plantation for future sawlog production. A study of the plantation site shows that the soil is shallow, poorly drained, and of low fertility. A dense cover of shrubs and alders already is growing on the site. Before even planting the trees, the owner must spend a considerable amount of money to put in drainage ditches, to clear the brush, and to add fertilizer. After all that, pines will probably not grow well in the shallow soil. It would be best for the owner to choose objectives that are more suited to the capabilities of the land and that are affordable. Perhaps the area would be better managed to encourage wildlife. Hunting rights could then be leased for a small fee.

Having set the objectives, the forest manager than chooses the *silvicultural operations* (fig. 25)

Figure 25. Choice of silvicultural operations.

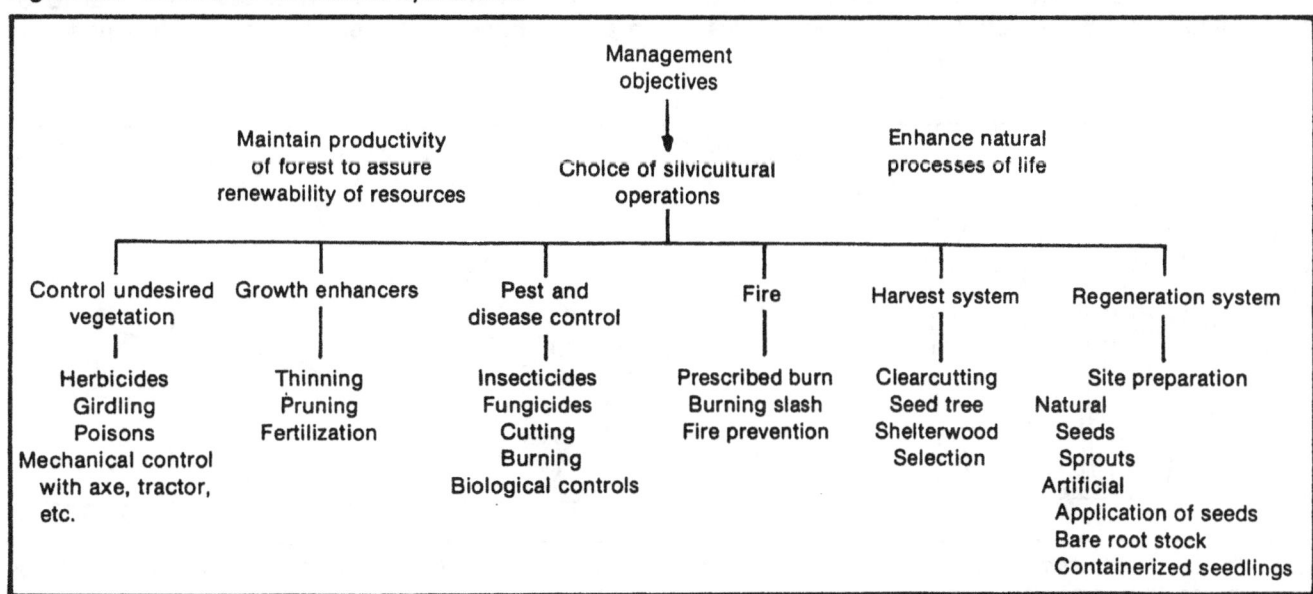

that will best meet the objectives but will not destroy the forest's productivity. Silvicultural operations include all the operations that go into developing and managing a forest stand. Questions a forest manager might ask in deciding which operations to use are: How can I manipulate the environment to favor the growth of the desired resources? What are the drawbacks of using these operations? What side effects will they have on the forest ecosystem? Are these methods socially, environmentally, and economically realistic?

Whole textbooks have been devoted to the topic of silviculture. A brief description of only the major silvicultural operations is provided below.

Control of Undesirable Vegetation

Shrubs, trees, and forbs competing with the desired vegetation for sun, nutrients, space, and other requirements should be controlled. Herbicides may be applied to kill or stunt the competing plants. Weed trees often are girdled, that is, a ring of bark is removed completely from the trunk. This cuts off the phloem and does not allow sugars to reach the roots. The tree in most cases dies. Poison can be injected to kill trees or sprouts and is sometimes combined with girdling. Bulldozers equipped with cutters or rakes are often used to destroy competing brush. An axe is a simple but effective tool for controlling undesirable vegetation.

Growth Enhancers

Growth of desired vegetation can be enhanced by thinning, pruning, and fertilizing. These silvicultural techniques are mainly applied to timber stands, although they can aid the production of other forest resources.

The most valuable sawlogs are made from trees that have a straight, branchless trunk and are fairly large in diameter. This good quality tree form can be obtained by thinning to control the spacing between trees. Trees that are closely spaced must put energy into height growth to compete for light. Tall, straight, thin, and small-crowned trees result. Widely spaced trees tend to be shorter, larger in diameter, and have more branches. To encourage diameter growth but still maintain the branchless, straight trunk, these stands should be *thinned* to an ideal spacing (fig. 26). This spacing varies depending upon the species and the age of the trees. After thinning, the trees will grow quickly, but growth slows down as the trees begin to crowd again. The stand is therefore thinned periodically. Poorly formed trees and undesirable species are removed. The remaining well-formed "crop" trees grow faster. Thus, it takes less time to produce wood products, and, in the long run, more usable wood is produced.

The purpose of *pruning* is to produce quality sawlogs free of knots formed by branches. The lower branches of individual trees are periodically removed with a pruning saw. Care must be taken to leave no branch stubs and to avoid injury to the trunk. Otherwise the tree may not heal correctly and rot can occur. No more than one-third of the height of the tree should be pruned at any time. Because pruning costs time and money, usually only the best, high-value trees are pruned. Often the trees in a Christmas tree plantation are pruned, but in a slightly different manner. Here the crown is pruned to give it a full, nicely shaped Christmas tree form.

Fertilizing a forest that is lacking in nutrients will increase tree growth. Although seedlings are sometimes fertilized when first planted, the majority of timberlands in the United States are not fertilized. Fertilization is rather expensive, and it is not clear whether the cost is equal to or exceeds the value of the increased

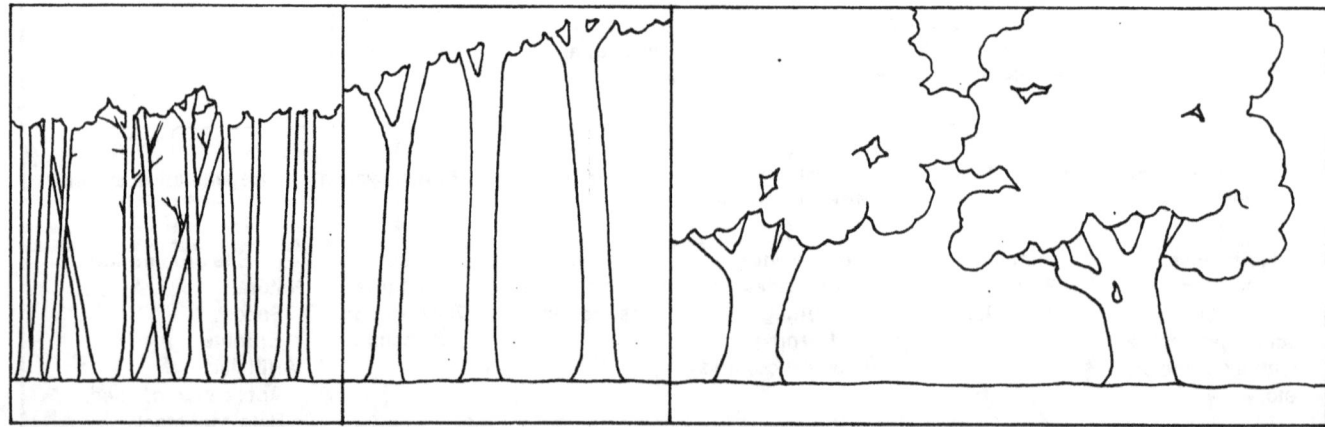

Figure 26. Thinning can produce an optimum density of trees for good growth and form: left — *too thick*; middle — *optimum density*; right — *too thin*.

growth. Perhaps an area that requires fertilization to produce timber would be better managed for a different forest resource.

Pest and Disease Control

Fungal diseases and damage by insects or other animals affect trees of all ages from seedling to mature tree. Diseases and pests become a problem that needs control when they cause wide-scale damage to forests or when they prevent the planned establishment of seedlings. Insecticide and fungicide sprays are commonly used for insect and fungal attacks. Epidemics can sometimes be controlled by cutting diseased trees and burning branches and logging residue that may harbor insects or diseases. Animal pests are usually controlled by extermination, by habitat destruction, or by methods to deter them. For example, in areas where regeneration is a problem, seedlings are often scented with unpleasing odors to discourage deer from eating them.

Fungicides and insecticides can create some problems while solving others. Organisms that are beneficial or neutral may be exterminated along with the target pest. The control is sometimes applied after the damage has already been done; it is therefore important to apply the control at the proper time.

Fire

Fire can play either a beneficial or an extremely destructive role in a forest. It has always been a part of the natural ecosystem. Certain organisms even depend on fire to survive. In the past, burns were sometimes frequent enough that the fuel load did not build up. "Cool" fires resulted, which could not burn through the thick bark of older trees. Many of the pine and redwood forests we have today are the result of periodic burns that killed the repeating crops of hardwood understory. Fires are destructive when they burn hot and completely destroy the forest. Repeated hot fires can "bake" the soil and turn a once forested land into a wasteland.

Every year, millions of acres of forested land are destroyed by "hot" wildfires. Forest managers work to prevent and suppress these burns. Because people cause 89 percent of wildfires, public education such as Smokey Bear campaigns are an important part of fire prevention. During periods of high fire danger, forested areas may be closed to public access. Other prevention techniques include building fire breaks and removing fuels in areas of high fire risk. The wildfires that do occur must be suppressed if they threaten to cause heavy damage to forest resources. Large crews of fire fighters are required to control the fire front and to mop up any hot spots after the fire has been contained. Often, air tankers and helicopters carrying flame retardants are used along with the fire crews. Federal, state, and local governments pool money to fight these costly battles. The complex science of firefighting must predict the fire's path and intensity, organize firefighters and equipment, and develop new tools and techniques to fight the fire.

Forest managers have recently been taking more advantage of the beneficial side of fire. In fact, the control or *prescribed burn* is often the easiest, most efficient management tool. Such fires are set in the proper place, under the right weather conditions, and under strict surveillance. Slash and other debris left over from logging can be burned to reduce the amount of fuel available to a wildfire. Seedbed preparation often includes a prescribed burn. Along with reducing weed competition to future seedlings and improving access for planting crews, a burn exposes bare mineral soil which enhances seed germination of certain important tree species. A prescribed burn can help to control undesirable vegetation, perhaps a hardwood understory in a pine forest. Despite their usefulness, prescribed burns can easily get out of control and should be attempted only by persons experienced in control burns.

Harvest Systems

Some forest resources, such as timber and firewood, must be removed or harvested from the forest to be used. Other resources, such as wildlife and recreation, can be maintained in the forest by periodic removal of trees. The method of tree removal is called the harvest system.

Harvest systems can be viewed as imitations of the continual harvest of trees in nature. In nature, insects, fungi, and old age sometimes cause the gradual death of trees scattered throughout the stand. This harvest is balanced by new growth. Natural harvest may also claim large tracts of forested land by windstorm, high intensity fire, or insect infestation. Unless excessive erosion, poor environmental conditions, or other factors interfere, a succession of plants and animals will invade the area and will gradually rebuild the forest. Periodic natural harvest helps maintain diversity and renews the vigor of the forest.

There are four main harvest systems used by people today: *clearcutting, seedtree, shelter-*

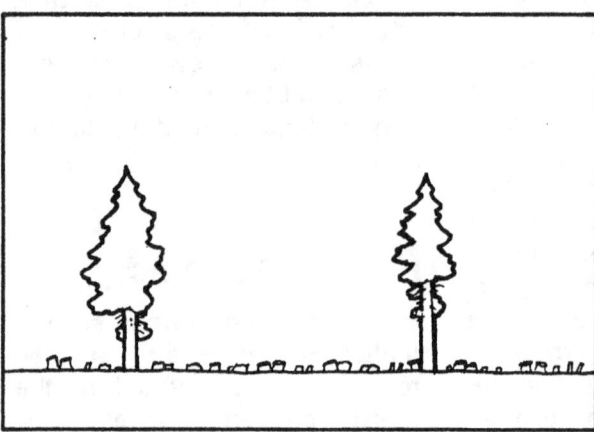
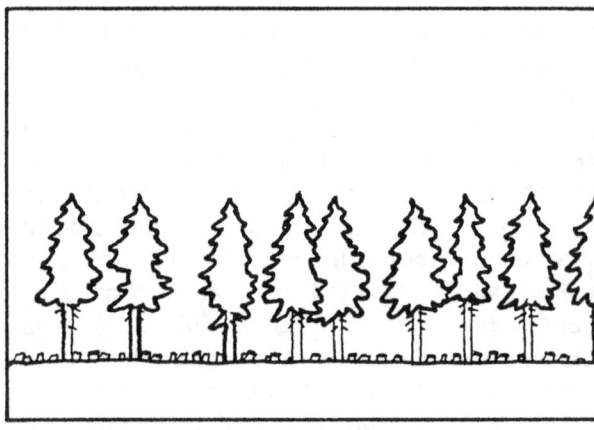

Figure 27. Schematic diagram of harvest systems.

wood, and *selection* (fig. 27). The system to be used is determined by the desired resource and its requirements for life. To assure the renewability of the resource, a regeneration method is combined with the harvest system. Regeneration is either artificial or natural. *Artificial regeneration* involves planting live seedlings or applying seeds. *Natural regeneration* relies on seeds from the surrounding forest or on sprouts for reproduction of the forest.

Clearcutting System

Clearcutting is best suited for intolerant trees, which require full sunlight for proper growth, or for shallowly rooted trees, which are subject to windfall if scattered individuals are left uncut. In this system, all trees in a block ranging from 4 to 40 hectares (10–100 acres) in size are cut. This cutting creates a large opening that many desirable and undesirable plants will invade. Sometimes the clearcut site must be prepared (burned, brush control) or even planted to favor the regeneration of the desired tree species. In responsible forest management, the cut must be followed with planned regeneration.

Other problems are also associated with clearcutting. Cutting large blocks of land on unstable soil can cause serious erosion, as can the presence of the skid trails and improperly constructed roads of any logging operation on such soil. Another problem is that at first clearcut is unsightly, and this causes a negative social reaction. Clearcuts, however, can be shaped with irregular borders and in other than square patterns to blend in with the natural landscape and reduce visual trauma. The site must be tailored correctly to meet the regeneration requirements of the desired tree species. If trees of intermediate tolerance are to be regenerated, the cut must not be too large. Clearcutting definitely is not satisfactory for tolerant trees. Methods of regeneration must also be considered. Planting, of course, poses no problem. However, to take best advantage of natural regeneration, the cut should be planned to coincide with a good seed fall. It should be also located in a good area and be of the right size to allow for seed fall over the whole site.

Although it is a very controversial harvest system, a well-planned clearcut is the most appropriate method of harvest and regeneration of some intolerant species.

Seed Tree System

In this sytem, the area is cut clear except for certain selected trees left standing singly or in groups. Trees of good form are carefully chosen as seed trees to furnish seed to restock the cut. After seedlings have become established, the seed trees may be removed in a second cutting or left indefinitely. The seed tree method of harvest is best suited for trees that develop strong root systems and need abundant sunlight to grow properly.

This system has many of the same disadvantages as clearcutting, to which it is quite similar. The seed trees relieve some of the problems of natural regeneration that occur with clearcutting; however, there is nothing to guarantee that the seed trees will have a good seed crop when desired. Sometimes seed trees are injured in the initial logging, and the removal of the seed trees themselves incurs additional expense and can cause harm to the newly established seedlings.

Of the methods of natural regeneration, however, the seed tree system allows the most control over species and quality of seed source.

Shelterwood System

In this system, a greater number of mature trees are left standing than in the seed tree system. These mature trees provide a seed source and protection for the next regeneration. After seedlings have become established and are well on their way, the mature sheltering trees are harvested. The new seedlings can then make full use of the growing space. The degree of shelter and exposure provided by the shelterwood can be adjusted to meet the environmental requirements of almost all species. Only intolerant species cannot be managed by this system.

The greatest disadvantage of this system is that the new generation of trees is susceptible to injury during the harvest of the shelterwood. Also, they can be in the way during harvest. However, regeneration is more certain and complete than with the previous two systems. There is also more protection of the site and of aesthetics. By creating openings rotated throughout the forest, the shelterwood system provides diversity, which is important for many of the nontimber resources.

Selection System

The selection system is designed to perpetuate a stand of trees varying greatly in age and size from seedling to mature trees. Under this system, individual, scattered mature trees or groups of them are harvested periodically. At the same time, undesirable trees are removed. The small openings created by harvest improve the growing conditions for the remaining trees. Within a few years, new trees are established on the soil disturbed by the logging operation, and other trees are mature and ready for harvest. This system favors trees that grow well in partial shade and is suited for trees with shallow root systems. Mutual protection prevents wind throw and exposure to the elements.

Logging under the selection system is both difficult and expensive. It requires frequent trips to the forest with heavy machinery, which can harm the remaining trees. It is unsuitable for intolerant species.

Of all the harvest systems, the selection system disrupts the forest and the aesthetics the least. It can provide a continuous supply of mature timber from a small tract of land.

Regeneration Methods

Regenerating a forest after harvest is the key to renewability. Removing trees makes extra space, nutrients, water, gases, and energy available to any organism. If left to nature, a succession of organisms will occupy the space. Trees will probably eventually become reestablished there as long as the site suffered no serious degradation. This natural succession may take too long for a forest managed to produce timber, and there is no guarantee that the desired trees will be among those ending up on the site. The forest manager may decide to speed up the establishment of desired species by using an appropriate method of regeneration.

Site preparation is often the first step to regeneration of a harvested area. Vegetation such as brush and grass occupying the site may prohibit or delay the prompt regeneration of trees. Logging debris and slash may physically inhibit the reproduction as well as be a fire hazard. Some forest soils are covered with a thick layer of duff, which prevents many seeds and seedlings from developing because of lack of water or presence of damping-off fungi. Site preparation methods such as prescribed burns and the use of herbicides and heavy machinery can modify these situations appropriately. The exact method used depends on the given ecological situation.

A forest can be regenerated in several ways. Natural methods of reproduction may be relied upon, or artificial measures may be used.

Natural Regeneration

Trees reproduce themselves naturally by seeds. Seed production, however, can be erratic, and not all crops are fertile. The forester cannot always depend on a good seed year to follow a harvest. This form of reproduction does not give complete control over which species will regenerate, over the desired mix and number of species, or over the location of seed fall. It is usually not suitable for intensive timber management.

Many hardwoods and a few conifers form root or stump sprouts that can become mature trees. In some cases, this type of vegetative reproduction, called the coppice system, creates the next forest. Because many sprouts tend to develop, one good sprout per stump is selected after a few years and all others are cut.

Sprouts have the advantage of a developed root system enabling them to grow faster than seedlings. As a result, the coppice system can produce more wood over a given time period than any other system. With age, however, the vitality of the root system decreases, and eventually a completely new forest must be established (fig. 28).

Artificial Regeneration

When natural methods of regeneration are not suitable, artificial means are used. Artificial measures cost more, but in the long run allow the forester more control over forest composition and tree quality. Applying seeds directly and planting tree seedlings are the methods used to artificially regenerate a forest.

The seed, which is usually spread by plane, is collected during years of abundant seed crop from high quality trees. When properly stored, the seed can remain viable for a number of years. Direct seeding, however, is not as common as it used to be. Because of high losses from predation, infection, poor environments, and other factors, large amounts of seeds are required to produce relatively few trees.

The seeds are better used if they are sown in a nursery to produce seedlings. The seedlings are grown in the nursery for a year or two and are then lifted and planted out in the field. Some seedlings are grown in individual tubes and are known as *containerized stock*. Although more expensive to produce than *bare root stock*, the containerized seedlings usually have a better field survival rate (fig. 29). Bare root stock must be planted with great care to prevent the roots from drying out or being damaged. Root damage is avoided with containerized seedlings because the soil around the roots remains intact during planting.

Figure 28. Regeneration by the coppice system permits development of one robust sprout per stump.

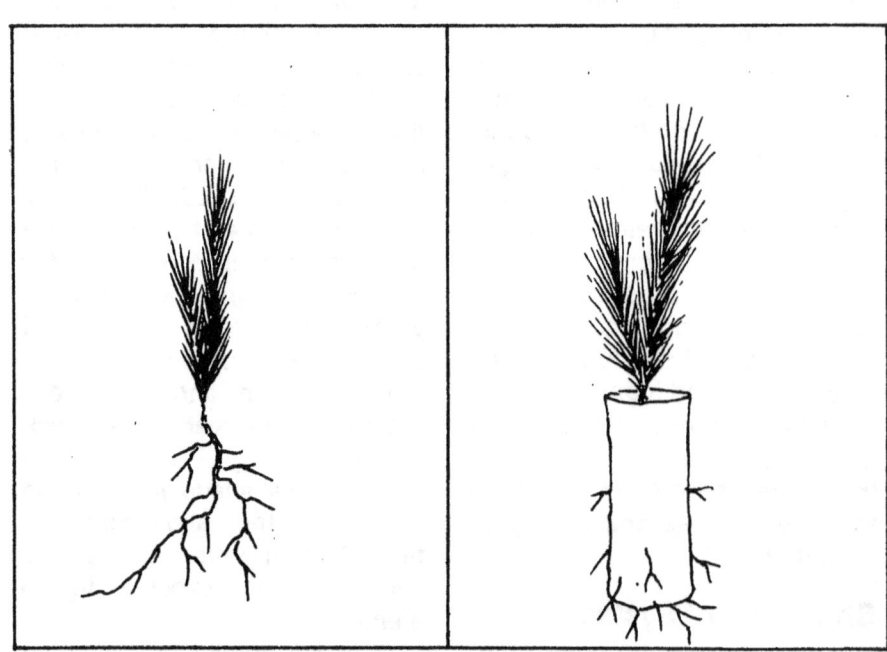

Figure 29. Bare root and containerized transplanting stock.

Exercise in Forest Management

This exercise is a followup to the forest inventory. It is designed as a discussion that, ideally, is conducted at the forest site you evaluated. Write up a summary of the main ideas you discuss.

Imagine that you own the land you inventoried. If necessary, imagine that the forest is large enough to be worth managing, and assume that the plots you measured are typical of this expanded forest. As the owner, you have decided to manage your forest. You are wealthy enough to carry out any practices that you desire. Where should you start?

1. Management Philosophy

Develop a management philosophy and a set of management objectives from the following questions.

A. Why do you want to manage your forest?
B. What resources do you desire from your forest? Look at the forest inventory to help you decide.
- What resources already exist in your forest?
- Are there any forest resources you would like that are not currently produced by your forest?
- Is it possible to produce them? (Can their requirements for production be met in your forest?)
For example, you may like to hunt grouse, but grouse are currently not found in the forest. If you were to create openings where aspen and shrubs can become established (to provide food and cover), you could be successful in attracting grouse to your land.
C. If you desire more than one resource from the forest, is their production compatible or mutually exclusive?
D. Do you wish to produce resources to sell? If so, is there a local market for these resources?
E. Are the resources you desire renewable? As a responsible forest owner, how will you assure the renewability of your forest?
F. Forests take a long time to grow, and it may take many years to reap the benefits of management. Do you wish to manage the forest just for yourself? Will you consider future generations?
G. How will your neighbors react to your plans for management? Your community?

2. Forest Management Recommendations

Obviously, you do not have the proper background to come up with a complex management plan. You will instead develop a set of management recommendations. Use your common sense, the knowledge you have gained, and your deductive ability.
Ask yourself:
- What are the requirements of the resources I desire?
- What can I do to enhance the production of the resources I desire?
- How can I provide the necessary requirements?
- What management tools can I use to create an environment that will enhance the desired resource(s)?
- What problems might I encounter, especially if I desire more than one resource?

In planning your recommendations, consider the following information about specific resources.

A. Water

Quality

Water is collected on the land and either runs over or seeps through the soil until it reaches an open body of water. As it passes through the soil, large particles, sediment, and impurities are filtered out of the water. Water that runs over the land may carry rocks, sediment, and debris if it is moving fast enough.

The forest cover and litter layer break the impact of water falling on the land and cause more of it to be filtered through the soil rather than run over the land. Roots also hold the soil in place and help prevent landslides and erosion that often occur on unforested slopes.

Special consideration should be given to how logging operations in the woods will affect water quality. Roads can be a major source of erosion and sedimentation if poorly built and improperly maintained. Doing sloppy logging jobs and skidding logs up streams can also cause erosion. Avoid logging close to open bodies of water, and provide proper bridge crossings for streams. Roads should be properly drained and maintained.

Quantity

Trees and vegetation remove water from the ground through their roots and transpire water through their leaves into the atmosphere. Thus, trees growing along a stream can influence the amount of water in the ground that will seep into streams and springs. Removal of trees can increase the water flow, and the establishment of trees can help to dry out a wet spot.

B. Recreation

Access to the location is important for recreation. If required, roads and parking layouts must be planned to enhance the recreational values. Their construction should cause the least environmental disruption possible (see water quality, above). Trails need to be carefully planned and clearly marked. They must be built properly to handle traffic without causing deterioration of the environment. Steepness and switchbacks should also be considered.

Location of any campsites should be planned to provide a balance of sun and shade, and a nearby water source is needed. Avoid swampy, insect-inhabited areas, and keep heavy camping at least 30 m (100 ft) from the water's edge.

C. Aesthetics

Areas may be cut to provide views. Trails may be built. Decide upon the aesthetic values you desire, and determine how to enhance them.

D. Wildlife

Requirements for cover, food, and habitat vary with different animals. The requirements of larger animals are more difficult to fulfill than those of smaller animals. For example, deer need a larger area and consume more food than birds.

An area of given size can only support a limited number of animals. This limit is called the carrying capacity of the area. If the population of animals goes beyond the carrying capacity, the animals will begin to destroy the area. They can no longer remain healthy, and many die through starvation or disease.

Wildlife can be pests, too, if they occur in large numbers and destroy things of value to people. Management practices such as trapping, hunting, or habitat destruction may be required to alleviate the problem.

E. Wood Products

The many wood products that can be obtained from our forest include sawlogs or timber for construction materials, pulpwood for paper products, firewood, cooperage stock, railroad ties, handle bolts, utility poles, and more. Several tree species may be suitable for producing a specific product, but those species with superior properties are more highly valued. They can be classified accordingly. On page 65 of *Know Your Trees,* species are listed by worth for timber, and *Conservation Circular* 6(1), "Wood for Fuel," compares the fuel values of various species. In managing for a specific wood product, the superior species are favored over the inferior.

The quality of an individual tree affects its value for certain wood products. A tall, straight tree with a clear trunk that branches only at the very top is worth more for sawtimber than a crooked, low-branched, and forked "wolf" tree of the same species. Trees free of rot bring a higher price, as do trees of larger diameter.

The key to successful management for wood products is to create the right growing environment for producing quality trees and to provide for regeneration of desired species. To reproduce quality trees, the life requirements of the desired species should be studied. The forest is then manipulated to produce a favorable environment for best growth of the desired species. Trees that are restricting the growth of good quality trees should be removed. As the crop trees are harvested, the valuable species must be regenerated immediately so as not to lose time between crops. Information on regeneration and life requirements of individual species may be obtained from *Silvics of Forest Trees of the United States,* USDA Forest Service, Agriculture Handbook 271.

Multiple Use

Forests can be managed to produce more than one resource at the same time. The combinations are numerous and depend on the individual situation. Low intensity timber management, for example, can be compatible with management for wildlife, recreation, aesthetics, and water. Brush and other wildlife encouragers can grow in openings created by harvests. These openings can also become camping spots. The thinning of a stand can be combined with clearing a trail for hiking, skiing, and snowshoeing. The views opened up by harvested areas and the openness created by thinning can add to the aesthetic appeal of an area that previously was a "dog's hair" thicket of trees. A forest cover helps maintain water quality. An area that is harvested does not necessarily decrease water quality if the roads and harvest are done with care and if the area is quickly regenerated with trees.

In some areas, certain uses are incompatible. Maple sirup production and timber production are examples of incompatible uses. The best trees for sap production are fully crowned, large trees. Tapping the tree causes the wood to stain. Such trees do not make good sawlogs because they will have too many knots and stained wood. The determined forester can get around the problem of mutually exclusive resources. The forest, if large enough, can be divided into compartments. Each compartment can then be managed intensely to produce one or more compatible resource.

Conclusion

You have gone through the steps of evaluating a forest. A forest should seem different to you now. It is alive, changing, and renewing itself. The many organisms living there depend on each other and the total forest environment to exist. Because it is dynamic, a forest can produce many renewable resources that people depend upon. Through careful planning and management, we can guide it to produce more of those resources we need without destroying its vitality. However, no matter how much forests are studied and used, there will always be a certain quality that cannot be described or measured. It is the magic possessed by a forest that has in the past and will continue in the future to enchant and enrich the lives of us all.

Glossary

aesthetics — visual beauty

allelopaths — chemical substances secreted by roots and toxic to plant species

artificial regeneration — the reestablishment of a forest by planting seedlings or applying seeds

aspect — the direction a particular location is facing; exposure

bare-root stock — seedlings grown in nursery beds and packaged without soil around the roots for planting

basal area — the amount of area occupied by the cross-sectional base of a tree

Biltmore stick — a device used to measure the heights and diameters of trees

blowdown — an uprooted tree that has been blown over by wind

browse — small bushes, sprouts, herbaceous plants, small trees, and other vegetation fed upon by wildlife

canopy — a collective term for the crowns of all the tallest trees in a forest

catface — partly healed fire scar or wound on a tree, usually at the base

clearcutting — the harvesting method in which all the trees in a particular area are cut; usually followed by some form of regeneration

climax forest — a forest maintained over a long period of time by natural forces that does not change in species composition

competition — struggle for survival that occurs between organisms making similar demands on the same environmental resources

containerized stock — seedlings grown in individual containers in nurseries to be planted in the field later

damping-off fungi — fungi that kill germinating seedlings; these fungi often grow in duff on the forest floor

DBH — the diameter of a tree at roughly breast height (4½ feet off the ground). This is a convenient height at which to measure a tree; moreover, many trees have large swells in the stem below this point which would add errors in computing tree volumes

duff — litter, humus, and decaying organic matter that makes up the top layer of the forest floor

edge — a wildlife management term referring to the division between forest cover and open clearings

forest ecosystem — a forest community in which all organisms interact with each other and their environment

forest inventory — a survey of forest land to determine area, condition, timber volume, and species for specific purposes such as timber purchase or forest management or as a basis for forest policies and programs

hardwood — flowering, dicotyledonous trees, usually broad-leaved; many are deciduous

horizons — distinct layers of soil as exposed in a pit; they differ in texture, color, composition, and other characteristics

hormone — a substance produced by the organism and transported by blood or fluids to produce a specific effect on the activity of cells remote from its source; plant growth hormones are called auxins

hypothesize — to make an educated guess based on scientific evidence

intolerant — term for a plant that does not grow well in the shade of other plants or trees and requires full sunlight to grow well

metabolism — all the chemical changes that occur in living matter

multiple use — the use of land for more than one product or benefit

mutually exclusive — two or more products or benefits that cannot be produced at the same time or in the same area

mycorrhizal fungi — fungi associated with roots that can benefit roots by increasing the absorption of essential minerals. They in turn absorb food from the roots

natural regeneration — reestablishment of a forest by seeds from neighboring trees transported without human help or by sprouts

overstory — the canopy formed by the tallest trees of a forest

photoperiod — the relative lengths of alternating periods of light and darkness

photosynthesis — the process by which green plants combine water and carbon dioxide to form glucose; oxygen is produced as a by-product

pruning — the cutting off of lower branches of trees to eliminate knots in the new growth or the shearing of a tree to produce a better shaped crown

relief — the elevations or inequalities of land's surface

renewable — able to be produced again

resource — tangible or intangible items of value and use to humans

respiration — the process by which cells consume oxygen and break down glucose to produce energy; carbon dioxide and water are the by-products

saprophytic — living on dead or decaying matter

sawlog — a log of suitable size for sawing into lumber

silvicultural operation — specific manipulations of forests, such as thinning and cuttings, with the purpose of improving growth and maintaining the forest's renewability

silviculture — the culture or tending of trees

site — specific location

slash — tops, branches, defective logs, and other wood debris left over from a logging operation

slope — the slant of land measured as the number of units of

rise or fall over a certain distance
snag — a standing dead tree
softwood — tree that usually bears its seeds in cones, has needlelike leaves that are usually evergreen.
static — showing little change
stratify — to store seeds in a cold, moist environment for a specific period of time
thinning — removal of selected trees in a grove to allow more space for the remaining trees
timber cruising — measuring trees to estimate the volume of valuable wood in a forest
tolerance — the relative capability of a plant to grow in varying amounts of light
tolerant — term for a plant that grows well in the shade of other vegetation
topography — configuration of the land's surface
tree crown — a collective term for the limbs, branches, and leaves of a tree
understory — all those trees in a forest that grow below the canopy
wolf tree — limby, gnarly, broad-trunked tree

Appendix 1. How to Construct and Use a Biltmore Stick

On a stick about the size of a yardstick (at least 82 cm [32.3 in] long), mark with a sharp knife and waterproof ink as shown in figure 30. Follow chart 1 in determining where to make the markings.

On the opposite side of the stick, mark as shown in figure 30. Follow chart 2 in making the marks.

Mark logs with Roman numerals every 5 meters as illustrated.

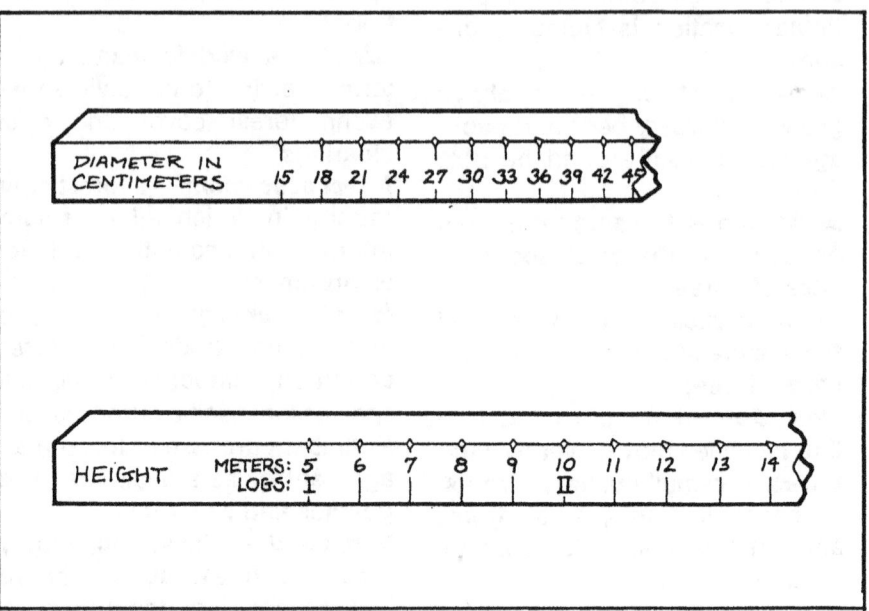

Figure 30. Biltmore stick design.

Chart 1.

Diameter of tree in cm	Distance to mark in cm from zero end of stick
15	13.46
18	15.85
21	18.15
24	20.38
27	22.54
30	24.63
33	26.66
36	28.63
39	30.56
42	32.43
45	34.25
48	36.04
51	37.78
54	39.48
57	41.14
60	42.77
63	44.37

Chart 2.

Height of tree in meters	Distance to mark in cm from zero end of stick
5	15
6	18
7	22
8	25
9	28
10	31
11	34
12	37
13	40
14	43
15	46
16	49
17	52
18	55
19	59
20	62
25	77

Using your Biltmore Stick.

To measure diameter (fig. 31):

1. Diameter is measured at what is called Diameter Breast Height (DBH). This is 1.37 m (4.5 ft) up the trunk from the ground. If the tree you are measuring is on a slope, diameter should be taken at 1.37 m on the uphill side of the tree.
2. Hold the Biltmore stick against the tree, 62 cm (24.4 in) from your eye. (If you make a mark 62 cm from the end on one side of your stick, you can check exactly where to hold the stick.) Make sure the edge of the stick that reads diameter is facing you.
3. Sight past the zero end of the stick and the edge of the tree.
4. Without moving your head, sight to other side of the tree and read the black diameter centimeter nearest to your line of sight.
5. Tree trunks usually are not round. If a trunk is very much out of round, you should measure wide and narrow diameters and take the average.

To measure height (fig. 32):

1. Stand 20.12 m (66 ft) from the tree so that —
- you are about on a level with the base of the tree. Walk out across slope instead of up or down slope from the tree.
- the tree is not leaning away from you.
- you can see the top up to its merchantable height. If you are measuring for sawlogs, the merchantable height is the point where the top is 15 cm in diameter. For pulpwood, merchantable height is to a top 9 cm in diameter; and for firewood, it is an 8-cm top. Practice estimating these top diameters by standing back from a tree with a known diameter of 15, 9, or 8 cm and comparing this to the tops of other trees.
2. Hold the stick vertically 62 cm from your eye.
3. Line up the zero end of the stick with the stump height — the height of the stump if the tree were cut. This is usually not more than .3 m (1 ft) from the ground.
4. Without moving your head or the stick, sight to the merchantable top.
5. The nearest meter or log mark is the merchantable height of the tree.

Practice measuring heights and diameters to develop your skill before recording actual measurements from your plot.

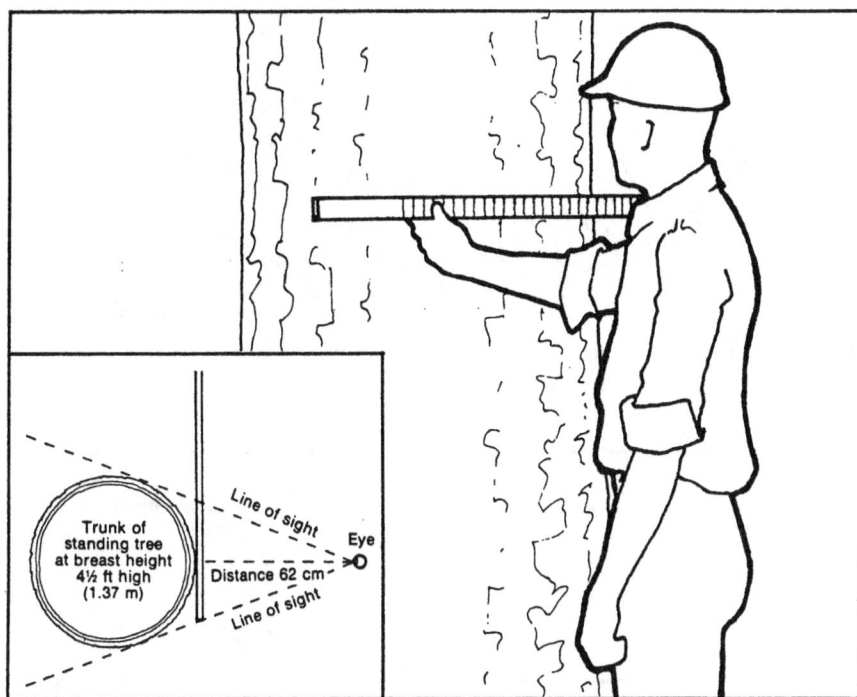

Figure 31. Using a Biltmore stick to find tree diameter.

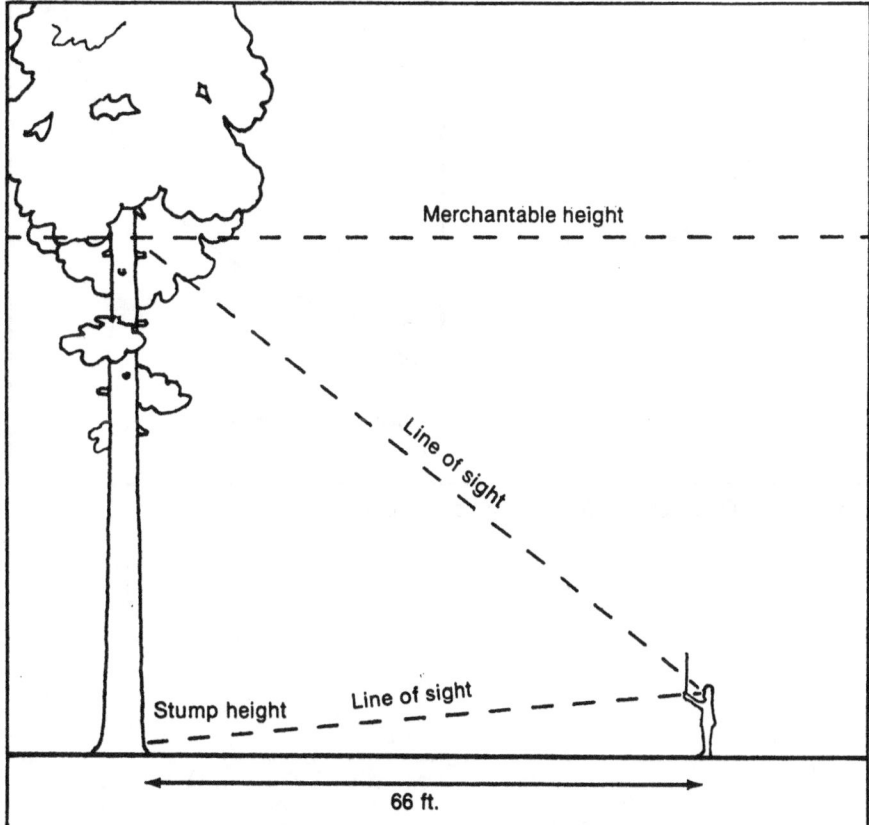

Figure 32. Measuring tree height with a Biltmore stick.

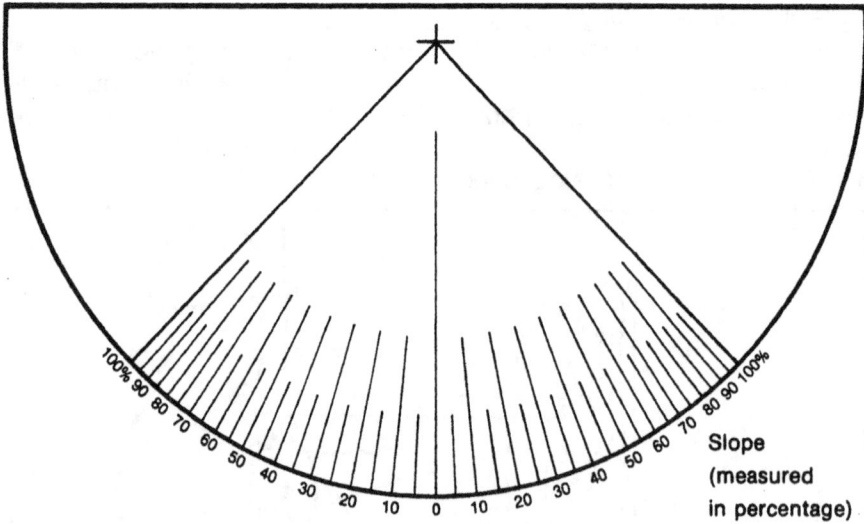

Figure 33. Clinometer scale for building your clinometer.

Appendix 2. How to Construct and Use a Clinometer

Glue a traced copy of the scale (fig. 33) on a piece of cardboard or thin wood cut to the same size and shape. Clear varnish or shellac may be applied for protection. Drive a thumb tack or small nail into the center, and to this attach a piece of string with a lead sinker weight on the end (fig. 34).

To measure slope with the clinometer (fig. 35):

1. Face across the slope. Line up the straight edge of the clinometer with the line of the slope of the hillside. Let the string hang freely.

2. Read the mark the string hangs closest to. This reading is the slope measured in percentage. It indicates how many meters the land rises for each hundred meters level.

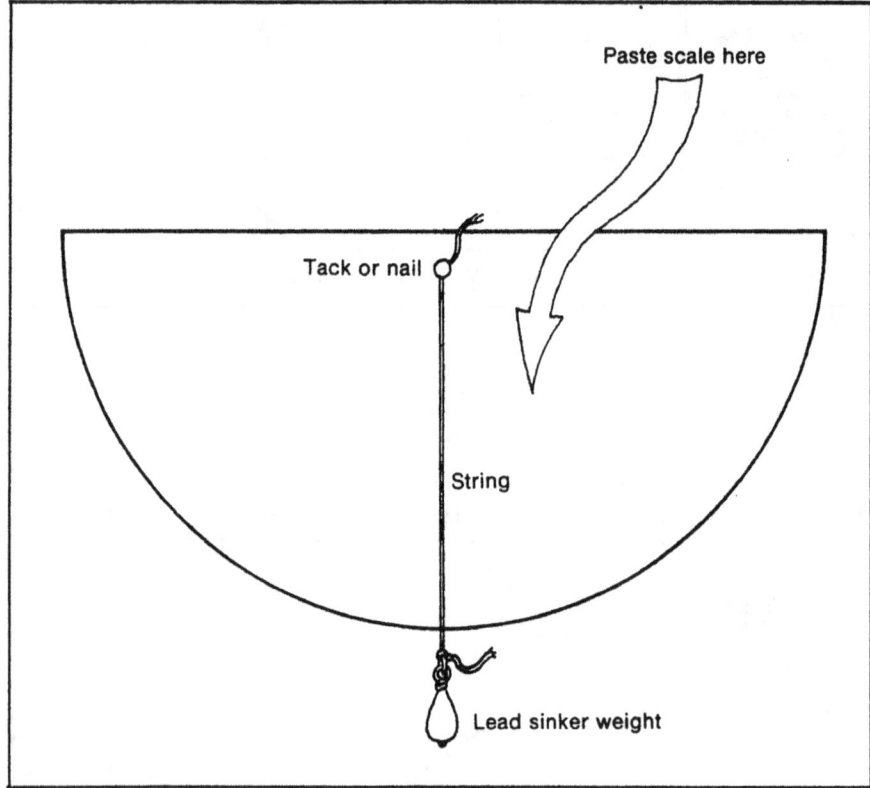

Figure 34. Diagram of clinometer construction.

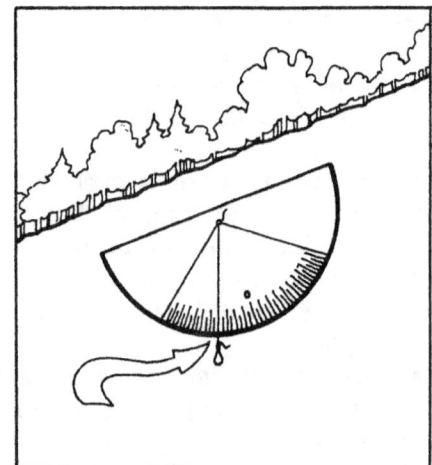

Figure 35. Using the clinometer to determine slope.

Appendix 3. Volume Tables

Appendix Table 1. Sawlog volumes in cubic meters

DBH	Volumes by 5-meter log intervals to a 15-cm top				
	1 log	2 logs	3 logs	4 logs	5 logs
cm					
30	0.26	0.44	0.62	0.79	0.97
33	0.30	0.51	0.73	0.94	1.16
36	0.34	0.60	0.85	1.11	1.37
39	0.38	0.69	0.99	1.29	1.59
42	0.43	0.78	1.14	1.48	1.84
45	0.48	0.88	1.29	1.69	2.10
48	0.54	0.99	1.45	1.92	2.38
51	0.59	1.11	1.63	2.15	2.67
54	0.66	1.24	1.82	2.41	2.99
57	0.72	1.37	2.02	2.67	3.32
60	0.79	1.51	2.23	2.95	3.67
63	0.87	1.66	2.45	3.25	4.04

Adapted from R. D. Hyland. 1977. *Cubic Volume Tables for Second-Growth Northern Hardwoods in New York Including English and Metric Units.* AFRI Research Report 35.

Appendix Table 2. Basal Areas

DBH cm	BA m^2	DBH cm	BA m^2
15	0.02	45	0.16
18	0.03	48	0.18
21	0.03	51	0.20
24	0.05	54	0.23
27	0.06	57	0.26
30	0.07	60	0.28
33	0.09	63	0.31
36	0.10	66	0.34
39	0.12	69	0.37
42	0.14	72	0.41

BA = 0.00007854 d^2

Appendix Table 3. Gross cubic meter volumes for pulpwood

DBH	Height in meters to a 9-centimeter top															
	5	6	7	8	9	10	11	12	13	14	15	16	17	18	19	20
cm																
15	0.06	0.07	0.08													
18	0.08	0.10	0.11	0.12	0.14	0.15										
21	0.11	0.13	0.14	0.16	0.18	0.20	0.21	0.23	0.25	0.27	0.28					
24	0.13	0.16	0.18	0.20	0.23	0.25	0.27	0.30	0.32	0.34	0.37	0.39	0.41	0.43	0.46	0.48
27	0.17	0.19	0.22	0.25	0.28	0.31	0.34	0.37	0.40	0.43	0.46	0.49	0.52	0.54	0.57	0.60
30	0.20	0.24	0.27	0.31	0.34	0.38	0.42	0.45	0.49	0.52	0.56	0.60	0.63	0.67	0.70	0.73
33	0.24	0.28	0.32	0.37	0.41	0.46	0.50	0.54	0.59	0.63	0.67	0.72	0.76	0.80	0.85	0.89
36	0.28	0.33	0.38	0.43	0.49	0.54	0.59	0.64	0.69	0.75	0.80	0.85	0.90	0.95	1.00	1.05
39	0.32	0.38	0.45	0.51	0.57	0.63	0.69	0.75	0.81	0.87	0.93	0.99	1.05	1.11	1.18	1.24
42	0.37	0.44	0.51	0.58	0.65	0.73	0.80	0.87	0.94	1.01	1.08	1.15	1.22	1.29	1.36	1.43
45	0.42	0.51	0.59	0.66	0.75	0.83	0.91	0.99	1.07	1.15	1.23	1.32	1.40	1.48	1.56	2.04
48	0.48	0.57	0.66	0.76	0.85	0.94	1.03	1.13	1.22	1.31	1.40	1.49	1.59	1.68	1.77	1.84
51	0.54	0.64	0.75	0.85	0.96	1.06	1.16	1.28	1.37	1.48	1.58	1.68	1.79	1.89	2.00	2.10

Adapted from R. D. Nyland. 1977. *Cubic Volume Tables for Second-Growth Northern Hardwoods in New York Including English and Metric Units.* AFRI Research Report 35.

Appendix Table 4. Gross volume in rough cords for firewood

DBH	Height in meters to an 8-cm top															
	5	6	7	8	9	10	11	12	13	14	15	16	17	18	19	20
10	0.00	0.00	0.00	0.01	0.01	0.01	0.01	0.01	0.01	0.01	0.01	0.01	0.01	0.01		
13	0.01	0.01	0.01	0.01	0.01	0.01	0.02	0.02	0.02	0.02	0.02	0.03	0.03	0.03		
15	0.02	0.02	0.02	0.02	0.02	0.02	0.02	0.03	0.03	0.04	0.04	0.04	0.04	0.05	0.05	0.05
18	0.02	0.02	0.03	0.03	0.03	0.04	0.04	0.04	0.05	0.05	0.05	0.06	0.06	0.06	0.07	0.07
21			0.03	0.04	0.04	0.05	0.05	0.06	0.07	0.07	0.08	0.08	0.09	0.09	0.10	0.11
24					0.07	0.07	0.08	0.09	0.10	0.10	0.11	0.12	0.13	0.14	0.15	0.16
27								0.12	0.13	0.14	0.15	0.16	0.17	0.18	0.19	0.20
30								0.14	0.15	0.16	0.18	0.19	0.20	0.21	0.23	0.24
33								0.17	0.18	0.20	0.21	0.22	0.24	0.25	0.27	0.30

Adapted from S. R. Gevorkiantz and L. P. Olsen. 1955. *Composite Volume Tables for Timber and Their Application in the Lake States.* U.S.D.A. Tech. Bul. 1104.

Glossary of Forestry Terms

CONTENTS

	Page
A Horizon .... Amendment	1
Amino acids ...... Basin irrigation	2
Basin listing ...... Capillary porosity	3
Capillary water ...... Clay loam	4
Clay mineral ...... Conveyance loss	5
Creep, soil ...... Drift material	6
Drop-inlet dam ...... Feldspars	7
Ferric iron ...... Genesis, soil	8
Gley soil ...... Igneous rock	9
Illite ...... Land	10
Land-capability classification ...... Macropore	11
Manure ...... Mor	12
Morphology, soil ...... Oxidation	13
Oxide ...... Porosity, soil	14
Prairie soils ...... Rendzina	15
Residual fertilizer ...... Sierozem soils	16
Silica ...... Soil, survey	17
Solonchak soils ...... Subsoiling	18
Substratum ...... Tracer techniques	19
Traffic pans ...... Yellow podzolic soils	20

Glossary of Forestry Terms

A HORIZON The surface horizon of a mineral soil having maximum biological activity, or eluviation (removal of materials dissolved or suspended in water), or both.

ABC SOIL A soil with a complete profile, including an A, a B, and a C horizon.

ABSORBING COMPLEX The materials in the soil that hold water and chemical compounds, mainly on their surfaces. They are chiefly the fine mineral matter and organic matter.

AC SOIL A soil with an incomplete profile, including an A and a C horizon, but no B horizon. Commonly such soils are young, like those developing from alluvium or on steep, rocky slopes.

ACID SOIL Generally, a soil that is acid throughout most or all of the parts of it that plant roots occupy. Commonly applied to only the surface-plowed layer or to some other specific layer or horizon of a soil. Practically, this means a soil more acid than pH 6.6; precisely, a soil with a pH value less than 7.0. A soil having a preponderance of hydrogen over hydroxyl ions in the soil solution.

ACTINOMYCETES A group of soil microorganisms which produce an extensive threadlike network. They resemble the soil molds in some respects but are more like the bacteria in size.

ADDITIVE A material added to fertilizer to improve its chemical or physical condition. An additive to liquid fertilizer might prevent crystals from forming in the liquid at temperatures where crystallization would normally take place.

ADSORB Removal of a substance in solution to a solid surface or a separate phase; to accumulate on a surface.

ADSORPTION The attachment of compounds or ionic parts of salts to a surface or another phase. Nutrients in solution (ions) carrying a positive charge become attached to (adsorbed by) negatively charged soil particles.

AERATION, SOIL The exchange of air in soil with air from the atmosphere. The composition of the air in a well-aerated soil is similar to that in the atmosphere; in a poorly aerated soil, the air in the soil is considerably higher in carbon dioxide and lower in oxygen than the atmosphere above the soil.

AEROBIC (1) Conditions with oxygen gas as a part of the environment. (2) Living or acting only in the presence of air or free oxygen. (3) Pertaining to the activity of organisms that grow under aerobic conditions, such as aerobic decomposition.

AGGREGATE (OF SOIL) Many fine soil particles held in a single mass or cluster, such as a clod, crumb, block, or prism. Many properties of the aggregate differ from those of an equal mass of unaggregated soil.

ALKALI SOIL Generally, a highly alkaline soil. Specifically, an alkali soil has so high a degree of alkalinity—pH 8.5 or higher—or so high a percentage of exchangeable sodium—15 percent or higher—or both, that the growth of most crop plants is reduced. (In former years this term was also applied loosely to both alkali and saline soils. The term is also applied by some to those uncommon soils that contain highly alkaline salts, such as sodium carbonate.)

ALKALINE SOIL Generally, a soil that is alkaline throughout most or all of the parts of it occupied by plant roots; although the term is commonly applied to only a specific layer or horizon of a soil. Precisely, any soil horizon having a pH value greater than 7.0; practically, a soil having a pH above 7.3.

ALLUVIAL SOILS Soils developing from transported and relatively recently deposited material (alluvium) with little or no modification of the original materials by soil-forming processes. (Soils with well-developed profiles that have formed from alluvium are grouped with other soils having the same kinds of profiles, not with the alluvial soils.)

ALLUVIUM Sand, mud, and other sediments deposited on land by streams.

ALUMINO-SILICATES Compounds containing aluminum, silicon, and oxygen atoms as main constituents.

AMENDMENT Any material, such as lime, gypsum, sawdust, or synthetic conditioners, that is worked into the soil to make it more productive. Strictly, a fertilizer is also an amendment, but the term "amendment" is used most commonly for added materials other than fertilizer.

Amino acids Amino acids are nitrogen-containing organic compounds, large numbers of which link together in the formation of a protein molecule. Each amino acid molecule contains one or more amino ($-NH_2$) groups and at least one carboxyl ($-COOH$) group. In addition, some amino acids (cystine and methionine) contain sulfur.

Ammonia A colorless gas composed of one atom of nitrogen and three atoms of hydrogen. Ammonia liquefied under pressure is used as a fertilizer.

Ammonification The formation by organisms of ammonium compounds from nitrogen-containing organic materials.

Ammonium ion The positively charged NH_4^+ ion. The form in which nitrogen occurs in many commercial fertilizers.

Anaerobic Living or functioning in the absence of air or free oxygen.

Anhydrous Dry, or without water. Anhydrous ammonia is water free; in contrast to the water solution of ammonia commonly known as household ammonia.

Anion An ion carrying a negative charge of electricity.

Anthropic soil A soil produced from a natural soil or other earthy deposit by the work of man that has new characteristics that make it different from the natural soil. Examples include deep, black surface soils resulting from centuries of manuring, and naturally acid soils that have lost their distinguishing features because of many centuries of liming and use for grass.

Antibiosis Opposed to living. Antibiotics suppress some micro-organisms.

Apatite A native phosphate of lime. The name is given to the chief mineral of phosphate rock and the inorganic compound of bone.

Aqua ammonia A water solution of ammonia.

Aquifer A water-bearing formation through which water moves more readily than in adjacent formations of lower permeability.

Arid climate A very dry climate like that of desert or semidesert regions where there is only enough water for widely spaced desert plants. The limits of precipitation vary widely according to temperature, with an upper limit for cool regions of less than 10 inches and for tropical regions of as much as 20 inches. (The precipitation-effectiveness index ranges from 0 to about 16.)

Arid region Areas where the potential water losses by evaporation and transpiration are greater than the amount of water supplied by precipitation. In the United States this area is broadly considered to be the dry parts of the 17 Western States.

Ash The nonvolatile residue resulting from the complete burning of organic matter. It is commonly composed of oxides of such elements as silicon, aluminum, iron, calcium, magnesium, and potassium.

Assimilation Conversion of substances taken in from the outside into living tissue of plants or animals.

Autotrophic Capable of using (oxidizing) simple chemical elements or compounds, such as iron, sulfur, or nitrates, to obtain energy for growth.

Auxins Organic substances which cause lengthening of the stem when applied in low concentrations to shoots of growing plants.

Available nutrient in soils The part of the supply of a plant nutrient in the soil that can be taken up by plants at rates and in amounts significant to plant growth.

Available water in soils The part of the water in the soil that can be taken up by plants at rates significant to their growth; usable; obtainable.

Azonal soils A general group of soils having little or no soil profile development. Most of them are young. In the United States, Alluvial soils, Lithosols, and Regosols are included in the azonal group.

B horizon A soil horizon, usually beneath an A horizon, or surface soil, in which (1) clay, iron, or aluminum, with accessory organic matter, have accumulated by receiving suspended material from the A horizon above it or by clay development in place; (2) the soil has a blocky or prismatic structure; or (3) the soil has some combination of these features. In soils with distinct profiles, the B horizon is roughly equivalent to the general term "subsoil."

Banding (of fertilizers) The placement of fertilizers in the soil in continuous narrow ribbons, usually at specific distances from the seeds or plants. The fertilizer bands are covered by the soil but are not mixed with it.

Base saturation The relative degree to which soils have metallic cations absorbed. The proportion of the cation-exchange capacity that is saturated with metallic cations.

Basin irrigation (or level borders) The application of irrigation water to level areas that are surrounded by border ridges or levees. Usually irrigation water is applied at rates greater than the water intake rate of the soil. The water may stand on uncropped soils for several days until the soil is well soaked; then any excess may be used on other fields. The water may stand a few hours on fields having a growing crop.

BASIN LISTING A method of tillage that creates small basins by damming lister furrows at regular intervals of about 4 to 20 feet. This method is a modification of ordinary listing and is carried out approximately on the contour on nearly level or gently sloping soils as a means of encouraging water to enter the soil rather than to run off the surface.

BC SOIL A soil with a B and a C horizon but with little or no A horizon. Most BC soils have lost their A horizons by erosion.

BEDDING SOIL Arranging the surface of fields by plowing and grading into a series of elevated beds separated by shallow ditches for drainage.

BEDROCK The solid rock underlying soils and other earthy surface formations.

BENCH TERRACES An embankment constructed across sloping soils with a steep drop on the downslope side.

BLOWOUT An area from which soil material has been removed by wind. Such an area appears as a nearly barren, shallow depression with a flat or irregular floor consisting of a resistant layer, an accumulation of pebbles, or wet soil lying just above a water table.

BOG SOIL An intrazonal group of soils with mucky or peaty surface soils underlain by peat. Bog soils usually have swamp or marsh vegetation and are commonest in humid regions.

BONDS Chemical forces holding atoms together to form molecules.

BORDER IRRIGATION Irrigation in which the water flows over narrow strips that are nearly level and are separated by parallel, low-bordering banks or ridges.

BROAD-BASE TERRACE A low embankment, with such gentle slopes that it can be farmed, constructed across sloping soils approximately on the contour. Broad-base terraces are used on pervious soils to reduce runoff and soil erosion.

BROWN FOREST SOILS An intrazonal group of soils that have dark-brown surface horizons, relatively rich in humus, grading through lighter colored soil into the parent material. They are characterized by a slightly acid or neutral reaction and a moderately high amount of exchangeable calcium. They are commonly developed under deciduous forests from parent materials relatively rich in bases, especially calcium.

BROWN PODZOLIC SOILS A zonal group of soils with thin mats of partly decayed leaves over thin, grayish-brown mixed humus and mineral soil. They lie over yellow or yellowish-brown, acid B horizons, slightly richer in clay than the surface soils. These soils develop under deciduous or mixed deciduous and coniferous forests in cool-temperate humid regions, such as parts of New England, New York, and western Washington.

BROWN SOILS A zonal group of soils having a brown surface horizon that grades below into lighter colored soil. These soils have an accumulation of calcium carbonate at 1 to 3 feet. They develop under short grasses, bunchgrasses, and shrubs in a temperate to cool semiarid climate.

BUFFER, BUFFERING Substances in the soil that act chemically to resist changes in reaction or pH. The buffering action is due mainly to clay and very fine organic matter. Highly weathered tropical clays are less active buffers than most less weathered silicate clays. Thus with the same degree of acidity, or pH, more lime is required to neutralize (1) a clayey soil than a sandy soil, (2) a soil rich in organic matter than one low in organic matter, or (3) a sandy loam in Michigan, say, than a sandy loam in central Alabama.

BUFFER STRIPS Established strips of perennial grass or other erosion-resisting vegetation, usually on the contour in cultivated fields, to reduce runoff and erosion.

BULK DENSITY The mass or weight of oven-dry soil per unit bulk volume, including air space. This mass in relation to the weight of a unit volume of water, was formerly called "apparent density" or "volume weight."

C HORIZON The unconsolidated rock material in the lower part of the soil profile like that from which the upper horizons (or at least a part of the B horizon) have developed.

CALCAREOUS SOIL A soil containing calcium carbonate, or a soil alkaline in reaction because of the presence of calcium carbonate. A soil containing enough calcium carbonate to effervesce (fizz) when treated with dilute hydrochloric acid.

CALICHE A broad term for the more or less cemented deposits of calcium carbonate in many soils of warm-temperate areas, as in the Southwestern States. When it is very near the surface or exposed by erosion, the material hardens. (Caliche is also used for deposits of sodium nitrate in Chile and Peru.)

CAPILLARY POROSITY The volume of small pores within the soil that hold water against the force of gravity.

CAPILLARY WATER The water retained in the fine pores in soil by surface tension that moves as a result of capillary forces.

CARBOHYDRATES Compounds containing carbon, hydrogen, and oxygen. Usually the hydrogen and oxygen occur in the proportion of 2 to 1, such as in glucose ($C_6H_{12}O_6$).

CARBON One of the commonest chemical elements, occurring in lampblack, coal, and coke in varying degrees of purity. Compounds of carbon are the chief constituents of living tissue.

CARBON DIOXIDE A colorless gas (CO_2) composed of carbon and oxygen and normally found in small amounts in the air. It is one of the end products of the burning (oxidation) of organic matter, or carbon-containing compounds.

CARBON-NITROGEN RATIO The ratio of the weight of organic carbon to the weight of total nitrogen in a soil or in an organic material.

CATALASE An enzyme capable of decomposing hydrogen peroxide into water and oxygen: $2H_2O_2 \rightarrow 2H_2O + O_2$.

CATALYST A material that increases the rate of a chemical reaction.

CATENA A group of soils, within a specific soil zone, formed from similar parent materials but with unlike soil characteristics because of differences in relief or drainage.

CATION An ion carrying a positive charge of electricity. The common soil cations are calcium, magnesium, sodium, potassium, and hydrogen.

CATION EXCHANGE The exchange of cations held by the soil-adsorbing complex with other cations. Thus if a soil-absorbing complex is rich in sodium, treatment with calcium sulfate (gypsum) causes some calcium cations to exchange with some sodium cations.

CATION-EXCHANGE CAPACITY A measure of the total amount of exchangeable cations that can be held by the soil. It is expressed in terms of milliequivalents per 100 grams of soil at neutrality (pH 7) or at some other stated pH value. (Formerly called base-exchange capacity.)

CELLULOSE The principal constituent of the cell walls of higher plants. It is made up of glucose molecules arranged in long chains and has the chemical formula $(C_6H_{10}O_5)_x$. The long molecules give it a fibrous nature. Cotton fibers are almost pure cellulose. Paper is mainly cellulose separated by chemical processes from wood or other plant remains.

CHELATES A type of chemical compound in which a metallic atom is firmly combined with a molecule by means of multiple chemical bonds. The term refers to the claw of a crab illustrative of the way in which the atom is held.

CHERNOZEM SOILS A zonal group of soils having deep, dark to nearly black surface horizons and rich in organic matter, which grades into lighter colored soil below. At 1.5 to 4 feet, these soils have layers of accumulated calcium carbonate. They develop under tall and mixed grasses in a temperate to cool subhumid climate.

CHERT A structureless form of silica, closely related to flint, which breaks into angular fragments. Soils developed from impure limestones containing fragments of chert and having abundant quantities of these fragments in the soil mass are called cherty soils.

CHESTNUT SOILS A zonal group of soils with dark-brown surface horizons, which grade into lighter colored horizons beneath. They have layers of accumulated calcium carbonate at 1 to 4 feet. They are developed under mixed tall and short grasses in a temperate to cool and subhumid to semiarid climate. Chestnut soils occur in regions a little more moist than those having Brown soils and a little drier than those having Chernozem soils.

CHISEL A tillage machine with one or more soil-penetrating points that can be drawn through the soil to loosen the subsoil, usually to a depth of 12 to 18 inches.

CHITIN A nitrogen containing polysaccharide found in the outer part of insects.

CHLOROPHYLL The constituent responsible for the green color of plants. Chlorophyll is important in photosynthesis in plants, the process by which sugar is manufactured.

CHLOROPLASTS Small bodies in cells of plants in which the green pigment chlorophyll is concentrated.

CHLOROSIS A condition in plants resulting from the failure of chlorophyll (the green coloring matter) to develop, usually because of deficiency of an essential nutrient. Leaves of chlorotic plants range from light green through yellow to almost white.

CLAY As a soil separate, the mineral soil particles less than 0.002 mm. in diameter. As a soil textural class, soil material that contains 40 percent or more of clay, less than 45 percent of sand, and less than 40 percent of silt.

CLAY LOAM Soil material that contains 27 to 40 percent of clay and 20 to 45 percent of sand.

Clay mineral Naturally occurring inorganic crystalline material in soils or other earthy deposits of clay size—particles less than 0.002 mm. in diameter.

Claypan A compact, slowly permeable soil horizon rich in clay and separated more or less abruptly from the overlying soil. Claypans are commonly hard when dry and plastic or stiff when wet.

Clod A mass of soil produced by plowing or digging, which usually slakes easily with repeated wetting and drying, in contrast to a *ped*, which is a natural soil aggregate.

Colloid, soil Colloid refers to organic or inorganic matter having very small particle size and a correspondingly large surface area per unit of mass. Most colloidal particles are too small to be seen with the ordinary compound microscope. Soil colloids do not go into true solution as sugar or salt do, but they may be dispersed into a relatively stable suspension and thus be carried in moving water. By treatment with salts and other chemicals, colloids may be flocculated, or aggregated, into small crumbs or granules that settle out of water. (Such small crumbs of aggregated colloids can be moved by rapidly moving water or air just as other particles can be.) Many mineral soil colloids are really tiny crystals and the minerals can be identified with X-rays and in other ways.

Colluvium Mixed deposits of soil material and rock fragments near the base of rather steep slopes. The deposits have accumulated through soil creep, slides, and local wash.

Companion crop A crop grown with another crop, usually a small grain with which alfalfa, clover, or other forage crops are sown. (Formerly such small grain crops were known as nurse crops, but because the small grain does not "nurse" the other crop this older term is being abandoned.)

Complex, soil An intimate mixture of tiny areas of different kinds of soil that are too small to be shown separately on a publishable soil map. The whole group of soils must be shown together as a mapping unit and described as a pattern of soils.

Compost A mass of rotted organic matter made from waste plant residues. Inorganic fertilizers, especially nitrogen, and a little soil usually are added to it. The organic residues usually are piled in layers, to which the fertilizers are added. The layers are separated by thin layers of soil. The whole pile is kept moist and allowed to decompose. The pile is usually turned once or twice. The principal purpose in making compost is to permit the organic materials to become crumbly and to reduce the carbon-nitrogen ratio of the material. Compost is sometimes called artificial or synthetic manure.

Concretions Hard grains, pellets, or nodules from concentrations of compounds in the soil that cement the soil grains together. The composition of some concretions is unlike that of the surrounding soil. Concretions can be of various sizes, shapes, and colors.

Conditioner (of fertilizer) A material added to a fertilizer to prevent caking and to keep it free flowing.

Conductance Conducting power, the reciprocal of resistance.

Conductivity, electrical A physical quantity that measures the readiness with which a medium transmits electricity. Commonly used for expressing the salinity of irrigation waters and soil extracts because it can be directly related to salt concentration. It is expressed in mhos per centimeter (or millimhos per centimeter or micromhos per centimeter at 25° C.).

Consistence The combination of properties of soil material that determine its resistance to crushing and its ability to be molded or changed in shape. Consistence depends mainly on the forces of attraction between soil particles. Consistence is described by such words as loose, friable, firm, soft, plastic, and sticky.

Consolidate (soil) To place into a compact mass and thus increase density and reduce pore space.

Consumptive use The water used by plants in transpiration and growth, plus water vapor loss from adjacent soil or snow, or from intercepted precipitation in any specified time. Usually expressed as equivalent depth of free water per unit of time.

Continental climate A general term for the climate typical of great land masses where wide ranges in temperature and other weather conditions occur because the area is not greatly influenced by nearness to the sea. Much of the United States has a continental climate.

Contour An imaginary line connecting points of equal elevation on the surface of the soil. A contour terrace is laid out on a sloping soil at right angles to the direction of the slope and level throughout its course. In contour plowing, the plowman keeps to a level line at right angles to the direction of the slope, which usually results in a curving furrow.

Contour basins Basins made by levees or borders built on contours with occasional cross levees.

Conveyance loss Loss of water from a conduit due to leakage, seepage, and evaporation.

CREEP, SOIL The downward mass movement of sloping soil. The movement is usually slow and irregular and occurs most commonly when the lower soil is nearly saturated with water.

CRUMB STRUCTURE Very porous granular structure in soils.

CRUST A thin, brittle layer of hard soil that forms on the surface of many soils when they are dry. An exposed hard layer of materials cemented by calcium carbonate, gypsum, or other binding agents. Most desert crusts are formed by the exposure of such layers through removal of the upper soil by wind or running water and their subsequent hardening.

CYTOCHROME An iron-containing pigment that plays a major role in respiration.

CYTOPLASM The portion of the protoplasm of a cell outside the nucleus.

D LAYER Any stratum underlying the soil profile that is unlike the material from which the soil has been formed.

DAMPING-OFF Sudden wilting and death of seedling plants resulting from attack by micro-organisms.

DEALKALIZATION Removal of exchangeable sodium (or alkali) from the soil, usually by chemical treatment and leaching.

DEEP PERCOLATION A general term for the downward movement of water beyond the reach of plant roots.

DEEP SOIL Generally, a soil deeper than 40 inches to rock or other strongly contrasting material. Also, a soil with a deep black surface layer; a soil deeper than about 40 inches to the parent material or to other unconsolidated rock material not modified by soil-forming processes; or a soil in which the total depth of unconsolidated material, whether true soil or not, is 40 inches or more.

DEFLOCCULATE To separate or to break up soil aggregates into the individual particles; to disperse the particles of a granulated clay to form a clay that runs together or puddles.

DEGRADATION (OF SOILS) The change of one kind of soil to a more highly leached kind, such as the change of a Chernozem to a Podzol.

DEHYDRATION Removal or loss of water.

DENITRIFICATION The process by which nitrates or nitrites in the soil or organic deposits are reduced to ammonia or free nitrogen by bacterial action. The process results in the escape of nitrogen into the air and is therefore wasteful.

DESALINIZATION Removal of salts from saline soil, usually by leaching.

DESERT SOIL A zonal group of soils that have light-colored surface soils and usually are underlain by calcareous material and frequently by hard layers. They are developed under extremely scanty scrub vegetation in warm to cool, arid climates.

DESILTING AREA An area used for removing the sediment from flowing water, especially by vegetation.

DESORPTION The removal of sorbed materials from surfaces.

DETAILED SOIL MAP A soil map showing the kinds of soil. The soil boundaries have been plotted on a base map or aerial photograph from observations made throughout their course and the kinds of soil are classified and the boundaries shown in all the detail significant to soil use and management. Most of the soils shown on such maps are phases of soil types.

DIFFUSION The transport of matter as a consequence of the movement of the constituent particles. The intermingling of two gases or liquids in contact with each other takes place by diffusion.

DIPOLAR Having two poles as a result of separation of electric charge. A dipolar molecule orients in an electric field.

DISPERSION OF SOIL Deflocculation of the soil and its suspension in water.

DIVALENT MANGANOUS ION The chemical element manganese (Mn^{+2}) in its lowest valence state.

DRAINAGE (A PRACTICE) The removal of excess surface water or excess water from within the soil by means of surface or subsurface drains.

DRAINAGE, SOIL (1) The rapidity and extent of the removal of water from the soil by runoff and flow through the soil to underground spaces. (2) As a condition of the soil, soil drainage refers to the frequency and duration of periods when the soil is free of saturation. For example, in well-drained soils, the water is removed readily, but not rapidly; in poorly drained soils, the root zone is waterlogged for long periods and the roots of ordinary crop plants cannot get enough oxygen; and in excessively drained soils, the water is removed so completely that most crop plants suffer from lack of water.

DRIFT Material of any sort deposited by geological processes in one place after having been removed from another. Glacial drift includes the materials deposited by glaciers and by the streams and lakes associated with them.

Drop-inlet dam A dam through which overflow water is carried through a shallow, sloping pipe in order to drop water from one level to another for gradient control and for stabilization of a waterway.

Drought A period of dryness, especially a long one. Usually considered to be any period of soil moisture deficiency within the plant root zone. A period of dryness of sufficient length to deplete soil moisture to the extent that plant growth is seriously retarded.

Dry farming Generally, producing crops that require some tillage in subhumid or semiarid regions without irrigation. The system usually involves periods of fallow between crops during which water from precipitation is absorbed and retained.

Dry sands Sandy deposits, with low water-holding capacity, in which there has been no clear development of soil characteristics since deposition.

Dry weight percentage (of water in soil) The weight of water expressed as a percentage of the ovendry weight of soil.

Duff The matted, partly decomposed organic surface layer of forested soils.

Dune A mount or ridge of loose sand piled up by the wind. Occasionally during periods of extreme drought, granulated soil material of fine texture may be piled into low dunes, sometimes called clay dunes.

Dust mulch A loose, dry surface layer of a cultivated soil, formerly thought to be effective in reducing the loss of moisture from the underlying soil.

Ecology The branch of biology that deals with the mutual relations among organisms and between organisms and their environment.

Effluent The outflowing of water from a subterranean storage space. (Also used generally for gases and other liquids.)

Electrolyte Any conductor of electric current in which chemical change accompanies the passage of the current and the amount of the change is proportional to the amount of current passed. Usually electrolytes are solutions of substances in a liquid, such as salt in water. A substance that forms a conductor of electricity when added to a solvent. Thus, common table salt becomes an electrolyte when added to water.

Eluviation The movement of material from one place to another within the soil in either true solution or colloidal suspension. Soil horizons that have lost material through eluviation are said to be eluvial; those that have received material are illuvial. With an excess of rainfall over evaporation, eluviation may take place either downward or laterally according to the direction of water movement. The term refers especially to the movement of soil colloids in suspension; leaching refers to the removal of soluble materials such as salt in true solution.

Environment All external conditions that may act upon an organism or soil to influence its development, including sunlight, temperature, moisture, and other organisms.

Enzymes Substances produced by living cells which can bring about or speed up chemical reaction. They are organic catalysts.

Equilibrium A state of balance between opposing soil forces or actions.

Erodible (soil) Soil susceptible to erosion.

Erosion The wearing away of the land surface by detachment and transport of soil and rock materials through the action of moving water, wind, or other geological agents.

Erosive (wind or water) Used in reference to wind or water having sufficient velocity to cause erosion. Not to be confused with erodible as a quality of soil.

Evapotranspiration The loss of water from a soil by evaporation and plant transpiration.

Exchange capacity (See cation-exchange capacity.)

Exchangeable This word describes the ions in the absorbing complex of the soil that can be exchanged with other ions. For example, when acid soils are limed, calcium ions exchange for hydrogen ions in the complex; when alkali soils are treated with gypsum, calcium ions exchange for sodium ions that can be leached away.

Exchangeable sodium Sodium that is attached to the surface of soil particles which can be exchanged with other positively charged ions in the soil solution, such as calcium and magnesium.

Fallow Cropland left idle in order to restore productivity, mainly through accumulation of water, nutrients, or both. Summer fallow is a common stage before cereal grain in regions of limited rainfall. The soil is tilled for at least one growing season to control weeds, to aid decomposition of plant residues, and to encourage the storage of moisture for the succeeding grain crop. Bush or forest fallow is a rest period under woody vegetation between crops.

Feldspars Primary alumino-silicate minerals having a three-dimensional framework structure.

Ferric iron An oxidized or high-valence form of iron (Fe^{+3}) responsible for red, yellow, and brown colors in soils. Fe^{+++}.

Ferrous iron A reduced or low-valence form of iron (Fe^{+2}), imparting a blue-gray appearance to some wet subsoils on long standing.

Fertility, soil The quality of a soil that enables it to provide compounds, in adequate amounts and in proper balance, for the growth of specified plants, when other growth factors such as light, moisture, temperature, and the physical condition of the soil are favorable.

Fertilizer Any natural or manufactured material added to the soil in order to supply one or more plant nutrients. The term is generally applied to largely inorganic materials other than lime or gypsum (mineral fertilizers) sold in the trade.

Fertilizer grade An expression that indicates the percentage of plant nutrients in a fertilizer. Thus a 10–20–10 grade contains 10 percent nitrogen (N), 20 percent phosphoric oxide (P_2O_5), and 10 percent potash (K_2O). This convention is in common use even though the nitrogen, phosphorus, and potassium are present in other forms.

Field capacity The amount of moisture remaining in a soil after the free water has been allowed to drain away into drier soil material beneath; usually expressed as a percentage of the ovendry weight of soil or other convenient unit. It is the highest amount of moisture that the soil will hold under conditions of free drainage after excess water has drained away following a rain or irrigation that has wet the whole soil. For permeable soils of medium texture, this is about 2 or 3 days after a rain or thorough irrigation. Although generally similar for one kind of soil, values vary with previous treatments of the soil.

Field moisture The water that soil contains under field conditions.

Film water The water held on the surfaces of soil particles that does not drain away, although it moves rapidly under suction gradients. Most of it is available to plant roots.

Fine-textured soil Roughly, clayey soil containing 35 percent or more of clay.

First bottom The normal flood plain of a stream, subject to frequent or occasional flooding.

Fixation (in soil) The conversion of a soluble material, such as a plant nutrient like phosphorus, from a soluble or exchangeable form to a relatively insoluble form.

Flocculate To aggregate or clump together individual tiny soil particles, especially fine clay, into small groups or granules. The opposite of deflocculate, or disperse.

Flood irrigation Irrigation by running water over nearly level soil in a shallow flood.

Flood plain The nearly flat lands along streams that overflow during floods.

Fluorapatite A member of the apatite group of minerals, rich in fluorine. Most common mineral in raw rock phosphate.

Foliar diagnosis Estimation of the plant-nutrient status of plant or the plant-nutrient requirements of a soil for producing a crop through chemical analyses or color manifestations of plant leaves or by both methods together.

Foliar fertilization Fertilization of plants by applying chemical fertilizers to their foliage.

Food, plant The organic compounds elaborated by a plant within its cells. (Sometimes used loosely for plant nutrients.)

Forage Unharvested plant material which can be used as feed by domestic animals. Forage may be grazed or cut for hay.

Forest land Land bearing a stand of trees at any age or stature, including seedlings, and of species attaining a minimum of 6 feet average height at maturity; or land from which such a stand has been removed but on which no other use has been substituted. The term is commonly limited to land not in farms; forests on farms are commonly called woodland or farm forests.

Fragipans Dense and brittle pans or layers in soils that owe their hardness mainly to extreme density or compactness rather than to high clay content or cementation. Removed fragments are friable, but the material in place is so dense that roots cannot penetrate and water moves through it very slowly because of small pore size.

Free Often said of silica, ferric oxide, or calcium carbonate. The condition of the substance within a mixture when it is not chemically combined with the other components of the mixture. For example, iron oxide in soils may be by itself as free iron oxide, or it may be combined with other elements in a mineral.

Fungi Forms of plantlife, lacking chlorophyll and unable to make their own food.

Genesis, soil The mode of origin of the soil, with special reference to the processes responsible for the development of the solum, or true soil, from the unconsolidated parent material.

GLEY SOIL A soil horizon in which waterlogging and lack of oxygen have caused the material to be a neutral gray in color. The term "gleyed" is applied, as in "moderately gleyed soil," to soil horizons with yellow and gray mottling caused by intermittent waterlogging.

GRANULAR, FERTILIZER A fertilizer composed of particles of roughly the same composition, about one-tenth inch in diameter. This kind of fertilizer contrasts with the normally fine or powdery fertilizer.

GRANULAR STRUCTURE Soil structure in which the individual grains are grouped into spherical aggregates with indistinct sides. Highly porous granules are commonly called crumbs. A well-granulated soil has the best structure for most ordinary crop plants.

GRAVITATIONAL WATER IN SOILS The water in the large pores of the soil that drains away under the force of gravity with free underdrainage. Well-drained soils have such water only during and immediately after rains or applications of irrigation water. In poorly drained soils, this water accumulates in the pores at the expense of air. Under such conditions, the soil lacks oxygen for the roots of most crop plants and is said to be waterlogged.

GRAY-BROWN PODZOLIC SOILS A zonal group of soils having thin organic coverings and thin organic-mineral layers over grayish-brown leached layers that rest upon brown B horizons richer in clay than the soil horizon above. These soils have formed under deciduous forests in a moist temperate climate.

GREAT SOIL GROUP Any one of several broad groups of soil with fundamental characteristics in common. Examples are Chernozem, Gray-Brown Podzolic, and Podzol.

GROUND WATER Water that fills all the unblocked pores of underlying material below the water table, which is the upper limit of saturation.

GROUND-WATER PODZOL An intrazonal group of soils, developed from imperfectly drained sandy deposits in humid regions, with thin organic and organic-mineral layers over light-gray or white leached layers that rest on dark-brown B horizons irregularly cemented with iron, organic matter, or both.

HARDPAN A hardened or cemented soil horizon or layer. The soil material may be sandy or clayey and may be cemented by iron oxide, silica, calcium carbonate, or other substances.

HEAD Difference in elevation of water-producing discharge. (Sometimes used incorrectly for the size of irrigation streams.)

HEAVY SOIL An old term formerly used for clayey or fine-textured soils. (The term originated from the heavy draught on the horses when plowing.)

HORIZON SOIL A layer of soil, approximately parallel to the soil surface, with distinct characteristics produced by soil-forming processes.

HUMIC ACIDS Alkali soluble end products of the decomposition of organic matter in soil and in composts. The term sometimes is used interchangeably for humus.

HUMID CLIMATE A climate with enough precipitation to support a forest vegetation, although there are exceptions where the plant cover includes no trees, as in the Arctic or high mountains. The lower limit of precipitation may be as little as 15 inches in cool regions and as much as 60 inches in hot regions. The precipitation-effectiveness index ranges between 64 and 128. A climate having a high average relative humidity.

HUMIFICATION A process or condition of decay in which plant or animal remains are so thoroughly decomposed that their initial structures or shapes can no longer be recognized.

HUMUS The well-decomposed, more or less stable part of the organic matter in mineral soils.

HYDRAULIC EQUILIBRIUM (OF WATER IN SOIL) The condition for zero flow rate of liquid or film water in soil. This condition is satisfied when the pressure gradient force is just equal and opposite to the gravity force.

HYDRONIUM IONS The predominant form of occurrence of hydrogen ions in solution, each hydrogen ion being associated with a single water molecule; H_3O^+.

HYDROUS Containing water.

HYDROXYAPATITE A member of the apatite group of minerals rich in hydroxyl groups. A nearly insoluble calcium phosphate.

HYGROSCOPIC Capable of taking up moisture from the air.

HYGROSCOPIC COEFFICIENT The amount of moisture in a dry soil when it is in equilibrium with some standard relative humidity near a saturated atmosphere (about 98 percent), expressed in terms of percentage on the basis of ovendry soil.

IGNEOUS ROCK Rock produced through the cooling of melted mineral matter. When the cooling process is slow, the rock contains fair-sized crystals of the individual minerals, as in granite.

ILLITE A series of micalike, nonexpandable, or slightly expandable alumino-silicate clay minerals in which two silica layers alternate with one alumina layer; also called hydrous micas.

ILLUVIATION An accumulation of material in a soil horizon through the deposition of suspended mineral and organic matter originating from horizons above. Since at least part of the fine clay in the B horizons (or subsoils) of many soils has moved into them from the A horizons above, these are called illuvial horizons.

IMMATURE SOIL A soil lacking clear individual horizons because of the relatively short time for soil-building forces to act upon the parent material since its deposition or exposure.

IMMOBILIZATION (OF PLANT NUTRIENTS) The conversion of an available plant nutrient in the soil from an inorganic to an organic form in living tissue. Thus the addition of fresh straw or sawdust to the soil may greatly increase the number of bacteria. These remove available nitrogen and phosphorus from the soil and immobilize them within their cells.

IMPERVIOUS SOIL A soil through which water, air, or roots penetrate slowly or not at all. No soil is absolutely impervious to water and air all the time.

INHERITED SOIL CHARACTERISTICS Any characteristic of a soil that is due directly to the nature of the material from which it formed, as contrasted to the characteristics that are wholly or partly the result of soil-forming processes acting on parent material. For example, some soils are red because the parent material was red; although the color of most red soils is due to soil-forming processes.

INORGANIC Refers to substances occurring as minerals in nature or obtainable from them by chemical means. Refers to all matter except the compounds of carbon, but includes carbonates.

INORGANIC NITROGEN Nitrogen in combination with mineral elements, not in animal or vegetable form. Ammonium sulfate and sodium nitrate are examples of inorganic nitrogen combinations, while proteins contain nitrogen in organic combination.

IN PLACE (*in situ*) (1) Formed or accumulated on the spot. A rock may decay and break down into small particles where it is first exposed in the land surface. It is then said to have weathered in place or in situ. (2) As a mass appears in the soil before any disturbance. For example, the deeper part of a profile may be massive and show no signs of structure in place but break down into lumps of regular size and shape when removed.

INTAKE RATE The rate, usually expressed in inches per hour, at which rain or irrigation water enters the soil. This rate is controlled partly by surface conditions (infiltration rate) and partly by subsurface conditions (permeability). It also varies with the method of applying water. The same kind of soil has different intake rates under sprinkler irrigation, border irrigation, and furrow irrigation.

INTERTILLED CROP A crop having or requiring cultivation during growth.

INTRAZONAL SOIL Any one of the great groups of soils having more or less well-developed soil characteristics that reflect a dominating influence of some local factor of relief or of parent material over the normal influences of the climate and the vegetation on the soil-forming processes. Such groups of soils may be geographically associated with two or more of the zonal groups of soils having characteristics dominated by the influence of climate and vegetation.

ION An electrically charged particle. As used in soils, an ion refers to an electrically charged element or combination of elements resulting from the breaking up of an electrolyte in solution. Since most soil solutions are highly dilute, many of the salts exist as ions. For example, all or part of the potassium chloride (muriate of potash) in most soils exists as potassium ions and chloride ions. The positively charged potassium ion is called a cation and the negatively charged chloride ion is called an anion.

ISOTOPE One of two or more forms of a chemical element having the same atomic number and position in the periodic table of elements, but distinguishable by differences of weight.

KAOLIN MINERALS A group of nonswelling clay minerals in which one layer or sheet of silicon and oxygen alternates with a sheet made up of aluminum, oxygen, and hydrogen.

LACUSTRINE DEPOSITS Materials deposited from lake water. Many nearly level soils have developed from such deposits from old lakes that have long since disappeared.

LAND The total natural and cultural environment within which production takes place. Land is a broader term than soil. In addition to soil, its attributes include other physical conditions such as mineral deposits and water supply; location in relation to centers of commerce, populations, and other land; the size of the individual tracts or holdings; and existing plant cover, works of improvement, and the like. Some use the term loosely in other senses: As defined above, but without the economic or cultural criteria, especially in the expression "natural land"; as a synonym for "soil"; for the solid surface of the earth; and also for earthy surface formations, especially in the geomorphological expression "land form."

LAND-CAPABILITY CLASSIFICATION A grouping of kinds of soil into special units, subclasses, and classes according to their capability for intensive use and the treatments required for sustained use.

LANDSCAPE The sum total of the characteristics that distinguish a certain kind of area on the earth's surface and give it a distinguishing pattern in contrast to other kinds of areas. Any one kind of soil is said to have a characteristic natural landscape, and under different uses it has one or more characteristic cultural landscapes.

LAND-USE PLANNING The development of plans for the uses of land that, over long periods, will best serve the general welfare, together with the formulation of ways and means for achieving such uses.

LATTICE The structural framework of a clay mineral which is made up by the orderly arrangement of the various ionic components of the mineral. The mineral is held together by the chemical bonds exerted toward each other by the various ions in the mineral. The structural pattern repeats itself indefinitely and regularly; the atoms are linked according to definite angles and distances. For example, micas and alumino-silicate clay minerals have layer lattices consisting of alternate silica and alumina layers.

LEACHING The removal of materials in solution by the passage of water through soil.

LEVEL TERRACE A broad surface channel or embankment constructed across sloping soil on the contour, as contrasted to a graded terrace, which is built at a slight angle to the contour. A level terrace can be used only on soils that are permeable enough for all of the storm water to soak into the soil so that none breaks over the terrace to cause gullies.

LEVELING (OF LAND) The reshaping or modification of the land surface to a planned grade to provide a more suitable surface for the efficient application of irrigation water and to provide good surface drainage.

LEY A term used in English writing for pastures or meadows. A short ley is roughly equivalent to our "rotation" pasture or meadow, and a long ley to our "longtime" pastures and meadows, often incorrectly called permanent.

LIGHT SOIL An old term formerly used for sandy or coarse-textured soils.

LIGNIN An organic substance that incrusts the cellulose framework of plant cell walls. It is made up of modified phenyl propane units. It is dissolved only with difficulty and is more inert chemically and biologically than other plant constituents. Lignin increases with age in plants.

LIME Generally the term lime, or agricultural lime, is applied to ground limestone (calcium carbonate), hydrated lime (calcium hydroxide), or burned lime (calcium oxide), with or without mixtures of magnesium carbonate, magnesium hydroxide, or magnesium oxide, and materials such as basic slag, used as amendments to reduce the acidity of acid soils. In strict chemical terminology, lime refers to calcium oxide (CaO), but by an extension of meaning it is now used for all limestone-derived materials applied to neutralize acid soils.

LIME REQUIREMENT The amount of standard ground limestone required to bring a 6.6-inch layer of an acre (about 2 million pounds in mineral soils) of acid soil to some specific lesser degree of acidity, usually to slightly or very slightly acid. In common practice, lime requirements are given in tons per acre of nearly pure limestone, ground finely enough so that all of it passes a 10-mesh screen and at least half of it passes a 100-mesh screen.

LITHOSOL A soil having little or no evidence of soil development and consisting mainly of a partly weathered mass of rock fragments or of nearly barren rock.

LOAM The textural class name for soil having a moderate amount of sand, silt, and clay. Loam soils contain 7 to 27 percent of clay, 28 to 50 percent of silt, and less than 52 percent of sand. (In the old literature, especially English literature, the term "loam" applied to mellow soils rich in organic matter, regardless of the texture. As used in the United States, the term refers only to the relative amounts of sand, silt, and clay; loam soils may or may not be mellow.)

LOAMY SOIL A general expression for soils of intermediate texture between the coarse-textured or sandy soils, on the one hand, and the fine-textured or clayey soils on the other. Sandy loams, loams, silt loams, and clay loams are regarded as loamy soils.

LOESS Geological deposit of relatively uniform, fine material, mostly silt, presumably transported by wind. Many unlike kinds of soil in the United States have developed from loess blown out of alluvial valleys and from other deposits during periods of aridity.

LUXURY CONSUMPTION The intake by a plant of an essential nutrient in amounts exceeding what it needs. Thus if potassium is abundant in the soil, alfalfa may take in more than is required.

MACROPORE Large or noncapillary pores. The pores, or voids, in a soil from which water usually drains by gravity. Is differentiated from micropore, or capillary pore, space, which consists of voids small enough that water is held against gravity by capillarity. Sandy soils have a large macropore, or noncapillary, pore space and a small micropore, or capillary, pore space. Nongranular clayey soils are just the reverse.

MANURE Generally, the refuse from stables and barnyards, including both animal excreta and straw or other litter. In some other countries the term "manure" is used more broadly and includes both farmyard or animal manure and "chemical manures," for which the term "fertilizer" is nearly always used in the United States.

MARL An earthy deposit, consisting mainly of calcium carbonate commonly mixed with clay or other impurities. It is formed chiefly at the margins of fresh-water lakes. It is commonly used for liming acid soils.

MATURE SOIL Any soil with well-developed soil horizons having characteristics produced by the natural processes of soil formation and in near equilibrium with its present environment.

MECHANICAL ANALYSIS The physical analysis of soil materials to determine the amounts of the various soil separates, or grain-size fractions.

MECHANICAL STABILITY Resistance of soil to breakdown by mechanical forces such as tillage or abrasion from windborne soil particles; strength of coherence; mechanical strength.

MEDITERRANEAN CLIMATE A general term for warm-temperature climates that are dry in the warm season and moist in the cool season.

MELLOW SOIL A porous, softly granular soil easily worked without becoming compacted.

METABOLISM Life functions that are a result of building up foods within the living body and using the foods for energy sources for various life processes. The synthesis of foods and their use as sources of energy.

METAMORPHIC ROCK A rock that has been greatly altered from its previous condition through the combined action of heat and pressure. For example, marble is a metamorphic rock produced from limestone, gneiss is one produced from granite, and slate is produced from shale.

METHOXYL A chemical grouping composed of a carbon atom linked to an oxygen atom and 3 hydrogen atoms. The conventional symbol is —OCH_3.

MICAS Primary alumino-silicate minerals in which two silica layers alternate with one alumina layer. They separate readily into thin sheets or flakes.

MICRO- A prefix meaning very small, as in micro-organism; one-millionth of something; that which makes use of a microscope, as in microbiology. Macro- implies large.

MICROCLIMATE The local climatic condition near the ground resulting from the modification of the general climatic condition by local differences in relief, exposure, and cover.

MICRONUTRIENTS Nutrients that plants need in only small, trace, or minute amounts.

MICRO-ORGANISMS Forms of life too small to be seen with the unaided eye, or barely discernible.

MICRORELIEF Small-scaled differences in relief, such as small mounts, swales, or pits that are a few feet across and have differences in elevation of a few inches to around 3 feet that are significant to soil-forming processes, to growth of plants, or to preparing the soil for cultivation.

MILLIMHOS Units of conductance.

MINERAL SOIL A general term for a soil composed chiefly of mineral matter, in contrast to an organic soil, which is composed chiefly of organic matter.

MINERALIZATION The release of mineral matter from organic matter, especially through microbial decomposition.

MOISTURE STRESS The tension at which water is held by the soil.

MOISTURE TENSION The force at which water is held by soil; usually expressed as the equivalent of a unit column of water in centimeters; 1,000 cm. equal 1 atmosphere equivalent tension. Moisture tension increases with dryness and indicates the degree of work required to remove soil moisture for use by plants.

MOLECULE A group of atoms bonded together in a characteristic pattern.

MONOVALENT CATIONS Ions having a single positive charge; having a deficiency of one electron from the neutral state.

MONTMORILLONITE A finely platy, alumino-silicate clay mineral that expands and contracts with the absorption and loss of water. It has a high cation-exchange capacity and is plastic and sticky when moist.

MOR Raw humus; a type of forest humus layer of unincorporated organic material, usually matted or compacted or both; distinct from the mineral soil, unless the latter has been blackened by washing in organic matter.

MORPHOLOGY, SOIL The constitution of the soil including the texture, structure, consistence, color, and other physical, chemical, and biological properties of the various soil horizons that make up the soil profile.

MOTTLED Soil horizons irregularly marked with spots of color. A common cause of mottling is imperfect or impeded drainage although there are other causes, such as soil development from an unevenly weathered rock. Different kinds of minerals may cause mottling.

MUCK Highly decomposed organic soil material developed from peat. Generally, muck has a higher mineral or ash content than peat and is decomposed to the point that the original plant parts cannot be identified.

MULCH A natural or artificially applied layer of plant residues or other materials on the surface of the soil. Mulches are generally used to help conserve moisture, control temperature, prevent surface compaction or crusting, reduce runoff and erosion, improve soil structure, or control weeds. Common mulching materials include compost, sawdust, wood chips, and straw. Sometimes paper, fine brush, or small stones are used.

MULCH TILLAGE Tillage of the soil and treatment of crop residues in ways to leave plant materials within or on the soil surface to form a mulch.

MULL A humus-rich layer of forested soils consisting of mixed organic and mineral matter. A mull blends into the upper mineral layers without an abrupt change in soil characteristics.

MYCELIA The threadlike bodies of simple organisms, such as the common bread mold.

MYCORHIZA (MYCORRHIZA) The morphological association, usually symbiotic, of fungi and roots of seed plants. The feeding roots are enshrouded and partially penetrated by fine filaments of fungi; such roots commonly are more branched and lose their root hairs.

NECROSIS Death associated with discoloration and dehydration of all or parts of plant organs, such as leaves.

NEMATOCIDE Any substance that can be used to kill nematodes.

NEMATODES Very small worms abundant in many soils and important because many of them attack and destroy plant roots.

NEUTRAL SOIL A soil that is neither significantly acid nor alkaline. Strictly, a neutral soil has pH of 7.0; in practice, a neutral soil has a pH between 6.6 and 7.3.

NITRIFICATION The formation of nitrates and nitrites from ammonia (or ammonium compounds), as in soils by micro-organisms.

NITROGEN FIXATION Generally, the conversion of free nitrogen to nitrogen combined with other elements. Specifically in soils, the assimilation of free nitrogen from the soil air by soil organisms and the formation of nitrogen compounds that eventually become available to plants. The nitrogen-fixing organisms associated with legumes are called symbiotic; those not definitely associated with the higher plants are nonsymbiotic.

NORMAL SOIL A soil having a profile in near equilibrium with its environment; developed under good but not excessive drainage from parent material of mixed mineral, physical, and chemical composition. In its characteristics it expresses the full effects of the forces of climate and living matter.

NUCLEIC ACIDS Complex compounds found in the nuclei of plant and animal cells and usually combined with proteins as nucleoproteins.

NUTRIENT, PLANT Any element taken in by a plant, essential to its growth, and used by it in elaboration of its food and tissue.

ORDER The highest category in soil classification. The three orders are zonal soils, intrazonal soils, and azonal soils.

ORGANIC SOIL A general term applied to a soil or to a soil horizon that consists primarily of organic matter, such as peat soils, muck soils, and peaty soil layers. Organic in chemistry refers to the compounds of carbon.

OSMOTIC A type of pressure exerted in living bodies as a result of unequal concentration of salts on both sides of a cell wall or membrane. Water will move from the area having the least salt concentration through the membrane into the area having the highest salt concentration and, therefore, exerts additional pressure on this side of the membrane.

OXIDATION A chemical change of an element or compound involving the addition of oxygen or its chemical equivalent. A chemical change that involves an increase of positive valence or a decrease of negative valence. For example, if iron is changed from the ferrous state (in which it has 2 positive valences) to the ferric state (in which it has 3 positive valences), the iron is said to be oxidized. The reverse process is reduction. During the burning of fuel, oxygen is added to carbon to form carbon dioxide; in the rusting of iron, the addition of oxygen forms a red iron oxide.

Oxide A compound of any element with oxygen alone.

Pan A layer or soil horizon within a soil that is firmly compacted or is very rich in clay. Examples include hardpans, fragipans, claypans, and traffic pans.

Parent material The unconsolidated mass of rock material (or peat) from which the soil profile develops.

Parts per million (p.p.m.) A notation for indicating small amounts of materials. The expression gives the number of units by weight of the substance per million weight units of ovendry soil. The term may be used to express the number of weight units of a substance per million weight units of solution.

Peat Unconsolidated soil material consisting largely of undecomposed or only slightly decomposed organic matter accumulated under conditions of excessive moisture.

Ped An individual natural soil aggregate such as a crumb, prism, or block, in contrast to a clod, which is a mass of soil brought about by digging or other disturbance.

Pedology The science that treats of soil.

Percolation The downward movement of water through soil.

Permanent pasture Pasture that occupies the soil for a long time in contrast to rotation pasture, which occupies the soil for only a year or two in a rotation cycle with other crops. As used in the humid parts of the United States, the term "permanent pasture" is equivalent to the European "long ley."

Permeability, soil The quality of a soil horizon that enables water or air to move through it. It can be measured quantitatively in terms of rate of flow of water through a unit cross section in unit time under specified temperature and hydraulic conditions. Values for saturated soils usually are called hydraulic conductivity. The permeability of a soil may be limited by the presence of one nearly impermeable horizon even though the others are permeable.

pH A numerical designation of relatively weak acidity and alkalinity as in soils and other biological systems. Technically, pH is the common logarithm of the reciprocal of the hydrogen-ion concentration of a solution. A pH of 7.0 indicates precise neutrality, higher values indicate increasing alkalinity, and lower values indicate increasing acidity.

Phase, soil The subdivision of a soil type or other classificational soil unit having variations in characteristics not significant to the classification of the soil in its natural landscape but significant to the use and management of the soil. Examples of the variations recognized by phases of soil types include differences in slope, stoniness, and thickness because of accelerated erosion.

Photosynthesis The process of conversion by plants of water and carbon dioxide into carbohydrates under the action of light. Chlorophyll is required for the conversion of the light energy into chemical forms.

Pitting The making of shallow pits in the soil to retain rainwater of snowmelt. In shortgrass rangelands pitting is done mainly with an offset disk or pitting machine.

Planosol An intrazonal group of soils with eluviated surface horizons underlain by claypans or fragipans, developed on nearly flat or gently sloping uplands in humid or subhumid climates.

Platy soil structure Soil aggregates with thin vertical axes and long horizontal axes. Flat, tabular; a three-dimensional object that has one dimension much smaller than the other two.

Plow layer Equals surface soil.

Podzol A zonal group of soils having surface organic mats and thin, organic-mineral horizons above gray leached horizons that rest upon illuvial dark-brown horizons developed under coniferous or mixed forests or under heath vegetation in a cool-temperate, moist climate.

Podzolic soil Soils that have part or all of the characteristics of the Podzol soils, especially leached surface soils that are poorer in clay than the B horizons beneath.

Podzolization The process by which soils are depleted of bases, become more acid, and have developed leached surface layers from which clay has been removed.

Polynutrient fertilizer A fertilizer containing more than one major plant nutrient.

Polysaccharides Compounds formed by chemical union of two or more simple sugars.

Pore space The fraction of the bulk volume or total space within soils that is not occupied by solid particles.

Porosity, soil The degree to which the soil mass is permeated with pores or cavities. Porosity can be generally expressed as a percentage of the whole volume of a soil horizon that is unoccupied by solid particles. In addition, the number, sizes, shapes, and distribution of the voids is important. Generally, the pore space of surface soil is less than one-half of the soil mass by volume, but in some soils it is more than half. The part of the pore space that consists of small pores that hold water by capillary is called capillary porosity.

PRAIRIE SOILS A zonal group of soils having dark-colored surface horizons grading through brown soil material to lighter colored parent material at 2 to 5 feet, formed under tall grasses in a temperate, humid climate. The term has a restricted meaning in soil science and does not apply to all soils developed in treeless landscapes.

PRECIPITATION-EFFECTIVENESS (P-E) INDEX The sum of the 12 monthly quotients of precipitation divided by evaporation.

PRIMARY MINERAL A mineral which occurs, or originally occurred, in igneous rocks; examples are micas and feldspars.

PRISMATIC SOIL STRUCTURE Prismlike structural aggregates with the vertical axes of the aggregates longer than the horizontal axes.

PRODUCTIVITY (OF SOIL) The present capability of a kind of soil for producing a specified plant or sequence of plants under a defined set of management practices. It is measured in terms of the outputs or harvests in relation to the inputs of production factors for a specific kind of soil under a physically defined system of management.

PROFILE (SOIL) A vertical section of the soil through all its horizons and extending into the parent material.

PROTEIN Any of a group of nitrogen-containing compounds that yield amino acids on hydrolysis and have high molecular weights. They are essential parts of living matter and are one of the essential food substances of animals.

PROTOPLASM The basic, jellylike substance in plant and animal cells; it carries out all their life processes.

PUDDLED SOIL Dense, massive soil artificially compacted when wet and having no regular structure. The condition commonly results from the tillage of a clayey soil when it is wet.

PULVERANT A term applied to ungranulated fertilizers, those which are largely powdered. Pulverant fertilizers are dusty and blow readily.

PURINES A group of closely related compounds containing carbon, hydrogen, and nitrogen. Uric acid, an example, is formed from proteins as an end product of animal metabolism. Uric acid is the chief nitrogenous compound in the excrement of birds.

QUICK TESTS Simple and rapid chemical tests of soils designed to give an approximation of the nutrients available to plants. Interpretations of results depend upon previous standardization with field trials of fertilizers and vary among different kinds of soil.

RADIATION The propagation of energy in the form of waves.

RANGE (or rangeland) Land that produces primarily native forage plants suitable for grazing by livestock, including land that has some forest trees.

REACTION, SOIL The degree of acidity or alkalinity of a soil mass, expressed in either pH value or in words, as follows:

	pH
Extremely acid	Below 4.5.
Very strongly acid	4.5–5.0.
Strongly acid	5.1–5.5.
Medium acid	5.6–6.0.
Slightly acid	6.1–6.5.
Neutral	6.6–7.3.
Mildly alkaline	7.4–7.8.
Moderately alkaline	7.9–8.4.
Strongly alkaline	8.5–9.0.
Very strongly alkaline	9.1 and higher.

RED PODZOLIC SOILS Formerly used for a zonal group of soils having thin organic and organic-mineral horizons over a yellowish-brown leached horizon that rests upon an illuvial red horizon developed under deciduous or mixed deciduous and coniferous forests in a warm to warm-temperate humid climate. These are now placed in the Red-Yellow Podzolic group.

REDUCTION Any chemical change involving the removal of oxygen or its chemical equivalent. A chemical change involving a decrease of positive valence or an increase of negative valence. The reverse of oxidation.

REGOLITH The unconsolidated mantle of weathered rock and soil material on the earth's surface; the loose earth materials above solid rock. Only the upper part of this, modified by organisms and other soil-building forces, is regarded by soil scientists as soil. In soil mechanics, however, most American engineers speak of the whole regolith, even to great depths, as "soil."

REGOSOL An azonal group of soils that includes those without definite genetic horizons developing from deep unconsolidated or soft rocky deposits.

RELIEF Elevations or inequalities of the land surface, considered collectively.

RENDZINA An intrazonal group of soils, usually with brown or black friable surface horizons, underlain by light-gray or pale-yellow soft calcareous material, developed under grass vegetation or mixed grass and forest vegetation, in humid and semiarid regions.

Residual fertilizer The amount of fertilizer that remains in the soil after one or more cropping seasons.

Residual material Unconsolidated and partly weathered parent material for soils presumed to have developed from the same kind of rock as that on which it lies. The term "residual" is sometimes incorrectly applied to soils, but it can be applied correctly only to the material from which soils are formed.

Rhizobia The bacteria that can live in symbiotic relations with leguminous plants within nodules on their roots. The normal result of the association is the fixation of nitrogen from the air into forms that can be used by living plants.

Rhizosphere The bounding surface of plant roots. The soil space in the immediate vicinity of the plant roots in which the abundance and composition of the microbial population are influenced by the presence of roots.

Root zone The part of the soil that is invaded by plant roots.

Runoff The surface flow of water from an area; or the total volume of surface flow during a specified time.

Saline soil A soil containing enough soluble salts to impair its productivity for plants but not containing an excess of exchangeable sodium.

Saline-alkali soil A soil having a combination of a harmful quantity of salts and either a high degree of alkalinity or a high amount of exchangeable sodium, or both, so distributed in the soil profile that the growth of most crop plants is less than normal.

Saltation The movement of soil and mineral particles by intermittent leaps from the ground when the particles are being moved by wind or water.

Salts The products, other than water, of the reaction of an acid with a base. Salts commonly found in soils break up into cations (sodium, calcium, etc.) and anions (chloride, sulfate, etc.) when dissolved in water.

Sand Individual rock or mineral fragments in soils having diameters ranging from 0.5 mm to 2.0 mm. Usually sand grains consist chiefly of quartz, but they may be of any mineral composition. The textural class name of any soil that contains 85 percent or more of sand and not more than 10 percent of clay.

Sandy clay Soil of this textural class contains 35 percent or more of clay and 45 percent or more of sand.

Sandy clay loam Generally, soil of this textural class contains 20 to 35 percent clay, less than 28 percent silt, and 45 percent or more of sand.

Sandy loam Generally, soil of the sandy loam class of texture has 50 percent sand and less than 20 percent clay.

Sandy soils A broad term for soils of the sand and loamy sand classes; soil material with more than 70 percent sand and less than 15 percent clay.

Sedimentary rock A rock composed of particles deposited from suspension in water. Chief groups of sedimentary rocks are conglomerates, from gravels; sandstones, from sand; shales, from clay; and limestones, from soft masses of calcium carbonate. There are many intermediate types. Some wind-deposited sands have been consolidated into sandstones.

Seepage The escape of water through the soil, or water emerging from an area of soil along an extensive line of surface, in contrast to springs where the water emerges from a local spot.

Semiarid climate A climate characteristic of the regions intermediate between the true deserts and subhumid areas. In the semiarid climate the precipitation-effectiveness (P–E) index ranges between 16 and 32. The upper limit of the average annual precipitation in cool semiarid regions is as low as 15 inches and in warm regions as much as 45 inches. The vegetation is close-growing or scattered short grass, bunchgrass, or shrubs. Soils in such regions that can take in nearly all of the rain that falls and that can hold it for crop plants can be used for crops under dry-farming methods but irrigation is common where water is available.

Separate, soil One of the individual-size groups of mineral soil particles—sand, silt, or clay.

Series, soil A group of soils that have soil horizons similar in their differentiating characteristics and arrangement in the soil profile, except for the texture of the surface soil, and are formed from a particular type of parent material. Soil series is an important category in detailed soil classification. Individual series are given proper names from place names near the first recorded occurrence. Thus names like Houston, Cecil, Barnes, and Miami are names of soil series that appear on soil maps and each connotes a unique combination of many soil characteristics.

Serpentine rocks Rocks consisting of acid magnesium silicate.

Sesquioxides Oxides of trivalent cations, such as iron and aluminum.

Sierozem soils A zonal group of soils having brownish-gray surface horizons that grade through lighter colored material into accumulated calcium carbonate, developed under mixed shrub vegetation in a temperate to cool-arid climate.

Silica An important soil constituent composed of silicon and oxygen. The essential material of the mineral quartz.

Silica-sesquioxide ratio The ratio of the number of molecules of silica to the number of molecules of alumina plus iron oxide in a soil or in the clay fraction of a soil. The more highly weathered materials of warm-temperate humid regions and especially of the Tropics generally have low ratios. The clay in soils with low ratios usually are less active, physically and chemically, than those with high ratios.

Silt (1) Individual mineral particles of soil that range in diameter between the upper size of clay, 0.002 mm., and the lower size of very fine sand, 0.05 mm. (2) Soil of the textural class silt contains 80 percent or more of silt and less than 12 percent of clay. (3) Sediments deposited from water in which the individual grains are approximately of the size of silt, although the term is sometimes applied loosely to sediments containing considerable sand and clay.

Silt loam Soil material having (1) 50 percent or more of silt and 12 to 27 percent of clay or (2) 50 to 80 percent of silt and less than 12 percent of clay.

Silty clay Soil of this textural class has 40 percent or more of clay and 40 percent or more of silt.

Silty clay loam Soil of this textural class has 27 to 40 percent of clay and less than 20 percent of sand.

Single grain soil A structureless soil in which each particle exists separately, as in dune sand.

Slick spot A small area of "alkali" or Solonetz soil.

Slip The downslope movement of a mass of soil under wet or saturated conditions; a microlandslide that produces microrelief in soils.

Slope The incline of the surface of a soil. It is usually expressed in percentage of slope, which equals the number of feet of fall per 100 feet of horizontal distance.

Soil (1) The natural medium for the growth of land plants. (2) A dynamic natural body on the surface of the earth in which plants grow, composed of mineral and organic materials and living forms. (3) The collection of natural bodies occupying parts of the earth's surface that support plants and that have properties due to the integrated effect of climate and living matter acting upon parent material, as conditioned by relief, over periods of time.

A soil is an individual three-dimensional body on the surface of the earth unlike the adjoining bodies. (The area of individual soils ranges from less than one-half acre to more than 300 acres.)

A kind of soil is the collection of soils that are alike in specified combinations of characteristics. Kinds of soil are given names in the system of soil classification. The terms "the soil" and "soil" are collective terms used for all soils, equivalent to the word "vegetation" for all plants.

Soil association A group of defined and named kinds of soil associated together in a characteristic geographic pattern. Except on detailed soil maps, it is not possible to delineate the various kinds of soil so that on all small-scale soil maps the areas shown consist of soil associations or two or more kinds of soil that are geographically associated.

Soil characteristic A feature of a soil that can be seen and/or measured in the field or in the laboratory on soil samples. Examples include soil slope and stoniness as well as the texture, structure, color, and chemical composition of soil horizons.

Soil climate The moisture and temperature conditions existing within the soil.

Soil conservation The efficient use and stability of each area of soil that is needed for use at its optimum level of developed productivity according to the specific patterns of soil and water resources of individual farms, ranches, forests, and other land-management units. The term includes the positive concept of improvement of soils for use as well as their protection and preservation.

Soil management The preparation, manipulation, and treatment of soils for the production of plants, including crops, grasses, and trees.

Soil population The group of organisms that normally live in the soil.

Soil quality An attribute of a soil that cannot be seen or measured directly from the soil alone but which is inferred from soil characteristics and soil behavior under defined conditions. Fertility, productivity, and erodibility are examples of soil qualities (in contrast to soil characteristics).

Soil survey A general term for the systematic examination of soils in the field and in the laboratories, their description and classification, the mapping of kinds of soil, and the interpretation of soils according to their adaptability for various crops, grasses, and trees, their behavior under use or treatment for plant production or for other purposes, and their productivity under different management systems.

SOLONCHAK SOILS An intrazonal group of soils with high concentrations of soluble salts in relation to those in other soils, usually light colored, without characteristic structural form, developed under salt-loving plants, and occurring mostly in a subhumid or semiarid climate. In soil classification, the term applies to a broad group of soils and is only approximately equivalent to the common term "saline soil."

SOLONETZ SOILS An intrazonal group of soils having surface horizons of varying degrees of friability underlain by dark-colored hard soil, ordinarily with columnar structure (prismatic structure with rounded tops). This hard layer is usually highly alkaline. Such soils are developed under grass or shrub vegetation, mostly in subhumid or semiarid climates. This term is used for a broad group of soils that include many so-called alkali soils in the western part of the United States. (Where the hard, clayey layer is overlain with a light-colored leached layer, the soils are called solodized Solonetz.)

SOLUM The upper part of a soil profile, above the parent material, in which the processes of soil formation are active. The solum in mature soils includes the A and B horizons. Usually the characteristics of the material in these horizons are quite unlike those of the underlying parent material. The living roots and other plant and animal life characteristic of the soil are largely confined to the solum.

SPECIFIC HEAT The amount of heat required to change the temperature of unit mass 1 degree.

SPECIFICITY Limited to a particular organism, compound, or set of conditions.

SPHAGNUM A group of mosses which grow in moist places. By annual increments of growth, deep layers of fibrous and highly absorbent peat may be built up. Sphagnum grows best in cool, humid regions.

STORAGE CAPACITY The amount of water that can be stored in the soil for future use by plants and evaporation.

STRATIFIED Composed of, or arranged in, strata, or layers, such as stratified alluvium. The term is confined to geological materials. Layers in soils that result from the processes of soil formation are called horizons; those inherited from the parent material are called strata.

STRESS (SOIL MOISTURE) A term used for the total energy with which water is held in the soil, including tension of soil moisture and additional effects of salts in the soil water. It can be expressed in any convenient pressure unit.

STRIPCROPPING The practice of growing crops in a systematic arrangement of strips, or bands. Commonly cultivated crops and sod crops are alternated in strips to protect the soil and vegetation against running water or wind. The alternate strips are laid out approximately on the contour on erosive soils or at approximate right angles to the prevailing direction of the wind where soil blowing is a hazard.

STRUCTURE, SOIL The arrangement of primary soil particles into compound particles or clusters that are separated from adjoining aggregates and have properties unlike those of an equal mass of unaggregated primary soil particles. The principal forms of soil structure are platy, prismatic, columnar (prisms with rounded tops), blocky (angular or subangular), and granular. Structureless soils are (1) single grain—each grain by itself, as in dune sand, or (2) massive—the particles adhering together without any regular cleavage as in many claypans and hardpans. ("Good" or "bad" tilth are terms for the general structural condition of cultivated soils according to particular plants or sequences of plants.)

STUBBLE MULCH A mulch consisting of the stubble and other crop residues left in and on the surface of the soil as a protective cover during the preparation of a seedbed and during at least part of the growing of the succeeding crop.

SUBHUMID CLIMATE A climate intermediate between semiarid and humid with sufficient precipitation to support a moderate to heavy growth of short and tall grasses, or shrubs, or of these and widely spaced trees or clumps of trees. The precipitation-effectiveness (P-E) index ranges from about 32 to 64. The upper limit of rainfall in subhumid climates may be as low as 20 inches in cold regions and as high as 60 inches in hot regions.

SUBIRRIGATION Irrigation through controlling the water table in order to raise it into the root zone. Water is applied in open ditches or through tile until the water table is raised enough to wet the soil. Some soils along streams are said to be naturally "subirrigated."

SUBSOIL The B horizons of soils with distinct profiles. In soils with weak profile development, the subsoil can be defined as the soil below the plowed soil (or its equivalent of surface soil), in which roots normally grow. Although a common term, it cannot be defined accurately. It has been carried over from early days when "soil" was conceived only as the plowed soil and that under it as the "subsoil."

SUBSOILING The tillage of the soil below the normal plow depth, usually to shatter a hardpan or claypan.

SUBSTRATUM Any layer lying beneath the solum or true soil. It is applied to both parent materials and to other layers unlike the parent material, below the B horizon or the subsoil.

SUBSURFACE TILLAGE Tillage with a sweep-like plow or blade that does not turn over the surface cover or incorporate it into the lower part of the surface soil.

SUCTION (OF SOIL WATER) The equivalent negative pressure in soil water. It is the pressure reduction required to extract water from soil. Suction, measured in pressure units, indicates the tenacity with which water is held by surface force action in soil. Experimentally, the suction of water in soil is the pressure difference required across a permeable membrane to produce hydraulic equilibrium between water in soil that is subject to surface force action and free water in bulk on the other side of the membrane. Also, soil suction; soil moisture suction.

SUPPLEMENTAL IRRIGATION A general term sometimes used for irrigation during dry periods in regions where normal precipitation supplies most of the moisture for crops.

SURFACE SOIL The soil ordinarily moved in tillage, or its equivalent in uncultivated soil, about 5 to 8 inches in thickness.

SYMBIOSIS The living together of two different organisms with a resulting mutual benefit. A common example includes the association of rhizobia with legumes; the resulting nitrogen fixation is sometimes called symbiotic nitrogen fixation. Adjective: Symbiotic.

SYNTHESIS Combination of simple molecules to form another substance—for example, the union of carbon dioxide and water under the action of light in photosynthesis.

TENSIOMETER A device for measuring the tension with which water is held in the soil. It is a combination of a porous cup and a vacuum gage.

TENSION, SOIL-MOISTURE The equivalent negative pressure of suction of water in soil.

TERRACE An embankment or ridge constructed across sloping soils on the contour or at a slight angle to the contour. The terrace intercepts surplus runoff in order to retard it for infiltration into the soil and so that any excess may flow slowly to a prepared outlet without harm.

TERRACE (GEOLOGICAL) A nearly flat or undulating plain, commonly rather narrow and usually with a steep front, bordering a river, a lake, or the sea. Although many old terraces have become more or less hilly through dissection by streams, they are still regarded as terraces.

TEXTURAL CLASS Kinds of soil material according to the proportions of sand, silt, and clay. The principal textural classes in soil, in increasing order of the amount of silt and clay, are as follows: Sand, loamy sand, sandy loam, loam, silt loam, silt, sandy clay loam, clay loam, silty clay loam, sandy clay, silty clay, and clay. These class names are modified to indicate the size of the sand fraction or the presence of gravel, cobbles, and stones. For example, terms such as loamy fine sand, very fine sandy loam, gravelly loam, stony clay, and cobbly loam, are used on detailed soil maps. These terms apply only to individual soil horizons or to the surface layer of a soil type, as in the name "Miami silt loam." Commonly the various horizons of any one kind of soil belong in different soil textural classes.

TEXTURE, SOIL The relative proportions of the various size groups of individual soil grains in a mass of soil. Specifically, it refers to the proportions of sand, silt, and clay.

TILLAGE The operation of implements through the soil to prepare seedbeds and rootbeds.

TILTH, SOIL The physical condition of a soil in respect to its fitness for the growth of a specified plant or sequence of plants. Ideal soil tilth is not the same for each kind of crop nor is it uniform for the same kind of crop growing on contrasting kinds of soil.

TOPOGRAPHY The shape of the ground surface, such as hills, mountains, or plains. Steep topography indicates steep slopes or hilly land; flat topography indicates flat land with minor undulations and gentle slopes.

TOPSOIL A general term used in at least four different senses: (1) A presumed fertile soil or soil material, usually rich in organic matter, used to topdress roadbanks, lawns, and gardens; (2) the surface plow layer of a soil and thus a synonym for surface soil; (3) the original or present dark-colored upper soil, which ranges from a mere fraction of an inch to 2 or 3 feet on different kinds of soil; and (4) the original or present A horizon, varying widely among different kinds of soil. Applied to soils in the field, the term has no precise meaning unless defined as to depth or productivity in relation to a specific kind of soil.

TRACE ELEMENTS An old term used for the elements found in plants in only small amounts, including several that are essential to plant growth, others that are essential to animals even though not to plants, and others having no known biological functions. (See micronutrients.)

TRACER TECHNIQUES The use of small amounts of radioactive isotopes to follow normal elements. The tracer is readily detected and measured by its radioactivity.

Traffic pans Subsurface layers in soil that have been so compacted by the application of weight (e. g., by machines, tractors, etc.) that the penetration of water and roots is interfered with. Because the traffic of machines is not the only cause of these pans, some persons call them pressure pans.

Transpiration Loss of water vapor from the leaves and stems of living plants to the atmosphere.

Type, soil A subgroup or category under the soil series based on the texture of the surface soil. A soil type is a group of soils having horizons similar in differentiating characteristics and arrangement in the soil profile and developed from a particular type of parent material. The name of a soil type consists of the name of the soil series plus the textural class name of the upper part of the soil equivalent to the surface soil. Thus Miami silt loam is the name of a soil type within the Miami series.

Unhumified Organic matter prior to its decomposition into humus.

Upland soils High ground; ground elevated above the lowlands along rivers or between hills.

Valence The combining capacity of atoms or groups of atoms. Sodium (Na^+) and potassium (K^+) are monovalent, while calcium (Ca^{++}) is divalent.

Virgin soil A soil that has not been significantly disturbed from its natural environment.

Viscosity, of fluid Property of stickiness of liquid or gas due to its cohesive and adhesive characteristics.

Volatilization The evaporation or changing of a substance from liquid to vapor.

Water ratio (in soil) The fraction of the total bulk volume of soil that is filled with water.

Water requirement (of plants) Generally, the amount of water required by plants for satisfactory growth during the season. More strictly, the number of units of water required by a plant during the growing season in relation to the number of units of dry matter produced. The water requirement varies with climatic conditions, soil moisture, and soil characteristics. Factors unfavorable to plant growth, such as low fertility, disease, and drought, increase the water requirement.

Water retention The physical property of soil that is based on surface force action and that makes it necessary to do work in order to remove water from soil pores and from soil surface.

Water table The upper limit of the part of the soil or underlying rock material that is wholly saturated with water. In some places an upper, or perched, water table may be separated from a lower one by a dry zone.

Water-holding capacity The capacity (or ability) of soil to hold water; field capacity is the amount held against gravity or 1 atmosphere tension or pF 2.7. The moisture-holding capacity of sandy soils is usually considered to be low while that of clayey soils is high. Often expressed in inches of water per foot depth of soil.

Waterlogged A condition of soil in which both large and small pore spaces are filled with water. (The soil may be intermittently waterlogged because of a fluctuating water table or waterlogged for short periods after rain.)

Watershed In the United States, the term refers to the total area above a given point on a stream that contributes water to the flow at that point. Synonyms are "drainage basin" or "catchment basin." In some other countries, the term is used for the topographic boundary separating one drainage basin from another.

Weathering The physical and chemical disintegration and decomposition of rocks and minerals.

Wilting point (or permanent wilting point) The moisture content of soil, on an ovendry basis, at which plants (specifically sunflower plants) wilt and fail to recover their turgidity when placed in a dark humid atmosphere. The percentage of water at the wilting point approximates the minimum moisture content in soils under plants in the field at depths below the effects of surface evaporation.

Yellow Podzolic soils Formerly used for a zonal group of soils having thin organic and organic-mineral layers over grayish-yellow leached horizons that rest on yellow B horizons, developed under coniferous or mixed coniferous and deciduous forests in a warm-temperate to warm, moist climate. These soils are now combined into the Red-Yellow Podzolic group.